FISCAL FEDERALISM IN INDIAN UNION

About the Author

Udai Bhan Singh (*b.* 1953) Ph.D. on Human Resource Development, fellowship under Colombo Plan at the University College, London (U.K.), Life Member of Indian Institute of Public Administration, Indian Public Administration Association and Indian Political Science Association. A senior member of the faculty of Regional Centre for Urban & Environmental Studies, University of Lucknow, has undertaken a number of research studies on different aspects of public administration; a prolific writer on urban administration and management; has contributed a number of articles to various journals; a unique combination of a trainer, researcher and teacher. His other publications are:

1. Commentary on U.P. Municipalities Act, 1916
2. Human Resource Development
3. U.P. Centralised Service Rules
4. Urban Local Government
5. Administrative System in India
6. Urban Local Governance in North Eastern Region
7. Functioning Local Government in South India
8. Privatisation of Municipal Services (ed.)
9. Assessing Training Needs in Urban Administration (In Press)
10. Revitalising Urban Administration in India (In Press)

FISCAL FEDERALISM IN INDIAN UNION

UDAI BHAN SINGH

CONCEPT PUBLISHING COMPANY, NEW DELHI-110059

ISBN : 81-7022-982-0

First Published 2003

Published and Printed by
Ashok Kumar Mittal
Concept Publishing Company
A/15-16, Commercial Block, Mohan Garden
New Delhi-110059 (INDIA)

Phone : 25351460, 25351794
Fax : 091-11-25357103
Email : publishing@conceptpub.com

PREFACE

The functional and financial domains of urban local bodies in India, have undergone radical changes in post 74th Amendment to the Constitution period. The historic amendments (73rd and 74th) to the Constitution have established three layer governments —Union, State and Local with certain ambiguities. India, the Union of States, now has one Union Government, several State Governments and thousands Local Governments within the State network. The third partner in the Union enjoys constitutionally limited autonomy but fully dependant upon States, the creator. Unlike functional clarity between the Union and the States, there is confusion between State and its constituents. The Local Government units, although recognised as third layer government in Indian (Federal) structure are deprived of deriving functions and finances directly under the Constitution.

In pursuance of the Constitutional obligations, the States have legislated conformity laws. The functions have been generously transferred to urban local bodies. The State Finance Commissions have been set up. Most of them have formulated the principles of devolution of finances to the grassroot institutions. Others are in offing. Thus, the Indian Constitution envisages three-layer government with Finance Commissions at two levels, the higher level still interested in financially strengthening the third partner. The President of India set up the Eleventh Finance Commission (July 3, 1998) in pursuance of the provisions of Article 280 of the Constitution. The interest of the Union Government in local government units reflected fully in terms of references framed for the Central Commission. Among others, the Commission was asked to make recommendations to "the measures needed to augment the Consolidated Fund of a State to supplement resources of the Panchayats and to Municipalities in the State on the basis of the recommendations made by the Finance Commission of the State". Moreso, the notification added that in the case of local bodies:

"(a) the Commission shall take into account the recommendations of the State Finance Commissions, and

(b) where the State Finance Commissions have not been constituted as yet, or have not submitted their report giving recommendations, the Commission will make its own assessment about the manner and extent of augmentation of Consolidated Fund of the State to supplement to resources of the Panchayats and Municipalities in the State. While making such assessment, the Commission —

(i) shall take into account the provisions required to be made for the emoluments and terminal benefits of the employees of local bodies including those of teachers,

(ii) shall take into account the existing powers of the Panchayats and Municipalities to raise financial resources including those by way of raising additional taxes by the Panchayats and Municipalities, and

(iii) the powers, authority and responsibility transferred to Panchayats and Municipalities under Articles 243 G and 243 W of the Constitution read with Schedules Eleven and Twelve".

This clearly signifies that the Central Finance Commission had to suggest the measures to augment the Consolidated Fund of a State, so that the State can devolve adequate finances to local bodies. The Commission to arrive at any measure was to assess and evaluate the extent of fiscal devolution from the State to local units. A State, thus, will be entitled to the transfer in proportion to the fiscal devolution made by the State to local bodies. In other words, to get more from Union, the States have to give proportionately to local bodies. This infers the adoption of indirect measures by the Union Government to financially strengthen the local government units, a State subject.

In these trivial circumstances, I have attempted to assess the functional domain and financial health of urban local bodies in most of the States where the Commissions have submitted their report. The taxation powers have also been discussed at length alongwith the changing urban scenario. The recommendations by the State Finance Commissions in the respective States have been analysed for the better appreciation of the subject. The analysis has been grouped mainly as augmenting existing sources—tax and non-tax, assignment of tax sources, sharing, grants-in-aid and miscellaneous.

The endeavour is divided into three parts. The PROLOGUE highlights the present urban scenario and conceptualises the principles of decentralisation in the historical perspective. It touches upon the challenges before the First State Finance Commissions. The following part consists of the analysis—State-wise. It contains in brief the urban scenario in respective States, Urban administration and functional jurisdiction have been discussed followed by the recommendations of the State Finance Commissions in fulfilment of the constitutional obligations.

In completing this work, I received encouragement and assistance from various corners. At the outset, I would like to express my sincere gratitude to the Secretary to various State governments for making the respective SFC report available. I am grateful to Prof. Gangadhar Jha, NIUA, New Delhi; Prof. S.K. Singh, Lucknow University; Dr. M.S. Verma, Member, First UPSFC; Sri S.K. Sinha, Patna; Dr. B. Mohanty, Utkal University, Bhubaneswar; Dr. S. Chandran, Madras University, Chennai; Prof. K.S.R.N. Sarma, IIPA, New Delhi and many others for encouragement in this venture. I am thankful to Dr. R.K. Trivedi, Assistant Librarian for rendering assistance in finalising the manuscripts and for other academic inputs, to Ms. N. Kamla Kumari for shaping the manuscripts and to Mr. Nimish Gupta for preparing computer floppy.

I express my thanks to M/s Concept Publication Co., New Delhi for publishing the book in a record time.

Kartik Purnima, 1999 U.B. SINGH
Lucknow.

CONTENTS

PROLOGUE

India has geo-political and historical characteristics which have few parallels. Its size and population, geographical, linguistic, religious, racial and other diversities give it the character of a sub-continent. But its natural boundaries marked by mountains and seas, serve to identify it as a separate geographical entity. This insularity over the years led to the evolution of a composite cultural unity, a feeling of common heritage and a pervasive under current of oneness. Another significant fact that stands out in India's history is that the provinces and the local institutions in various empires from Mauryas to the Mughals enjoyed considerable degree of autonomy. The British also, at the commencement of their regime tried to centralise all powers. But they soon realised that it was not possible to rule without progressive decentralisation of powers to the Provinces and local bodies. Too centralised an administration was found to be incompatible with the size and diversity of the country. It bred administrative inefficiency and local discontent. Hence some decentralisation was thought inevitable.

DECENTRALISATION TREND

The first small but significant step in the direction of decentralisation was taken by the Indian Council Act, 1861. It provided for participation by non-officials in the Legislative Council of the Governor-General. An important factor which helped and sustained the evolution of a dispersed political system in India, was the decentralisation of finances. This process started with the Mayo Scheme in 1871.

Until 1871, the Provincial Governments had no independent sources of revenue and they received fixed grants from the Central Government to meet their public expenditure. The first step by which the Provinces were given some heads of revenue was taken in 1871 when income from certain heads like registration, police, jails, medicine, education, roads and civil works was handed over to them. But because of obvious inadequacy, the system of lump sum grants still continued. It was only in 1904 that a system of divided heads of revenue was adopted on a quasi-permanent basis and was made permanent in 1912. In the scheme, some taxes like land revenue, irrigation, excise duties and stamp duties were shared between the Centre and the Provinces. This system was accompanied with that of grants from the Centre.

The Government of India Act, 1919, ushered in the first phase of responsible government in India. It demarcated the sphere of Provincial Governments from that of the Centre. By the Devolution Rules framed under the Act, powers were delegated to the provinces not only in the administrative but also in the legislative and financial spheres. For this purpose, separate Central and Provincial Lists of subjects were drawn up. There was also a third List regarding taxation powers of local bodies.

Under the Act, various matters of regional and local importance went to the Provincial Governments. This scheme, however, lacked a close correspondence between the functions and resources assigned to them. The resources given to them were relatively inelastic and inadequate while the functions assigned to them were of expanding nature.

Under the Government of India Act, 1935, the functions of the Central and Provincial Governments were classified such that the Federal Legislative List contained 59 entries, the Provincial Legislative List consisted of 94 entries, and a third list having the concurrent legislative powers had 36 entries. In the same way, the financial resources were also divided into three categories, namely (a) Federal, (b) Provincial, (c) Jointly Federal and Provincial. The third list covered those taxes and duties which could be levied only by the Central Government but the revenue from which were to be shared between the Central and Provincial governments.

The Government of India Act, 1935, thus, was an important milestone in the history of constitutional devolution of powers, particularly from two stand points. Firstly, it constitutionally distributed powers between the Centre and the Provinces. Secondly, subject to certain safeguards, it introduced representative government at the provincial level responsible to the Provincial Legislature.

POST-INDEPENDENCE SCENARIO

The Constitution of free India came into force in 1950. It followed more or less the pattern laid down in the Government of India Act, 1935. The Constitution envisages India as a 'Union of States'. The member-States have the Union or Central Government for the whole country and there are State governments for parts of the country. The 73rd and 74th Amendments to the Constitution have provided for constituting local government in the country. In this set-up then, more than one government are found for each State. To put it differently, in our set-up, there are three layers of government. The topmost layer is the Union Government, and below it lies the State governments which have local government units therein.

The Constitution divides the functions of the government at upper two layers into Union and State spheres together with concurrent areas. The Seventh Schedule lays down the respective functions and financial resources and contains three lists. The Union List consists of 97 entries, the State List has 66 entries and the Concurrent List with 47 entries. The Constitution also allots separate legislative heads of taxation to the Union and States. There are no taxes in the sphere of their concurrent jurisdiction. As regards functions pertaining to the third layer government i.e. the local governments, the subject is included in the State List and the States have been empowered to entrust the functions to local government units out of the functions enumerated for them. Interestingly, two Schedules (XI and XII) are also appended in the Constitution containing a list of functions which may be assigned to the local government units. The identical situations replicates in respect of taxation power as well. Thus it seems that Indian federal structure is the result of gradual evolution from the centralised authority (from Union to States and States to local government units). This differentiates the Indian federation from other federations and makes a structure uni-federal one-federal in general and unitary in emergent situations.

In this historical backdrop it becomes a necessity to introduce the new partner to the Indian uni-federal structure. The new partner is evidently not a new one but has been an inseparable existent over the empires. The newness is in the sense of identity, stability, continuity, responsibility, authority etc. This third entrant in our uni-federal framework is 'local government'. Interestingly, the number of local governments is very high. It includes units of local self governance in rural as well as in urban areas. The scope for this venture being limited, the discussion centres around the urban local government only.

MUNICIPAL GOVERNANCE

The modern municipal governments have been in existence in India since 1687 when the first municipality was set up in Madras (now Chennai). The municipalities in Calcutta (Kolkata) and Bombay (now Mumbai) were established in 1726. In the early nineteenth century, municipal governments were established in other towns as well. These municipal governments had members nominated by the provincial governments. The foundation of democratic form of local government in India was laid in 1882 with Lord Ripon's Resolution on Local Self Government. The Government of India Act, 1919, incorporated the essence of the Resolution and powers of the democratically elected governments were laid down. Under the Government of India Act, 1935, the local governments were brought within the purview of the provincial government. The Constitution of free India in the Directive Principles of State Policy (Art. 40) provided that the State shall take steps to organise village panchayats and endow them with such powers and authority as may be necessary to enable them to function as units of self government. There was no mention for constituting urban local bodies although they were in existence. The municipal governments continued to derive their functional and fiscal powers from State Legislations.

K.M. Raipuria distinguishes three main lines of relations between the State government and the local authorities. Firstly, the powers and functions of local bodies are defined by the State. Secondly, the State acts as a watchdog so far as the financial administration is concerned. Thirdly, the State is responsible to provide finances to meet the assigned functions to them either through shared taxes or shared tax receipts or direct grants and loans. Thus, the Zakaria Committee feels that "In State local government relations, local government must inevitably be in the position of the junior partner". But the importance of the local bodies as 'primary schools of democracy' in India implies strong and independent minded local authorities. They serve at the cutting edge of administration in close association with the electorate whom they provide the merit goods. U. Hicks suggests that "optional relationship would be partnership of two active and cooperative members though the State government will remain the senior partner". But over the passage of time, the State governments reduced functional domain of these bodies by establishing parastatal agencies. The State governments also eroded their financial base by abolishing buoyant sources of their revenue and by appropriating some other resources. In addition, the State governments also superseded local governments and did not hold elections for many years.

As a result of functional and financial erosion, the urban local governments were unable to respond to the needs of the people. The heavy dependence on the State for financial resources resulted in progressive erosion of jurisdiction, authority and initiative of these grassroots level institutions in their own sphere.

The Constitution (74th Amendment) Act, 1992 is a landmark in the history of municipal governance in the country. The Act consists of mandatory as well as discretionary provisions. Uniformity in constitution, representative in composition, fixed life, assured financial base, integrated planning, decentralisation are the main mandatory provisions. The Act ensures democratic decentralisation besides providing stability of tenure to these grassroot institutions. It brings the administration nearer to the people, makes it accountable to the people and representative in nature. It provides an institutional framework for the efficient delivery of urban services and sensitise to the problems of weaker sections and women. The Act envisages a systematic change in municipal governance in the country.

Thus, this enactment has elevated "Local Bodies" to "Local Self Governments". In pursuance, the attempts are being made for strengthening local governments. More money and staff have to be put at their disposal to make the strengthening possible. Indeed, a government at any level should have adequate resources—human as well as financial to discharge its responsibilities properly.

For better appreciation of distribution of revenue resources in such a unique structure, functional responsibilities of the governments at different layers deserve special appraisal. The Constitution clearly delineates the functional domains of Union and State governments on the basis of three lists contained in it. The case however in respect of the third layer is somewhat ambiguous.

FUNCTIONAL DOMAIN

As discussed earlier, the Constitution clearly divides the functional powers into Union and State governments. Article 246 grants the Parliament exclusive power to make laws in respect to matters enumerated in List I (Union List) and, limited powers in respect of matters given in List III (Concurrent List). It further authorises the legislature of a State exclusively to enact laws for matters mentioned in List II (State List). The State has powers to make laws in respect of matters enumerated in the Concurrent List. The Union has the residuary powers of legislation. The Parliament is even empowered (Article 249) to legislate with respect to a matter in the State List in the national interest. Thus the functions enumerated in the Seventh Schedule are clearly divided by the Constitution (Articles 245-255). There is no such earmarking of functions for local government units. The 73rd and 74th Amendments to the Constitution annex separate Schedules (Eleventh for rural and Twelfth for Urban) with the clear provisions in Articles 243G and 243W respectively. Our concern being the urban local bodies, the respective provision reads as under :

> "*243W. Powers, authority and responsibilities of Municipalities, etc.—subject to the provisions of this Constitution, the legislature of a State may, by law endow*
>
> (a) the municipality with such powers and authority as may be necessary to function as institutions of self government and such law may contain provisions for the devolution of powers and responsibilities upon municipalities, subject to such conditions as may be specified therein, in respect to
>
> (i) the preparation of plans for economic development and social justice,
>
> (ii) the performance of functions and the implementation of schemes as may be entrusted to them including those in relation to the matters listed in the Twelfth Schedule.
>
> (b) the Committees with such powers and authority as may be necessary to enable them to carry out the responsibilities conferred upon them including those in relation to the matters listed in the Twelfth Schedule".

Thus, the Constitution delineates guidelines for the State Government to entrust functions to urban local bodies. Consequently, there is no uniformity in the States in transferring the functions to the municipalities. The municipal laws all over the country illustrate the enthusiasm of the State governments in transferring varied functions to municipal institutions. In practice, however, the situation is somewhat disappointing. It is surprising that the functions transferred to and made obligatory for local bodies in the laws in many States are actually being performed by other agencies. Thus, only incorporation of functions in municipal laws is not going to functionally strengthen the urban local bodies, rather it may create a confusing state of affairs. Further, the level of technical and administrative competence of municipal staff may not be commensurate to as required in performing most of functions assigned to them. There is a need for removing ambiguities and clarifying the assignment of functions to municipalities. The assignment of municipal finances and enforcement of managerial accountability cannot be meaningful without the clarity in functions.

POWER OF TAXATION

The Constitution clearly divides the resource base of the Union and the State governments. The perusal of the concerned provisions (Articles 268-272) shows that the actual levying and collection of taxes follows the dictates of administrative and financial efficiency, while the allocation of proceeds follows the relative needs of various governments. On this basis, the tax-revenue of the country may be divided into following categories :

(i) The first category contains those taxes which are levied by the Central Government but are collected and retained by the States (Article 268).
(ii) The second category has those taxes which are levied and collected by the Central Government but are wholly assigned to the States (Article 269).
(iii) The third category is of those taxes which are levied and collected by Union Government but are shared with the States (Article 270).
(iv) In the fourth category are those taxes which are levied and collected by the Union and may be distributed between the Union and States (Article 272).
(v) The last category contains those taxes which are levied, collected and retained by the States.

For determining the shares of the Union and the States, the Constitution envisages the setting up of a Finance Commission every fifth year by the President (Article 280). The duty of the Commission is "to make recommendations to the President as to the distribution between the Union and the States the net proceeds of taxes which are to be or may be divided between them and the allocation between the States of the respective shares".

These provisions clearly demarcate the taxation powers between the two upper layers of government i.e. the Union and the States. Contrarily, the Constitution is not clear about the taxation powers of the local bodies. They derive their powers out of the State laws. Traditionally, urban local bodies in the country accrue their income through tax and non-tax sources. The sources are mainly :

1. House Tax/ Property Tax
2. Octroi
3. Water Tax
4. Drainage Tax
5. Sewerage Tax
6. Tax on Vehicles and animals
7. Tax on Advertisements
8. Lighting Tax
9. Profession Tax
10. Betterment Tax
11. Fire Tax
12. Theatre Tax
13. Passenger Tax
14. Pilgrims Tax
15. Duty on Transfer of Properties
16. License Fees
17. Fee on markets
18. Fee on dogs
19. Fee on boats and animals
20. Toll
21. Betterment Tax
22. Water Cess/Charge/Rate
23. Fee on Pilgrims
24. Parking Fee
25. Fee on building plans, etc.

In addition, the local bodies have been favoured with grants-in-aid from the Union and State governments generously.

Thus, it is found that local bodies are left with the most inelastic and trivial sources of taxation. In view of this, it is generally accepted that local bodies should be helped with adequate funds from above. The Union Government allots funds for special programmes and the State governments launch various development activities. However, there has been an air of uncertainty. Now that the local bodies have been given the status of self government, these uncertainties should end. At least, it should end substantially. A local government unit must have access to some funds which will have the status of entitlement. With this end in view, the Constitution delineates the taxation powers of urban local bodies.

While providing for resource base to urban local bodies the Constitution (74th Amendment) in Article 243(X) reads as under:

> "*243-X. Power to Impose Taxes by and Funds of the Municipalities*—The Legislature of a State may, by law
>
> (a) authorise a Municipality to levy, collect and appropriate such taxes, duties, tolls and fees in accordance with such procedure and subject to such limits;
> (b) assign to a Municipality such taxes, duties, tolls and fees levied and collected by the State government for such purposes and subject to such conditions and limits;
> (c) provide for making such grants-in-aid to the Municipalities from Consolidated Fund of the State, and
> (d) provide for constitution of such Funds for crediting all moneys received, respectively, by or on behalf of the Municipalities and also for the withdrawal of such moneys therefrom, as may be specified in the law".

The analysis of Municipal Acts of the States depicts the taxation powers of municipalities. It is seen that the taxes relating to buildings and lands are mainstay of the municipalities. House tax, Water Tax, Latrine Tax, Light Tax, Entertainment Tax are the major taxes left with the urban local bodies. Octroi is imposed only in a few States. The property tax is the single most important local government tax. It is, however, not necessarily the best revenue raising instrument for a city because it is very difficult to administer efficiently, can have undesirable land-use effects and is very unpopular with the payers. Yet local governments often have few other sources of revenue and important studies have been made toward improving the fairness and revenue productivity of property taxation.

According to conventional wisdom, there are three basic forms of property taxation. The property tax may be levied on the annual rental value of the property, the capital value of the land and improvements or the site value of the land. The annual value form may be seen as an attempt to tax the yearly income from properties, whereas the capital and site value forms are partial Wealth taxes. The common feature of annual value system is property assessment according to some estimates of rental value or net rent. Rental value assessment schemes have been criticised in the past on grounds that they ignored variations in the quality of rented premises, such as location by floor in a building or exposure to breezes, factors which surely affect market rent.

The studies have found that property taxation suffers from various malpractices resulting into the under-exploitation. The Government of India has issued guidelines to reform the administration of property taxes. The State governments should adopt the new procedure for better outcome of this major source of income of municipalities. Erosion in tax sources leads more dependence on non-tax revenue sources and grants-in-aid from the State.

As regards powers to levy and revise the rates, municipalities in majority of the States are not empowered to reimpose, increase or modify the rates and the approval of the State government is necessary for the purpose. This increases dependence of municipalities on the State government.

Actually, K.M. Raipuria feels that the tax systems of local bodies present the situation of lost opportunities. There is no list of taxes reserved for them. The utilisation of buoyant taxes by State is justified on the ground of increasing demand made by the requirements of the plans. But it is equally justified to assign some buoyant taxes exclusively to the local bodies to meet their financial requirements.

The Constitution, thus, puts the units of local government totally on the mercy of the State government, whereas there is clear demarcation of taxation powers between the Union and States. The provision leaves every scope of bias on the part of the State government to devolve the financial powers to municipalities. This necessitates a fresh consideration in view that with the transfer of functions as mentioned in the Twelfth Schedule, the needs of municipalities have increased tremendously on account of increasing responsibilities, but their revenue resources not so buoyant and widen. Generally speaking, local governments any where on the globe are not self-sustaining. They need subventions in various forms from above. One may also note that people living in these localities are taxed by the Union and State governments in the form of income tax, wealth tax, excise duties, sales tax etc. and thus, the cream is skimmed off.

FISCAL DECENTRALISATION

The historical Amendments to the Constitution have facilitated the decentralisation—democratic, administrative and financial. The current structure of local government reflects commitment of Central and State governments to decentralisation. A development strategy of decentralisation, however, does not necessarily mean that local government will finance and deliver more services. Many countries have come to realise that strengthening local governments by granting them some fiscal autonomy is an important component of decentralisation.

Three general agreements might be given in support of fiscal decentralisation :

(i) if the expenditure mix and tax rates are determined closer to the people, local public services will improve and local residents will be more satisfied with government services,

(ii) stronger local governments will contribute to nation building because people can identify more closely with local than State and Central governments,

(iii) overall resource mobilisation will be increased because local governments can tax and fast growing parts of their economic base more easily than can the State and Central governments.

The third argument is particularly important and ultimately may make the strongest case for fiscal decentralisation. As the economies of rural areas and secondary cities develop, their taxable capacity and willingness to purchase public services will also develop. It will be very difficult for State and Central governments to capture much of this fiscal surplus because neither income nor consumption taxes typically reach outside the larger cities, local government business and occupation licences, sales taxes, permits and property taxes have a much better chance. The Constitution, therefore, makes provision for assured fiscal decentralisation by way of State Finance Commission.

STATE FINANCE COMMISSION

On the pattern of a Finance Commission being set up under Article 280, the Constitution also provides for constituting Finance Commissions under Articles 243 I (for PRIs) and Article 243 Y (for Urban Local Bodies). Both the Articles read as under :

"243 I. *Constitution of Finance Commission to review financial position*—(1). The Governor of the State shall as soon as may be within one year from the commencement of the Constitution (Seventy-Third Amendment) Act, 1992, and thereafter at the expiration of every fifth year, constitute a Finance Commission to review the financial position of the Panchayats and to make recommendations to the Governor as to—

(a) the principles which should govern—

(i) the distribution between the State and the Panchayats of the net proceeds of taxes, duties, tolls and fees leviable by the State, which may be divided between them under this Part and the allocation between the Panchayats at all levels of their respective shares of such proceeds;

(ii) the determination of taxes, duties, tolls and fees which may be assigned to, or appropriated by, the Panchayats;

(iii) the grants-in-aid to the Panchayats from the Consolidated Fund of the State;

(b) the measures needed to improve the financial position of the Panchayats;

(c) any other matter referred to the Finance Commission by the Governor in the interests of sound finance of the Panchayats.

(2) The legislature of a State may, by law, provide for the composition of the Commission, the qualifications which shall be requisite for appointment as members thereof and the manner in which they shall be selected.

(3) The Commission shall determine their procedure and shall have such powers in the performance of their functions as the Legislature of the State may, by law, confer on them.

(4) The Governor shall cause every recommendation made by the Commission under this article together with an explanatory memorandum as to the action taken thereon to be laid before the Legislature of the State".

Article 243 Y reads as under :

"243Y. *Finance Commission*—The Finance Commission constituted under Article 243I shall also review the financial position of the Municipalities and make recommendations to the Governor as to :

(a) the principles which should govern :

(i) the distribution between the State and the Municipalities of the net proceeds of the taxes, duties, tolls and fees leviable by the State, which may be divided between them under this Part and the allocation between the Municipalities at all levels of their respective shares of such proceeds;

(ii) the grants-in-aid to the Municipalities from Consolidated Fund of the State;

(b) the measures needed to improve the financial position of the Municipalities;

(c) any other matter referred to the Finance Commission by the Governor in the interests of sound finance of the Municipalities.

(2) The Governor shall cause every recommendation made by the Commission under this article together with an explanatory memorandum as to the action taken thereon to be laid before the Legislature of the State".

A comparison of these three Articles of the Constitution reveals the difference on strategy at both the levels. The fundamental difference between the Central Finance Commission and the State Finance Commissions lies in the Constitution itself. While Article 280 envisages the Central Finance Commission to make "distribution of net proceeds of taxes" and also determine the respective shares of such proceeds, the State Finance Commissions set up under Article 243 I and 243 Y are to "formulate the principles which should govern the distribution of net proceeds of taxes" between the State and Local bodies. The principles may only provide a framework for financial devolution rather than suggesting direct devolution. Despite all such lacunae, having emerged in view of the local governments falling in State List but provided an entry into the Constitution by the Union Government, the creation of State Finance Commission is a revolutionary mechanism in the fiscal relationship between the States and the local government units. In absence of any procedure at this intermediary level, the State Finance Commissions were to base on the devolution formulae as having been adopted by successive Central Finance Commissions.

PRINCIPLES OF DEVOLUTION

Historically, 'derivation' and 'need' have been the most common basis of fiscal transfers. Derivation refers to the origin of certain sources of revenue entrusted to the federal government.

The objectives of fiscal transfers depend upon the means

through which they are effected. There are various ways to do this e.g. through revenue sharing, revenue assignment, tax-rental agreement, tax-base sharing, grants-in-aid and other grants and loans and so on. These various means differ in their nature and implications.

Tax base sharing is not applicable in India. Under this system one common base is competitively exploited by both e.g. sharing of tax base of income tax in the U.S.A.

Tax Assignment

In tax assignment, Union Government does not get any share from the tax proceeds, though it levies and collects the revenue. The basic reason for such arrangements is to have some uniformity with respect to the tax-structure and rates and administrative convenience and minimisation of inter-State controversies.

Assignment of tax means transfer of taxation power from a higher level to a lower level of government. Taxation power includes the right to levy the tax, collect the tax and appropriate the proceeds from the tax. Thus, there can be three interpretations of assignment of a tax. In the first case, the higher level government may levy and collect but hand over the entire proceeds to a lower level government. Secondly, the higher level government may levy a tax but allow the lower level government to collect it and retain fully the proceeds therefrom. Finally, the higher level government may transfer a tax to a lower level government, lock, stock and barrel. This is the situation which defines assignment of a tax in its strictest sense. Assignment of a tax however should not be unconditional.

Tax Sharing

In revenue sharing, the Union Government levies and collects the revenues and its net proceeds are shared with the States on some common basis. In India, taxes on Income are compulsorily shared with the States and the Union Excise Duties are voluntarily shared.

Revenue sharing is a coordination device. Provision for such arrangement is founded on the recognition that the most efficient tax-collecting unit may be in many cases considerably larger than the most efficient public spending unit. One of the important problems with respect to tax sharing pertains to working out a generally accepted sharing formula and the delineation of criteria upon which the revenues shall be distributed among the subordinate units. The nature of revenue sharing is different from 'agreed' or 'assigned' taxes and duties.

Transfers

Transfers are used to correct vertical fiscal imbalances. However, before such transfers are effected, it should be ensured that taxes, duties and levies assigned to the lower level government are being optimally tapped. The need for transfers arises because the own revenues of a lower government are generally insufficient to meet the expenditure required for providing services by it. Transfers from the higher level to a lower level of government are made in the form of tax sharing, grants and loans. There are two types of tax sharing mechanism. Under the first method, called global sharing, the whole of the tax revenues forms a pool for sharing with the lower level government. A certain percentage of the total tax revenue is allocated to the constituents. The second method, called scheduler of itemised sharing, involves sharing of revenue from individual higher level taxes. Tax sharing may take the form of a fixed amount or a fixed proportion of tax revenue.

In revenue sharing, tax is certainly collected, not purely for reasons of administrative efficiency but also because certain other national objectives are to be furthered in sharing. There are some differences between revenue sharing and grants. The grant is given out of the total sums raised through all types of tax and non-tax resources considered as a group, while revenue sharing applies to specified taxes and duties or a group of taxes. The second difference lies in the fact that grants are made at the discretion of the grantor with the main purpose of bringing down horizontal fiscal imbalances. Under revenue sharing, all the units where these taxes are levied are entitled to get a share in the net proceeds of specified or all taxes. The main purpose of revenue sharing is to bring down vertical fiscal imbalances and in this process the distribution *inter se* may aim at bringing down horizontal fiscal imbalances also. While under grants-in-aid the grantor government can discriminate between the units under revenue sharing system, all units have to be given their dues on some uniform principles. Barring some of the essential points of differences, the basic objective of achieving vertical and horizontal fiscal equalisation remains common to revenue sharing and grants of unconditional nature, though the relative emphasis on the two objectives differs.

Grants-in-Aid

A vicious circle of weak finances and limited low level services prevails at the local level. Local bodies are caught between two conflicting forces; insistence on a high level of services and precarious finances. They have to depend on the States for funds due to their weak finances. The Zakaria Committee thus finds that "the system of grants-in-aid to local authorities to perform their functions, has developed out of necessity. As the Central and State governments burden the local authorities with more and more functions, they have a moral obligation to assist them to carry out these functions particularly when the principal sources of revenue have already been tapped by them".

Grants are given mainly for the purpose of equalisation though they are often given to further the objectives and priorities of the higher level government. Keeping in mind the criteria of fiscal equity and efficiency, three types of grants may be given. General purpose or unconditional grants are given to offset fiscal disadvantages arising from lower taxable capacity and/or higher unit cost of the services provided. Such equalising grants have to be general and their basic purpose is to enable different local bodies to come up to a minimum standard of services provided. The specific purpose or conditional grants are tied to the achievements of specific objectives. They may be with or without matching requirements. They are used to ensure minimum levels of specified public services to be provided by municipalities. The incentive grants are given for the purpose of encouraging constituents to streamline their operations.

Thus, the designing of sound system of transfers is of vital importance in the context of financial discipline and promotion of local initiatives. The scheme of transfers should be based on well defined objective criteria so that financially weak units are adequately assisted. These may include size of population, level of economic development, availability of infrastructure and minimum service standards. The system of transfers should be so designed that municipalities are not discouraged to mobilise resources on their own. The system should contain inbuilt mechanism to promote internal mobilisation of resources and their judicious management. For this purpose, additional criteria of tax effort, adoption of sound financial management, innovation in the provision of public services and economy in expenditure are adopted and given due weightage. The amount and frequency of transfers should be reasonably predictable. They should be pre-determined.

CHALLENGES BEFORE SFC

At the time of these historic enactments, it was observed that there was a huge municipal deficit that hindered effective delivery of even core municipal services according to established norms of spending for such services. Even after stretching their efforts, the local bodies could not meet the deficit all by themselves.

The past experience of State assistance to local bodies brought with the deficiency of completely ignoring the resource needs and potentials of these institutions. Their increasing demand for resources had no consideration and there was no flexibility in flow of funds in this pattern of assistance. There was no objective assessment of financial requirements and resource rich and resource poor local institutions resulting in serious imbalances in the development of towns and villages and in services rendered by them.

In such a scenario, the Constitution necessitates the setting up of State Finance Commissions every five years. As required under the Constitution, all State governments set up Finance Commissions. These State Finance Commissions were expected to strengthen the local bodies so that they may function as democratic units for the socio-economic development of urban and rural areas in the country. The National Commission on Urbanisation (1988) also felt that "even without an amendment of the Seventh Schedule, a provision to constitute Finance Commission would at least ensure that there is a statutory uniform procedure for devolution of State funds to local bodies. But more important still, this Commission (State Finance Commission) would also have to suggest how there can be additionality of resources. In the ultimate analysis it is generation of new resources which will help in funding urban development rather than merely dividing an inadequate cake between several hungry mouths".

In a developing country like ours mere equalisation of needs is not sufficient, there is every need to promote resource mobilisation efforts and hence the fiscal transfers scheme has to make due allowance for the incentive factor. The State Finance Commission has to keep in mind that the quantum of funds annually devolved to the lower units should not be static or erratic because uncertain State assistance is one of the important reasons for their poor performance. Thus, the pattern of State's funding should be dynamic at least to partially account for the increasing funds requirements of these units. Thus, the task of the First Finance Commission of a State was difficult and arduous in the absence of precedence and it was expected to make *suo motu* all such studies in areas which never existed before. Nevertheless, the work of the First Finance Commission was crucial because it had to pave the way for subsequent Commissions.

While determining the principles for governing the "distribution of the net proceeds of the taxes, duties, tolls and fees leviable by the State", the State Finance Commissions had multipronged challenges before them. They were supposed to "distribute" the "taxes of the State" and for the purpose it was necessary that the Finance Commission should have reviewed the financial position of the State Government. Such a review only was to pave the way for devolving net proceeds of State taxes. It was a virgin area. There have been devolutions between Union and States. But now the Constitution provides for formulating basic principles for fiscal transfers from State to local units, without any precedence. Hence, an arduous task and challenging exercise before the State Finance Commissions.

Further the Tenth Finance Commission forewarned the forthcoming State Finance Commissions in its remarks. The Central Finance Commission feels that "it is necessary to guard against generation of dependency for resources at each sub-national level. The three-tier structure with two layers of Finance Commissions, may generate expectations that in the end it will be the responsibility of the Centre to channel resources through State governments to the Panchayats and urban local bodies. The fiscal system can scarcely meet such expectations. Panchayats and urban local bodies need to have well-defined sources of income and taxing powers. They must be encouraged to exploit them to the full, relying on transfers from the above only at the margin and preferably on a matching basis".

In this backdrop, the succeeding chapters present an analysis of functional domain of urban local bodies, the taxation powers of municipalities and the approach, strategy and recommendations of the State Finance Commissions for bettering the fiscal health of this junior partner in the Indian uni-federal structure.

REFERENCES

Argal, *Municipal Government in India*, Agarwal Press, Allahabad, 1955.

Augmentation of Financial Resources of Urban Local Bodies (Zakaria Committee), 1963.

Background Material for Regional Meet on Devolution of Functional and Financial Powers to ULBs prepared by RCUES, Hyderabad and NIUA, New Delhi, 1998-99, Unpublished.

Bhargava, R.N., *Indian Public Finance*, George Allen and Unwin, London, 1969.

Buehler, A.G., *Public Finance*, McGraw Hill, New York, 1948.

Chelliah, R.J., *Fiscal Policy in Under Developed Countries*, George Allen and Unwin, London, 1969.

Chuge, V.B.(ed.), *States Taxation in Indian Federation*, Mehta Pub. House, Pune, 1979.

Dalton, H., *Principles of Public Finance*, Kegan, London, 1945.
Datta, A. (ed.), *Municipal and Urban India*, IIPA, 1980.
David, W.L. (ed.), *Public Finance, Planning and Economic Development*, Macmillan, London, 1973.
Eckstein,G., *Public Finance*, Prentice Hall of India Pvt. Ltd., New Delhi, 1975.
Hicks, U., *Development from Below*, Oxford, 1961.
Hicks, U.K., *Public Finance*, James Nisbet & Co. Ltd., 1961.
Joshi, M.D., *Mobilisation of State Resources*, Impex India Ltd., New Delhi, 1967.
Mehta, J.K., *Public Finance*, Kitab Mahal, Allahabad, 1972.
Musgrave, R. A., *The Theory of Public Finance*, Kogakusta Co. Ltd., 1959.
Musgrave, R.A. & Musgrave, P.B., *Public Finance in Theory and Practice*, McGraw Hill, Kogakusta, Tokyo, 1959.
Musgrave, R.A. & Peaode, A.T., (eds.), *Classics in the Theory of Public Finance*, St. Martin Press, New York, 1967.
Musgrave, R.A., *Fiscal System*, Yale University Press, 1969.
Nanjundappa, D.M., *Studies in Public Finance*, Asia, 1976.
Peacock, A. T. (ed.), *Public Finance as an Instrument for Economic Development*, OECD Press, 1965.
Prest, A. R., *Public Finance in Theory and Practice*, ELBS, 1975.
Prest, A. R., *Public Finance in Theory and Practice*, Weidenfield and Nicholson, 1968.
Raipuria, K.M., Municipal Finance : Time Rate of Growth, *The Economic Times*, 5th November, 1969.
Report of the National Commission on Urbanisation, Government of India, 1988.
Report of the Tenth Finance Commission, Government of India.
Sati Sahni (ed), *Centre-State Relation*, Vikas, New Delhi, 1984.
Sharma, K.S., *Public Finance*, McMillan, New Delhi, 1975 (Hindi).
Shultz, W. J. and Harriss, C.L., *American Public Finance*, Prentice Hall, New York, 1954.
Stanford, C.T., *Economics of Public Finance*, Pergamon, 1969.
Tripathi, R.N., *Public Finance in Under-developed Countries*, The World Press, Calcutta, 1968.
Tyagi, B.P., *Public Finance*, Jai Prakash Nath & Co., Meerut, 1975.
Venkataraman K., *Local Finance in Perspective*, Bombay, Asia Publishing House, 1964.
Wolfson, D. J., *Public Finance and Development*, John Hopkins University Press, 1979.

1

ANDHRA PRADESH

The word "Andhra" is used to denote a distinct linguistic region, the people of that region and the language spoken by them. It is also used synonymously with "Telugu or Tenugu". Andhra Desa is also known as Trilinga Desa, which means the land covered by the three famous seats of Lord Siva namely Srisailam, Kaleswaram and Draksharama.

The regular history of Andhra Desa begins with 236 B.C., the year of Ashoka's death. During the following centuries, Satavahanas, Sakas, Ikshvakas, Eastern Chalukyas, Kakatiyas ruled the Telugu country. Other dynasties which ruled over the area in succession were the kingdoms of Vijayanagar and Qutab Shahi followed by Mir Qumruddin and his successors, known as Nizams. Slowly and gradually from the 17th century onwards, the British annexed territories of the Nizam and constituted a single province of Madras. After Independence, Telugu speaking areas were separated from the composite Madras State and a new Andhra State came into being on 1st October, 1953.

The area in the State is politically, geographically and historically divided into three regions. The coastal districts (Coastal Andhra or the circars), Rayalseema and Telangana. The first two parts were in the Madras Presidency until October 1, 1953. The third region was in erstwhile State of Hyderabad. With the passing of the State Reorganisation Act, 1956, there was a merger of Hyderabad State and Andhra State and Andhra Pradesh came into being on 1st November, 1956. Before merger Kurnool was the capital and afterwards Hyderabad was made the capital of Andhra Pradesh. Telugu is the predominant language and the next important language is Urdu. Telugu is spoken by eighty per cent of the population, whereas Urdu is spoken by about seven per cent.

Andhra Pradesh is bounded on north by Orissa and Madhya Pradesh, on west by Maharashtra and Karnataka, on south by Tamil Nadu and on east by the Bay of Bengal. The total area of the State is about 275,068 sq. kms. and sea coast is about 974 kms. in length. The State is divided into 23 districts.

Agriculture is the main occupation of about 70 per cent of the people in Andhra Pradesh. About 40 per cent of cultivated area is irrigated. The State is surplus in foodgrains, particularly rice. Forest covers about 23 per cent of the State's area. Several major industries are in operation around Hyderabad and Visakhapatnam. They manufacture machine tools, synthetic, drugs, pharmaceuticals, ships, fertilizers etc. Andhra Pradesh has virtual monopoly of quality chrysolite asbestos in the country. It accounts for about 93 per cent of India's total production of barytes.

URBAN STATUS

Urbanisation in the State is consistently increasing. The State accounts for more than eight per cent urban population to the country's urban population (1991), whereas the proportion was less than eight (7.83 per cent) in 1981. However, the decennial growth rate of urban population decreased from 48.62 per cent in 1981 to 42.64 per cent in 1991, whereas proportion of urban population to total population recorded contrary. It increased from 23.32 per cent in 1981 to 26.84 per cent in 1991. The total number of town in the State was found decreasing, whereas number of class one towns increased over the decades. The population inhabiting in class one towns is alarming. About two-third (66.88 per cent) of urban population lives in these big towns, according to 1991 census. The proportion was a little more than half (53.76 per cent) in 1981, less than half (48.36 per cent) in 1971 and still less in previous decades.

Out of 23 districts in the State, Hyderabad district is an urban district accounting about 4.5 per cent of total population in the State. Rangareddy is another district having 47.1 per cent urban population and sharing 3.7 per cent of the total population. Two districts have urbanisation between 30-40 per cent accounting about more than one-tenth of the total urban population. About half of the districts (11) have level of urbanisation between 20-30, inhabiting more than half of the urban population. The eight districts are less urbanised (10-20 per cent) and account a little less than one-third (31.3 per cent) of the urban population.

Cuddapah and Ramagundam are two towns which show maximum growth rate (109 and 158 per cent respectively) in 1981-91, Hindupur (87.18%), Visakhapatnam (74.3%), Karimnagar (72.25%), Hyderabad (67%), Chittoor (54.5%), Tirupati (52.57%), Khammam (50.52%) and Ongole (50.21%) are other class one towns having recorded rapid urbanisation in 1991. While Ramagundam (159.7%), Nellore (77.5%), Karimnagar (76.1%), Khammam (73.5%), Tirupati (72.1%), Mehbubnagar (69.1%), Chirala (67.1%), Visakhapatnam (66.11%), Warangal (61.5%), Ongole (60.1%), Veemavaram (59.8%), Nizamabad (58.3%), Cuddapah (55.8%), Vijayawada (55.3%), Proddutur (51.2%) and Kurnool (51.0%) were the towns which showed tremendous increase in 1981. Kothagudam town recorded the lowest growth (7.55%) in 1991 while Tenali (15.9%) was less urbanised in 1981.

As regards urban literacy, the Sate commands appreciable position with 56.8 per cent in female population. Chittoor is the most literate district (62.9%), while Nizamabad is lowest with 50.1 per cent. In male literacy Chittoor (71.2%), Warangal (71.0%) and Visakhapatnam (70.4%) top the list, while nine other districts have more literacy in male population than that of the State. In female literacy Chittoor occupies the top position with 54.2 per cent followed by Visakhapatnam (52.5%), West Godavari (52.6%), Krishna (53.8%), Nellore (52%), Hyderabad (50.2%), Khammam (50.1%) and Nalgonda (50.1%) In urban centres Tirupati occupies the top place with 68.84 per cent literacy, followed by Karimnagar (67.48%), Chittoor (66.95%), Mehbubnagar (64.05%), Khammam (64%), Ongole (63.74%),

Visakhapatnam (63.22%), Machilipatnam (62.32%), Anantapur (61.82%), Warangal (61.43%), Vijayawada (60.60%), Nellore (60.15%) and Tenali (60.26%)

There are two Acts dealing with municipal affairs in the State i.e. the Municipal Corporations Act, 1956 and the Municipalities Act 1965.

FUNCTIONAL DOMAIN

The urban local bodies in the State are entrusted with a large number of obligatory as well as discretionary functions.

Municipal Corporation

Duties and Powers of Municipal Authorities

The Corporation has to make adequate provisions for :

(a) erection of substantial boundary marks,

(b) the watering, scavenging and cleansing of all public streets and places in the city and the removal of all sweeping therefrom,

(c) the collection, removal, treatment and disposal of sewage, offensive matter and rubbish and the preparation of compost manure from such sewage, offensive matter and rubbish,

(d) construction of drains and drainage works after collecting the prescribed fees fixed by the commissioner,

(e) maintenance and cleansing of drains and drainage works and the construction, maintenance and cleansing of public latrines, water-closets, urinals and similar conveniences,

(f) the lightening of public buildings vested in the corporation, public streets and municipal markets,

(g) the maintenance of a municipal office and of all public monuments and open spaces and other property vesting in the corporation,

(h) the naming or numbering of streets and of public places

in the corporation and the numbering of premises,

(i) the maintenance, change, regulation of places for disposal of dead and the provision of new places for the purpose and disposing of unclaimed dead bodies,

(j) the construction of acquisition and maintenance of public markets and slaughter houses and the regulation of all markets and slaughter houses,

(k) the construction and acquisition and maintenance of cattle pounds,

(l) public vaccination,

(m) the reclamation of unhealthy localities, the removal of noxious vegetation and generally the abatement of all nuisances,

(n) the registration of births and deaths,

(o) the construction, maintenance, alteration and improvement of streets, bridges, subways, culverts, causeways or the like,

(p) the removal of obstructions and projections in or upon streets, bridges and other public places,

(q) the management and maintenance of all municipal water works and the construction or acquisition of new works necessary for a sufficient supply of water for public and private purposes,

(r) preventing the spread of infectious diseases,

(s) the securing or removal of dangerous buildings and places,

(t) the improvement of the city,

(u) the provision of public parks, gardens, playgrounds and recreation grounds,

(v) the fulfilment of any obligation imposed upon it,

(w) the provision of relief to destitute persons in the city in times of famine and scarcity and the establishment and maintenance of relief works in such times,

(x) make payments for the maintenance and treatment in any institution suitable for anti-rabic treatment,

(y) make payments for the maintenance and treatment at any asylum, hospital or house suitable for lunatics.

Discretionary Duties

The corporation at its discretion may provide wholly or partly for all or any of the following matters :

- (a) the organisation, maintenance or management of institutions within or without the city for the care of persons who are infirm, sick or incurable or for the care and training of blind, deaf, mute or otherwise disabled persons or of handicapped children,
- (b) the organisation, maintenance or management of maternity and infant welfare homes or centres,
- (c) the provision of milk to expectant or nursing mothers, infants or school children,
- (d) the organisation, maintenance or management of chemical or bacteriological laboratories for the examination or analysis of water, food or drugs, for the detection of disease or for researches connected with public health,
- (e) dairies or farms for the supply, distribution and processing of milk products for the benefit of the residents,
- (f) the construction and maintenance in public streets or places of drinking fountains for human beings and water troughs for animals,
- (g) the planting and maintenance of trees on road sides and elsewhere,
- (h) the providing of entertainment in public places or places of public resorts,
- (i) the holding of exhibition, athletics or games,
- (j) the regulation of lodging houses, camping grounds, and rest-houses in the city,
- (k) the maintenance of ambulance service,
- (l) the construction, establishment and maintenance of theatres, places of entertainment, rest-houses and other public buildings,
- (m) the organisation or maintenance in times of scarcity of shops or stalls for the sale of necessities of life,

(n) the building or purchase and maintenance of dwellings for municipal officers and servants,

(o) the grant of loans to the municipal officers and servants for construction of houses and purchase of house sites and vehicles,

(p) the organisation, maintenance or management of transport facilities for the conveyance of the public goods,

(q) the furtherance of educational objects, and the making of grants to educational institutions,

(r) the establishment and maintenance or the aiding of libraries, museums and art galleries, botanical or zoological collections and the purchase or construction of building therefor,

(s) the destruction of vermins, birds or animals causing a danger or nuisance and the confinement of destruction of stray dogs,

(t) contribution towards any public fund raised for the relief of human suffering within the city,

(u) the granting of rewards for information for correct registration of vital statistics,

(v) the acquisition and the maintenance of grazing grounds and the establishment and maintenance of a stud farm,

(w) establishing and maintaining a farm or factory for the disposal of sewage,

(x) supplying, constructing and maintaining receptacles, fittings, pipes and other appliances on or for the use of premises receiving and conducting the sewage thereof into drains under the control of the Corporation,

(y) granting rewards for information regarding the infringement of any provisions of the Act, rules, laws, orders etc.,

(z) laying out new streets and acquiring land for that purpose or for the construction of buildings or cartilages thereof to abut on such streets,

(aa) the building or purchase and maintenance of suitable dwellings for the poor and working classes, (ab) the provision of shelter to destitutes or homeless persons and any form of poor relief,

(ac) the building or purchase and maintenance of sanitary stables or byres for horses, ponies, cattle used for hackney carriages or carts or for milchkine,

(ad) the surveying of buildings or lands,

(ae) taking measures to meet any calamity affecting the public in the city,

(af) the making of a contribution towards any public ceremony or entertainment in the city,

(ag) the construction, purchase, organisation, maintenance, extension and management of tramways, trackless trains, mechanically propelled transport facilities for the conveyance of the public,

(ah) the purchase, maintenance, management and conduct of any undertaking for the supply of electric energy or gas to the public or the subsidising of any such undertaking,

(ai) the acquisition of immovable or movable property for any purpose including payment of the cost of investigation, surveys or examinations in relation to or the construction or adaptation of buildings necessary for such purposes,

(aj) preparation and presentation of address to persons of distinctions,

(ak) maintaining, aiding and suitably accommodating schools for primary education,

(al) provide parking places, public landing places, halting places for vehicles including motor vehicles and levy fees for their use,

(am) the taking of any measures likely to promote public safety, health, convenience or instruction,

(an) swimming pools, public wash houses, bathing places and other institutions designed for the benefit of the residents.

MUNICIPALITIES

The municipalities are obliged to discharge following functions :

1. The council, so far as the funds at its disposal permit, causes the public streets to be lighted and for that purpose provides such lamps and works.
2. The council provides and maintains a sufficient system of drains,
3. The council has to make adequate arrangements for the regular sweeping and cleaning of streets and removal of sweepings therefrom.
4. The council causes the public streets and bridges to be maintained and repaired,
5. The council gives names to all public streets/roads.
6. The council causes a number to be affixed or painted to the side or outerdoor of any building or to some place at the entrance of the premises.
7. The council may, with the sanction of the Government, direct the construction of water-works and may cause existing works for the supply of water to be maintained and supplied with water.
8. The council registers all births and deaths occurring in the municipality.

TAX JURISDICTION

Municipal Corporation

The Corporation can impose the following taxes mandatorily :

(i) taxes on lands and buildings,
(ii) octroi,
(iii) taxes on vehicles,
(iv) taxes on animals and boats,
(v) taxes on advertisements, and
(vi) a tax on transfer of immovable property.

Optional Taxes

In addition to above, the corporation may impose any of the following taxes :

(i) taxes on entertainments, and
(ii) any other tax subject to the previous sanction of the Government.

Municipality

Every council has by resolution to levy the following obligatory taxes :

(i) A property tax,
(ii) A tax on carriages and carts, and
(iii) A tax on animals.

Optional Taxes

The Council may by resolution and with the previous sanction of the Government also levy :

(i) a tax on advertisement, and
(ii) duty on transfer of property.

FISCAL DEVOLUTION

The State Finance Commission in Andhra Pradesh was constituted as a sequel to the Constitution Amendments. The Governor constituted a five-member Commission on 21st June, 1994. It was headed by a former Registrar of a university and consisted of both bureaucrats as well as academicians. In making its recommendations, the commission had regard among other considerations to :

1. the resources of the State Government on account of expenditure on liabilities,

2. the maintenance and upkeep of capital assets like buildings, roads, water supply schemes by local bodies and the norms on the basis of which specified amounts are recommended for the maintenance of assets and the manner of monitoring such expenditure,
3. the requirements of local bodies for modernising of expenditure i.e. computerisation of accounts and upgrading the standards and non-developmental sectors, servicing and the manner in which such expenditure can be monitored,
4. the requirements of the local bodies for meeting the non-plan revenue expenditure on staff and administration etc. also keeping in view the potential for raising their resources.

The Commission utilised the services of a number of experts also. The Commission submitted its report in May 1997.

EXISTING RESOURCES

Motor Vehicles Tax

As regards the capital and maintenance requirements for municipal roads, the Commission recommends enhancement of Motor Vehicle Tax compensation to Municipal Bodies. As the enhanced amount would be available for roads, the Commission does not recommend any further grant for maintenance of municipal roads.

Water Rates

The Commission feels that the Municipalities should be able to meet the maintenance expenditure from the user charges i.e. Tap Rates etc. by increasing the rates. The rate of Rs. 40 per month fixed by Government towards Water Tap Charges is not sufficient in some cases. The Commission therefore recommends that Municipal councils may be empowered to enhance the rates to run the schemes at least on no profit and no loss basis.

Property Tax

The Commission recommends that there should not be any interference by Government in the matters relating to taxation where it adversely affects the revenues. The Commission further recommends that the general revision of taxes may be conducted once in three years.

No house however humble may be and should be exempted from the tax.

Entertainment Tax

Whenever exemptions or concessions are granted by the Government in Entertainment Tax, local bodies should be given compensation to that extent.

Stamp Duty

The rate of surcharge on stamp duty may be increased from 5 per cent to 10 per cent.

DEVOLUTION OF FUNDS

In the approach for devolution, the Commission identified the basic civic functions to be discharged by the local bodies and also the important developmental functions entrusted to them. The Commission therefore recommends an amount of Rs. 8 crore each to Municipal Corporations of Hyderabad, Visakhapatnam and Vijayawada and an amount of Rs. 5 crore to each of the remaining four Municipal Corporations as a block grant to be utilised for their felt needs.

Global Sharing

The Commission recommends an additional devolution of 10.93 per cent of the total Tax and Non-Tax revenues of the State. The percentage for Rural Bodies is 9.14 and that of Urban Bodies is 1.79.

Keeping in view the requirements of the local bodies for the core functions, the Commission arrives at the Divisible Pool as the modest one. The Commission recommends that 39.24 per cent of State's Revenue both from Taxes and Non-Taxes be entitled to the local bodies. This entitlement, in view of the Commission, would give a firm backing so that the local bodies can prepare perspective plans for the development of the areas. The devolution may be allocated on the basis of matching contribution from the local bodies.

Inter se Distribution

The Commission recommends to categorise Gram Panchayats as Advanced, Ordinary, Backward and Tribal. The amount may be distributed on the basis of the formula :

Ordinary	x
Advanced	2/3 x
Backward	5/3 x
Tribal	8/3 x

The amount to Mandals be allocated with reference to plinth area of the buildings (school) and mileage of roads.

Regarding Zila Parishads, the entitlement will have to be worked out in respect of increase of per capita grant, pension for non-teaching Panchayat Raj employees. The additional requirements for Rural Water Supply, Roads and roads maintenance etc. may be allocated with reference to the plinth area/length of roads and number of borewells and C.P.W.S. Schemes etc. in each district.

As regards urban local bodies, the Commission addresses the amount required for development activities and regular administration and identifies per capita grade-wise requirement as under :

Selection Grade	Rs. 62
Special Grade	Rs. 92
First Grade	Rs. 111

Second Grade	Rs. 125
Third Grade	Rs. 130

On this basis, the additional requirement is worked out to be Rs. 94 crore per annum. The *inter se* distribution of this amount among various Municipal Councils may be made as per the amounts indicated against each grade by giving the following weightage :

Population	40 per cent
Area (excluding slum area)	40 per cent
Area of slums in each Municipality	20 per cent

Assigned Revenue

The urban local bodies are assigned revenues by the State Government besides the payment of compensation. The entire five per cent surcharge on Stamp Duty and Entertainment Tax collected in urban areas are paid to Municipal Councils and Corporations after deducting collection charges. The urban local bodies are paid compensation towards Profession Tax and Motor Vehicle Tax besides a compensation for the abolition of Octroi in Telengana region.

The Commission recommends that the existing system of government collecting Profession Tax be continued.

The Commission recommends to pass on ten per cent of the receipts from the Betting Tax to the Hyderabad Municipal Corporation.

It recommends that five per cent of the amount collected may be deducted as collection charges and the balance of 95 per cent be transferred to local bodies. The amounts collected in urban areas may be allocated to Municipal Councils and Corporations on the basis of urban population. Similarly the amount collected in rural areas may be allocated to Panchayat Raj Institutions on the basis of rural population.

The Commission recommends to enhance the property tax compensation by five per cent every year.

The Commission recommends that the Octroi compensation

may be increased by ten per cent every year.

The Commission further recommends that an amount of Rs. 20 crore may be allocated as Motor Vehicle Tax compensation to the municipal bodies as an initial step.

Grants-in-Aid

In view of the increased responsibilities of the Municipalities, the Commission recommends that the per capita grant to Municipal Bodies may be increased from Rs. 4 to Rs. 8.

The Commission recommends the Government to consider sanction of incentive grant to the local bodies which helps in propagating family planning and achieving highest targets in a number of operations.

The Commission recommends an additional grant of Rs. 50,000 as and when a Gram Panchayat is converted into a Municipality and when a new Municipal Corporation is constituted, a special grant of Rs. 25 lakh is sanctioned to the Corporation.

TFC Award

The Commission recommends that Rs. 18 crore may be provided from 1997-98 onwards for water supply schemes in Municipal areas after setting off the Tenth Finance Commission grant.

Miscellaneous

1. It should be made compulsory for any person applying for a loan to Government or any Corporation or for any purpose including telephone, electricity, water tap or registration as a contractor or small scale industry etc. to submit a 'No-Tax Certificate' from the Panchayat/ Municipality alongwith the application.
2. At the earliest possible opportunity the State should transfer the functions contemplated in the Constitution to the local bodies. As and when the State Government decides to devolve any of the functions of Schedule

XII, the finances intended for the discharge of the functions should also be devolved on the Municipal Bodies alongwith the functionaries and empowerment in discharge of the responsibility.

3. Government may provide Rs. 31 crore per annum for the years 1998-99 and 1999-2000 for developmental works in the Municipal Bodies.
4. The Government should give grant-in-aid to the Municipal Bodies towards payment to the non-teaching Municipal Employees.
5. The Commission feels that designing correct computer programs for each type of locality is very essential. Hence, the Commission recommends computerisation of local bodies.
6. The possibilities of levying a fee of Rs. 50 per annum per phone by the local body concerned may be considered by the State Government and the matter be taken up with the Government of India to amend the concerned Acts if necessary.
7. Consequent to increase in the population of Scheduled Castes and Scheduled Tribes, the percentage of earmarking of funds for these weaker sections be increased to eighteen per cent and eight per cent respectively.
8. Government should take effective steps for preparing and publishing the consolidated annual administration reports on the accounts of local bodies.
9. Social Audit may be introduced in the local bodies.
10. Provisions relating to the percentage of devolution may be incorporated in the Acts.
11. The Government should see that rules relating to placing financial statements before the Standing Committee are followed. Effective steps should be taken to get the consolidated audit and review reports and the accounts are prepared and placed on the floor of the Assembly.
12. The Second Finance Commission to be appointed early

in 1998 much earlier to the appointment of the XI National Finance Commission so that the Second Finance Commission could give its report before XI National Commission starts functioning.

13. The Commission recommends the creation of a Cell in Secretariat to monitor the recommendations of the State Finance Commission.

It is observed that many major recommendations destined to better the fiscal health of local bodies are not accepted by the State Government. A few are still under consideration. The Second Commission has been constituted.

2

ASSAM

The political map of Assam has undergone several changes and as a result, Assam of today is a reduced region. It is remarkable that the people of Assam have reconciled to Union Government's bid to bring about integration in this region by fragmenting the State into several units.

Geographically, Assam is a shadow of its former self. It has been reduced to one-third of its original size in a few decades. In 1947, Assam had an area of over two lakhs sq. km., excluding the then North-East Frontier Agency, the present Arunachal Pradesh. Today, the area of Assam is only 78,523 sq. km. comprising 23 districts. The State covers about 2.39 per cent of the total area of the country.

Scholars are not agreed on the origin of the name 'Assam'. Some say that Assam is called so, because of its unequal terrain. During the epic period, Assam was known as Projyothis and later as Kamrupa. Guwahati, the pulsating centre of Assam is an ancient town whose history goes back to the Puranic days.

Assam, which is situated in the north-east corner of India is surrounded by Bhutan and Arunachal Pradesh on the north, Nagaland and Manipur on the east, Meghalaya and Mizoram on the south and Bangladesh, Tripura and West Bengal on the west. Only a narrow strip of sub-mountain region of Himalayas connects Assam with the Indian mainland. Assam is dominated by Brahmaputra river. It has 120 tributaries. Rainfall in Assam is one of the highest in the world.

The State is the largest one in the north east region. About eleven per cent of its population inhabits in 87 urban centres.

The State has been experiencing higher decennial growth. Four class one towns account for more than one-third of its total urban population. The State has been experiencing slow but steady increase in urban population. While the total population recorded an increase of more than 24 per cent in 1981-91 decade, the growth in urban population was increased to about 9 per cent during the period.

Municipal Administration

It was in the 1836 that a Town Improvement Committee was formed in Guwahati for the first time followed by Barpeta, Mangaldoi, Golaghat and North Lakhimpur. The sole objective of these Committees was sanitation. The Bengal Municipal Act, 1842 was not introduced in Assam and this Act was replaced in 1850 by the Town Improvement Act, 1850. In 1853, the Guwahati Municipal Board was constituted. The financial condition of the Board was not sound from the time of its establishment.

Thereafter, the District Improvement Act, 1864, and District Towns Act, 1863 were enacted repealing earlier enactments. The 1868 Town Act had the provision to constitute Town Committees where that Act was extended, whose main function was to advise the District Magistrate on general matters and express its opinion on the budget submitted to it by the District Magistrate. However, under 1868 Act only Guwahati Municipal Board and Sylhat Town Committee could be constituted. Since 1874 several Municipal Boards viz. Dibrugarh, Sylhet, Goalpara came into being.

Ripon Resolution in 1882 gave a thrust to the creation of Local Self Government in India. Government of Assam accepted some of the suggestions mentioned in the Ripon Resolution. Accordingly, the Boards which applied for such introductions were allowed to divide the Municipal area into wards for election of members and finally the Boards were permitted to re-elect their own Chairman.

In 1887, the Bengal Municipal Act, 1884 was adopted in Assam so as to obviate the constraints regarding imposition of water tax and latrine tax as the Act of 1876 did not empower the Board to levy these taxes. However, both these Acts of 1876 and 1884 remained operative in Assam till 1923.

However, the concept of Local Self Government in Assam can be said to have received its full meaning when the Assam Municipal Act, 1956 was enacted. This Act provides the State a more up-to-date scientific and suitable Municipal law to cope with the altered requirements of time after Independence. There is a separate Act, the Guwahati Municipal Corporation Act, 1969 for managing the local affairs in lone Guwahati Municipal Corporation area.

FUNCTIONAL DOMAIN

Urban local bodies in the State are entrusted a large number of mandatory as well as discretionary functions.

Municipal Corporation

The Guwahati Municipal Corporation has to perform following functions :

Obligatory

(a) the construction, maintenance and cleaning of drains and drainage works and public latrines, urinals and similar conveniences,
(b) the construction and maintenance of works and means for water supply,
(c) the scavenging, removal and disposal of filth, rubbish and obnoxious and polluted matters,
(d) the regulation of unhealthy localities,
(e) the reclamation of places for disposal of dead,
(f) the registration of births and deaths,
(g) public vaccination and inoculation,
(h) measures for preventing and checking the spread of dangerous and contagious diseases,
(i) the establishment and maintenance of hospitals,

dispensaries and maternity and child welfare centres,
- (j) the construction and maintenance of municipal markets and slaughter houses,
- (k) the regulation and abatement of offensive or dangerous trades or practices,
- (l) maintenance of fire brigade,
- (m) the securing or removal of dangerous buildings and places,
- (n) the construction, maintenance, alteration and improvement of public roads, streets, bridges, culverts, causeways etc.,
- (o) the removal of obstructions and projections and unauthorised occupation in or upon streets, bridges etc.,
- (p) the naming and numbering of streets and premises,
- (q) the maintenance of a municipal office, and of all public monuments,
- (r) the establishment and maintenance of cattle pounds,
- (s) the construction and maintenance of residential quarters for its staff,
- (t) the maintenance of ambulance service,
- (u) the provision of public parks, gardens, playgrounds and recreation grounds,
- (v) the lighting, watering and cleansing of public streets,
- (w) the provision of relief to destitute persons in times of famine and scarcity,
- (x) taking measures against food adulteration,
- (y) the fulfilment of any other obligation imposed.

Discretionary Functions

The Corporation may at its discretion make provisions for the following :

1. the establishment, aiding or maintenance of educational institutions, libraries, museums etc.
2. the establishment and maintenance of and aid to stadia, gymnasia and places for sports etc.
3. the planting and care of trees on road sides,

4. the survey of buildings and lands,
5. the registration of marriages,
6. the taking of a census of population,
7. the civic receptions to persons of distinction,
8. the providing of music or other entertainments,
9. the holding of fairs and exhibitions,
10. the organisation, maintenance or management of institutions for care of destitutes, infirms, sick etc.,
11. the organisation, maintenance or management of maternity and infant welfare houses,
12. the purchase and maintenance of dwelling houses for corporation employees,
13. any measures for the welfare of corporation employees,
14. the organisation and management of chemical or bacteriological laboratories or the examination or analysis of water, food adulteration etc.,
15. the establishment and maintenance of veterinary hospitals,
16. the organisation, construction, maintenance and management of swimming pools, public houses etc.,
17. dairies and farms for supply, distribution and processing of milk products,
18. the provision of milk to expectant or nursing mothers or infants or school children,
19. the construction and maintenance of drinking fountains,
20. the regulation of lodging houses, camping grounds etc.,
21. the construction, establishment and maintenance of theatres, cinemas, petrol pumps etc.,
22. the organisation and maintenance of shops or stalls,
23. the prevention of cruelty to animals,
24. contribution towards any public fund raised for human relief,
25. the acquisition and maintenance of grazing grounds,
26. establishing and maintaining farm or factory for sewage disposal,
27. the construction and maintenance of warehouses and godowns,

28. the construction and maintenance or regulation of garages, sheds and stands for vehicles etc.,
29. the organisation and management of cottage industries, handicraft centres etc.,
30. establishing labour welfare centres for its employees,
31. the maintenance of a band orchestra,
32. establishing or assisting in the establishment of information centres,
33. arranging for the publication of information or for the delivery of lectures etc.,
34. preparing or joining in the preparation of films, exhibitions etc.,
35. contributing towards the expenses of cooperative organisation for promoting and development of trade, industry etc.,
36. the acquisition of property,
37. any measures to improve public safety, health, welfare etc.,
38. the regulation of trade and commerce,
39. the regulation of the distribution of electric power,
40. the regulation of streams, nallas and pipes carrying water, rubbishes and effluents,
41. urban planning including town planning,
42. regulation of land-use and construction of buildings,
43. planning for economic and social development,
44. slum improvement and upgradation,
45. urban poverty alleviation.

MUNICIPALITIES

The municipalities are left to make provisions on their discretion for the following matters :

1. construction, maintenance and improvement of roads, tramways, bridges, squares etc.,
2. planning, preservation and felling of trees and bamboos,
3. supply of water, and the lighting and watering of roads,
4. erection and maintenance of town hall offices,

5. payment of gratuity to its staff,
6. establishment and maintenance of a market,
7. establishment and maintenance of schools, hostels etc.,
8. establishment and maintenance of poor houses, hospitals, dispensaries etc.,
9. payment of the expenses of poorer inhabitants for treatment of special diseases,
10. employment of public vaccinations and the promotion of free vaccination,
11. acquiring, keeping and equipping of open spaces for ventilation, public recreation etc.,
12. industrial and other technical training and employment of medical and veterinary practitioners,
13. establishment and maintenance of veterinary dispensaries,
14. payment of contribution towards public fund raised for human relief,
15. appointment and payment of qualified persons to prevent and treat diseases of horse, cattle etc.,
16. improvement of the breed of horses and cattle,
17. establishment and maintenance of or granting of aid to public libraries, reading rooms etc.,
18. payment of fire brigade services,
19. provision of burial and burning grounds,
20. taking of census,
21. holding of fairs and industrial exhibitions,
22. payment of rewards for the destruction of noxious animals or unclaimed dogs etc.,
23. preparation of compost manure,
24. prevention of the spread of dangerous diseases,
25. establishment and maintenance of dairies,
26. other work of public utility,
27. payment of contribution to other local authority,
28. payment for anti-malarial and other projects of social services

TAXATION POWERS

For carrying out the functions entrusted, the Corporation is empowered to impose following levy compulsorily :

(a) property taxes,
(b) a tax on draught animals, vessels and vehicles,
(c) a tax on advertisement,
(d) a duty on the transfer of property,
(e) a tax on profession, trades and callings.

In addition the Corporation may impose all or any of the followings :

(a) a betterment tax on properties whose value may have increased as a result of town planning scheme,
(b) a tax on dogs,
(c) a toll on vehicles and animals entering the city,
(d) market dues on persons exposing goods for sale,
(e) a drainage tax where a system of drainage has been introduced,
(f) a tax on pilgrims resorting periodically to a shrine,
(g) a tax on passengers and goods carried by roads or inland waterways,
(h) a toll on new bridges,
(i) octroi,
(j) any other tax with the prior approval of the State Government.

Municipalities

The Act authorises the municipalities to levy at their discretion following taxes, fees and tolls :

(a) a tax on holdings assessed on their annual value,
(b) a water tax,
(c) a lighting tax,
(d) a latrine tax,
(e) a drainage tax,
(f) a tax on private markets,
(g) licence fee on carts, carriages and animals used for

riding or burden,

(h) a fee on the registration of dogs and cattle,

(i) a fees on boats mooring within the limit,

(j) tolls on bridges,

(k) a betterment fee on holdings whose value has increased due to improvement schemes,

(l) fees for setting up and maintenance of fire brigade,

(m) fees for conducting any scheme of social service for the improvement of public health,

(n) licence fee on boats,

(o) any other tax, fee on the approval of the State government.

FISCAL DEVOLUTION

The Assam State Finance Commission was constituted on 23rd June, 1995 by a separate Act enacted by the State Legislative Assembly. The five-member Commission was headed by a retired bureaucrat and consisted of an advocate, a retired professor of commerce and a retired bureaucrat, besides the Secretary to the Government in the Department of Finance working as member-secretary. The Commission submitted its report on 28th February, 1996..

Reforms in Existing Sources

The Commission has given certain recommendations to optimise the existing sources.

Property Tax

The current tax domain of the local bodies is very narrow and relatively inelastic. Taxes levied and collected by the local bodies do not yield substantial revenue and, therefore, they depend on higher transfer from the Government. The property tax happens to be the most universal and stable local tax. This source so far has become not only buoyant but also has run into serious problems of record keeping, assessment, valuation, administration and enforcement resulting in decline in revenue. The Commission recommends a reform to it. The coverage of the building land tax where confined to residential structure should be extended to cover all structures. Taxes should be levied by area rather than at a flat rate per structure. The highest rate tax may be levied on the users of community halls, marriage halls, food and lodging establishments, shops and factories.

Fees

The Commission feels that the fees presently charged on licence etc. need rational revision taking into consideration the prevailing cost structure.

NEW TAX/CHARGES

Vacant Land

The Commission suggests that local bodies should levy tax on vacant land.

User Charges

The Commission recommends the levying of user charges for the services rendered by local bodies on parks, public toilets, public health centres etc.

Registration Fee

The Commission strongly recommends that issue of birth and death certificates should be the responsibility of the local bodies. They should issue the certificate on the basis of registration made by them and collect the registration fees.

TRANSFER OF FUNDS

Transfer of fund by the State government by way of share of State taxes plays a vital role in the functioning of the local bodies and constitutes a major component of the total revenues of the local bodies. The purpose of transfer is to provide a satisfactory level of services to the community. Share of taxes may not fulfil the needs of the local bodies and dependence of the local bodies on State government is also not desirable. It is necessary that the local bodies should explore all possibilities to generate their own resources and minimise their expenditure or revenue account maintaining optimum number of staff so that the expenditure can balance the earnings. A gap, if any, can only be partially met by the transfer of fund by way of share of State taxes to meet only the obligatory liabilities of the local bodies to cover services to the locality. The Commission therefore recommends that the present system of transfer of share of State taxes to local bodies may continue with a minor exception of allocating to rural local bodies a share of Motor Vehicle Tax to the extent of 10 per cent. In view of this the Commission recommends that the existing rate of 30 per cent of the net proceeds of Motor Vehicle Tax to be shared by the urban local bodies may be enhanced to 40 per cent to ccver the rural local bodies from the divisible pool. Out of the divisible pool, 75 per cent may be transferred to the local urban bodies and the balance 25 per cent may be transferred to rural local bodies.

The *inter se* distribution among the urban local bodies may be made on the basis of number of vehicles of each urban local body and among the rural local bodies as per population of the latest census. To sum up the total percentage of share of State Taxes for transfer to local bodies both urban and rural should be 2 per cent in each financial year. On this basis the year-wise amount for devolution of taxes to local bodies comes as under :

Year	*Share of Tax as to be provided for transfer to local bodies (in crore)*
1996-97	Rs. 17.83
1997-98	Rs. 20.06
1998-99	Rs. 22.50
1999-2000	Rs. 25.16
2000-2001	Rs. 28.20

Tenth Finance Commission

In order to distribute the award of the Tenth Finance Commission by the State government to the local bodies, the Commission recommends that the amount may be distributed on the basis of the population of each local body as per 1971 census. Further, an equivalent amount as in 1999-2000 may be made available for the first year of the subsequent Central Finance Commission i.e. for 2000-2001. This amount may be provided out of the State plan fund.

Maintenance of Data

The Commission feels that in order to make an assessment of the financial requirement and potentials of local bodies by the State government and also by the State Finance Commission, it is essential to maintain a reliable, systematic and regular data base with minimum level of information. Most of the informations may be available but since no standard format for data maintenance exists for the present, it becomes difficult to compile such information. Hence, the need was felt for standardised and comparable local finance data. Further, lack of uniformity in the maintenance of Accounts and the lack of regular audit of Accounts, also lead to complexities of available local finance data. Accountability is also one of the reason for having a sound data base. The Commission has suggested the nature of data to be compiled and has devised a set of formats and registers for the purpose. It is also of the view that massive efforts will be required on the part of local bodies in order to make the establishment of a Local Finance Data Base a reality and they would require fund for it. The Commission, therefore, recommends that the initial funding and technical expertise for the purpose be provided through a plan scheme of the State. Due to lack of infrastructure, it may not be possible to complete maintenance of the Registers. The Commission, however, suggests that these registers are maintained properly and effectively invariably from the beginning of the Ninth Plan. The initial expenditure for the purpose may be Rs. 1000 per local body for the first year and 50 per cent of this amount in subsequent years. This fund may be provided as grants to local bodies and by the State government within the plan outlay.

Provision of Services

It is the primary responsibility of the local bodies to provide and maintain certain basic infrastructure. After considering all the aspects, the Commission feels that a minimum physical standard of basic services should be attained by each local body. The Commission recommends that in order to implement the schemes, the staff of the concerned departments of the State government executing the schemes presently may continue to execute the schemes on behalf of the local bodies without their services being placed at the disposal of the local bodies so that the liability for their salary does not fall on the local bodies.

MINIMUM PHYSICAL STANDARD OF SERVICES

1.	Water Supply	100 per cent population to be covered	Piped water supply with sewerage 150 lpcd. Piped water supply without sewerage 70 lpcd. 40 lpcd with spot sources. Public stand posts in low revenue settlements. One source for 20 families within a walking distance of 10 mts.

2. Sanitation/Sewerage

(a) 100 per cent city area to be covered by sewer system with treatment facilities in large urban centres.

(b) Low cost sanitation method for other urban areas.

(c) In low income areas of large cities community latrines may be provided.

3.	Solid waste collection and disposal	All the solid wastes generated should be collected and disposed of. 100 per cent collection of generated wastes with its proper disposal. Hazardous waste must be incinerated in all areas.
4.	Primary Education	Fulfilment of national goal of universalisation of elementary education of children upto 14 years of age. Provisions of primary schools in all areas : (a) at least three large all weather rooms with teaching material. (b) at least one teacher per class room. (c) one primary school for every 3000-4000 population. (d) In order to improve environment at the upper primary stage, specially for girls the walking distance should normally be 2 km. In case of primary school, this standard is 1 km.
5.	Primary Health Centre	Fulfilment of national goal of health for all by 2000 A.D. 1 public health centre for 20,000-30,000 population. 1 sub centre for 3000-5000 population. 1 community health centre for 1 lakh population.

Miscellaneous

In addition, the Commission has made recommendations on various associated aspects. These are :

(a) The Commission recommends that outstanding State government loan to the Municipalities be consolidated into a single block loan to be repaid in 30 annual equal instalments with interest of 5 per cent per annum. Henceforth distribution of outlay between the loan component and non-loan component should be at the rate of 1:3.

(b) The Commission recommends that a high power Committee be constituted to review the flow of fund to the local bodies from the State government and utilisation thereof properly at least in every six months.

(c) The Commission also recommends that a permanent arrangement in the Finance Department may be made to monitor the follow-up action of the recommendations of the Commission and to maintain the records properly for the future Commission.

(d) It further feels that like Panchayats the services of minimum number of staff with a standard norm of the urban local bodies should also be provincialised and the cost of salary of these employees may be met by the State government out of State Plan Fund.

(e) Considering the present financial position of local bodies, the Commission recommends that no further recruitment should be made over the existing level of staff.

(f) The Commission further recommends to set up a Tariff Commission for formulation and streamlining the pattern of rates of taxes etc. for the local bodies. The Commission may also look into the service conditions, staffing pattern and other aspects of the employees of the urban local bodies.

(g) The Commission recommends that full time executive officer of appropriate rank should be posted to every urban local body for effective functioning of the local bodies.

The State Government has accepted all the major recommendations of the Commission.

3

KARNATAKA

Karnataka has a written history of more than 2000 years. After Independence, the new united Mysore State was created in 1956 and was renamed as Karnataka in 1973. It lies to the south of Goa and Maharashtra, to the west of Andhra Pradesh, to the north-west of Tamil Nadu and to the north of Kerala. It has a sea coast of nearly 267 km. Karnataka is predominantly rural and agrarian. Agriculture and allied activities account for nearly two-thirds of the workforce in the State. It is however, one of the leading industrialised States contributing four per cent of the national production in the industrial sector and 20 per cent to the State income. Karnataka has 1.34 lakh km. (1996-97) of motorable roads including 1997 km. of national highways. The surfaced road constituted 65 per cent of the total. Rail network in Karnataka is 3301 km. which includes broad gauge (2560 km.), metre gauge (388 km.) and narrow gauge (85 km.) There are four main airports and one all-weather sea port to cater the State. The State is divided into 20 districts.

URBAN SCENARIO

Although there is an increase in urban population, the share of urban population of the State to that of the country is found decreasing. The State accounted for 6.73 per cent of total urban population in 1981, while it reduced to 6.38 per cent in 1991. The decennial growth in 1981-91 also reduced from 50.65 in previous decade to 29.09 per cent. Contrarily, the number of towns is found increasing over the decades. So is the case with class one towns, whose number and population both recorded an increase. The proportion of population contained by class one towns was 51.32 per cent in 1971 increased to 58.66 per cent in 1981 and further to 64.60 per cent in 1991. However, the growth rate of population in these towns decreased to 42.1 per cent in 1991 from 72.2 per cent in 1981 and 67.7 per cent in 1971.

Among twenty districts Bangalore is the most urbanised district with 85.82 per cent of urban population, followed by Dharvad containing only 34.95 per cent of the urban content. All other districts have less than one-third of their population inhabiting in urban areas. Four districts have no class one towns. Three districts of Bangalore, Dharvad and Bellary have urban population more than thirty per cent. Thus, level of urbanisation in the State is not uniform. One district with 10.7 per cent of total population has urbanisation level of more than 80 per cent, while another one containing 7.8 per cent population records level between 30 and 40. The highest number of eleven districts with majority of the population (59.3 per cent) fall between 20-30 and the remaining seven with 22.2 per cent population comes into 10-20 per cent urbanisation.

As regards cities, Bangalore is the most populous one. It experienced a tremendous growth of 75.56 per cent in 1971-81. The cities of Dangere and Belary had more than 60 per cent growth. The city of Udupi with 12.30 per cent growth was at the bottom. In 1981-91, Harem Udupi faced the highest growth of 252.39 per cent. Bidar (65.88%) and Tumkur (65.18%) followed the suit. Hassan recorded 51.62 per cent and Gulbarga and Davangare had more than 40 per cent. Bangalore (39.87%), Mysore (36.15%), Mangalore (39.11%), Belgaum (33.71%), Bijapur (31.04%), Raichur (36.66%) and Chitradurga (38.57%) were the towns having growth rate of more than thirty per cent. Kolar Gold Fields was at the bottom with 8.32 per cent, preceded by Gadg Batigeri (14.10%), Bhadravati (14.18%) and Mandya (19.63%).

The evolution of urban local bodies in the State was patterned on the experience of the British Provinces. In the princely state of Mysore the first municipal organisation was created in 1897 for Bangalore Cantonment area where the British army was stationed. Subsequently, the Mysore City Municipalities Act of 1937 established the elected municipalities in Mysore and Bangalore. The other towns were governed by different legislations depending upon their location in the Bombay and Madras Provinces. After the reorganisation of the States, a comprehensive Municipal Act was passed in 1964 to create municipal bodies and to empower them to perform civic functions. Likewise, in 1976 a separate Act was passed, creating City Corporations. Today there are six Municipal Corporations, twenty Town Municipal Councils, one hundred thirty five Town Municipal Councils, forty eight Town Panchayats, a few Notified Area Committees and two Sanitary Boards. The total number of statutorily constituted urban local bodies in Karnataka today is two hundred and ten.

Among the City Corporations, Belgaum, Gulbarga and Hubli-Dharwad experienced much higher rate of growth of population than others. Mangalore City Corporation had lowest rate of 4.51 per cent only. In the case of City Municipal Councils, though the overall increase was 23.64 per cent, Chikmangalore experienced less than one per cent increase whereas Shimoga experienced 46 per cent followed by Bidar with 37 per cent. Among the Town Municipal Councils, Sindhanur experienced the highest population growth by almost doubling between 1981-91 and only a few Town Municipal Councils experienced single digit population growth. The negative growth rate was experienced by only four towns viz. Konnur, Terdal, Suratkal and Arasikere. Bangalore City Corporation accounted for about 19 per cent of the urban population and thus six per cent of total population of the State. Out of every five persons living in urban areas one is a Bangalorean. Out of 100 people living in urban areas, 18 live in City Municipal Councils, 27 in Town Municipal Councils, 34 in City Corporations and the remaining 21 live in other urban areas including Town Panchayats.

There are presently two Municipal Acts to govern the urban affairs in the State. The Karnataka Municipalities Act, 1964 regulates the management of municipal affairs in towns and cities. The municipal corporations in the State are managed by the Karnataka Municipal Corporations Act of 1976.

FUNCTIONAL DOMAIN

Both the Municipal Acts enumerate a bunch of functions — obligatory as well as discretionary assigned to the urban local government units in the State.

Municipal Corporations

Obligatory Functions

It is incumbent on the Corporation to make reasonable and adequate provisions for the following :

(a) erection of substantial boundary marks defining the limits of the city,

(b) the watering and cleansing of all public streets and public places and the removal of all sweepings therefrom,

(c) the collection, removal, treatment and disposal of sewage, offensive matters and rubbish and the preparation of compost manure from such sewage, offensive matters and rubbish,

(d) the construction, maintenance and cleaning of drains and drainage works and of public privies, water closets, urinals and similar conveniences,

(e) the maintenance of a Corporation office and of all public monuments and open space and other property vesting in the Corporation and keeping a true and correct account of all Corporation property,

(f) the naming or numbering of streets and of public places vesting in the Corporation and the numbering of premises,

(g) the regulation and abatement of offensive and dangerous trades or practices,

(h) the maintenance, change and regulation of places for the disposal of the dead and the provision of new places for the purpose and disposing of unclaimed dead bodies,

(i) the construction or acquisition and maintenance of public markets and slaughter houses and the regulation of all markets and slaughter houses,

(j) the maintenance of an ambulance service and service for conveying dead bodies to crematoriums,

(k) the destruction of birds or animals causing nuisance or of vermin and confinement or destruction of stray or ownerless dogs,

(l) laying out new public streets,

(m) maintaining or aiding schools for pre-primary education,

(n) the construction or acquisition and maintenance of cattle pounds,

(o) establishing and maintaining a system of public vaccination,

(p) the reclamation of unhealthy localities, the removal of noxious vegetation and generally the abatement of all nuisances,

(q) the planting and maintenance of trees on road sides and elsewhere,

(r) the construction, maintenance, alteration and improvement of public streets, bridges, subways, culverts, causeways and the like,

(s) the removal of obstruction and projections upon streets, bridges and other public places,

(t) the management and maintenance of all municipal water works and the construction or acquisition of new works necessary for a sufficient supply of water for public and private purposes,

(u) preventing and checking the spread of dangerous diseases,

(v) the lighting of public streets, municipal markets and places of resort vested in the Corporation,

(w) the securing or removal of dangerous buildings and places,

(x) the construction and maintenance of residential quarters for the *paura karmikas*,

(y) the provision of public parks, gardens, playgrounds and recreation grounds,

(z) the regulation of lodging houses, camping grounds and rest houses in the city,

(aa) establishing and maintaining compost plants for disposal of sewage,

(ab) supplying, constructing and maintaining in accordance with the general system approved by the Corporation, receptacles, fittings, pipes and other appliances whatsoever on or for the use of premises for receiving and conducting the sewage thereof into drains under the control of the Corporation,

(ac) vital statistics including registration of births and deaths,

(ad) regulation of tanneries,

(ae) taking measures to meet any calamity affecting the public,

(af) fulfilment of any obligation imposed by the Government,

(ag) subject to adequate provision being made for the matters, the provision of relief to destitute persons in the city in times of famine and scarcity and the establishment and maintenance of relief works in such times.

Discretionary Functions

The Corporation may, in its discretion, provide, either wholly or in part, for all or any of the following matters :

(a) the organisation, maintenance or management of institutions within or without the city for the care of persons who are infirm, sick or incurable, or for the care and training of the blind, deaf, mute or otherwise disabled, mothers or infants or school children,

(b) the organisation, maintenance or management of maternity and infant welfare homes,

(c) the provision of milk to expectant nourishing mothers or infants or school children,

(d) the organisation, maintenance or management of chemical or bacteriological laboratories for the examination or analysis of water, food or drugs for the detection of diseases or for research connected with public health,

(e) the organisation, maintenance or management of swimming pools, public wash houses, bathing places and other institutions designed for the improvement of public health,

(f) the construction and maintenance in public streets or places of drinking fountains for human beings and water troughs for animals,

(g) survey of buildings or lands,

(h) the provision of music for the people,

(i) encouraging the development of planning and maintenance of trees and plants on private lands and within private compounds,

(j) maintenance of health museums,

(k) construction and maintenance of infirmaries or hospitals for animals,

(l) the organisation and maintenance in times of scarcity of shops or stalls for the sale of necessities of life,

(m) the building or purchase and maintenance of residence for Corporation officers and servants,

(n) the grant of loans for building purposes to Corporation servants,

(o) any other measures for the welfare of Corporation servants,

(p) the establishment and maintenance or the aiding of museums and art galleries or zoological collections and the purchase or construction of buildings therefor,

(q) contribution towards public funds raised for the relief

of human suffering caused by natural calamities within the city or for the public welfare,

(r) the preparation or presentation of addresses to persons of distinction,

(s) granting rewards for information regarding the infringement of any provisions of the Act or of the rules etc.,

(t) the building or purchase and maintenance of suitable dwellings for the poor and working classes,

(u) the provision of shelter for destitute or homeless persons and any form of poor relief,

(v) slum improvements and upgradation,

(w) urban forestry, protection of the environment and promotion of ecological aspects,

(x) urban poverty alleviation,

(y) promotion of cultural, educational and aesthetic aspects,

(z) with the previous sanction of the Government, the making of a contribution towards any public ceremony or entertainment in the city,

(aa) any measures to promote public safety, health, convenience or instruction.

Municipalities

Obligatory Functions

It is incumbent on every council to make adequate provisions for following matters within the municipal area :

(a) lighting public streets, places and buildings,

(b) watering public streets and places,

(c) cleaning public streets, places and sewers, and all spaces not being private property, removing noxious vegetation and abating all public nuisances,

(d) extinguishing fires and protecting life and property when fire occurs,

(e) regulating or abating offensive or dangerous trades or practices,

(f) removing obstructions and projections in public streets, bridges and other public places,

(g) securing and removing dangerous buildings or places and reclaiming unhealthy locations,

(h) acquiring and maintaining, changing and regulating places for the disposal of dead,

(i) constructing, altering and maintaining public streets, culverts, municipal boundary marks, markets, slaughter houses, latrines, privies, urinals, drains, sewers, drainage works, sewage works, baths, washing places, drinking fountains, tanks, wells, dams and the like,

(j) obtaining supply of or an additional supply of water proper and sufficient for preventing damage to the health of the inhabitants,

(k) naming streets and numbering houses,

(l) registering births and deaths,

(m) public vaccination,

(n) providing suitable accommodation for calves, cows, or buffaloes required for the supply of animal lymph,

(o) maintaining schools for pre-primary education,

(p) arranging for the destruction or the detention and preservation of stray dogs,

(q) providing facilities for anti-rabic treatment and treatment of lepers and mental patients and meeting the expenses of indigent persons undergoing anti-rabic treatment within or outside the municipal limit,

(r) providing covered metallic receptacles mounted on wheels for use by the municipal council for the removal of night-soil and rubbish and, if so required by the Government, preparation of compost manure from night-soil and rubbish,

(s) providing accommodation for municipal sweepers and scavengers and granting of loans for construction of house,

(t) printing annual report on the municipal administration,

(u) paying salary and the contingent expenditure on account of police or guards required by the council,

(v) collecting vital statistics including registration of births and deaths,
(w) regulating tanneries,
(x) maintaining up-to-date records of all buildings and sites, and
(y) planning and maintaining of road-side trees.

Special Functions

Every municipal council has to make reasonable provisions for the following special matters :

(a) providing special medical aid and accommodation for the sick in time of dangerous diseases; and taking measures to prevent the outbreak as suppress and prevent the recurrence of the disease,
(b) giving relief to and establishing and maintaining relief works in times of famine or scarcity for destitute persons within the limits of the municipal area.

Discretionary Functions

Every municipal council may in its discretion provide either wholly or in part for all or any of the following matters :

(a) laying out public streets and acquiring the land for that purpose, including the land requisite for the construction of buildings or curtilages thereof to abut in such streets,
(b) constructing, establishing or maintaining public parks, gardens, libraries, museums, mental hospitals, halls, offices, *dharamshalas*, choultries, *musafirkhanas*, rest houses, homes for disabled and destitute persons and other public buildings,
(c) providing shelter for destitute women,
(d) constructing and maintaining suitable sanitary houses for the habitation of the poor and granting loans for construction of such houses or for effecting necessary

improvements connected therewith,

(e) providing accommodation for any class of servants other than sweepers and scavengers employed by the municipal council or granting loans to such servants for construction of houses,

(f) planting and maintaining roadside and other trees,

(g) taking statistics and granting rewards for information which may tend to secure the correct registration of vital statistics,

(h) making a survey,

(i) securing or assisting to secure suitable places for the carrying on of the offensive trades,

(j) supplying, constructing and maintaining receptacles, fittings, pipes and other appliances on or for the use of private premises for receiving and conducting the sewage thereof into a sewer under the control of the council,

(k) providing of music or other entertainments in public places or places of public resort,

(l) the promotion of public health or child welfare,

(m) contribution towards any public funds for the relief of human sufferings, within or without the municipal area,

(n) by a resolution passed at a general meeting and supported by one-half of the total number of councillors and with the previous sanction of the Deputy Commissioner, in the case of a town municipal council and, of the Commissioner, in the case of a city municipal council, organising any public reception, public ceremony, public entertainment or public exhibition within the municipal area,

(o) the organisation or maintenance during scarcity, of shops or stalls for the sale of necessities of life,

(p) housing and maintaining destitute orphans and destitute cripples,

(q) constructing, establishing and maintaining warehouses,

(r) establishment and maintaining of dairy farms and breeding studs,

(s) provision of transport facilities within the municipal area,
(t) maintenance of an ambulance service,
(u) supply of water beyond the limits of the municipal area,
(v) the acquisition and maintenance of grazing grounds,
(w) guaranteeing the payment of interest on money expended for the construction of a telephone line,
(x) promoting the well-being of municipal employees and/or class of municipal employees and their dependants,
(y) the construction, purchase, organisation, maintenance, extension and management of mechanically propelled transport facilities for the conveyance of the public,
(z) the construction, maintenance, repairs, purchase of any works for the supply of electrical energy,
(aa) making contributions towards the construction, establishment or maintenance of educational institutions including libraries and museum, any hospital, dispensary or similar institution providing for public medical relief, or any other institution of a charitable nature,
(ab) construction, maintenance and provision of public bathing houses,
(ac) revival or promotion of cottage industries,
(ad) improvement of cattle and livestock including construction and maintenance of veterinary hospitals,
(ae) maintenance of maternity houses and child welfare centres,
(af) maintenance of art galleries,
(ag) slum improvement and upgradation,
(ah) urban forestry, protection of environment and promotion of ecological aspects,
(ai) urban poverty alleviation,
(aj) promotion of cultural, education, and aesthetic aspects,
(ak) promotion, formation, extension or assistance of cooperative societies, and

(al) any other matter which is likely to promote education or public health, safety or general welfare or convenience or the advancement of the economic condition of the inhabitants.

TAXATION POWERS

The Corporations can, with the sanction of the Government and at rates not exceeding to the prescribed limit, levy any one or more of the following taxes :

(a) a tax on buildings, or lands or both situated within the city,
(b) a toll on vehicles, other than motor vehicles, entering the Corporation limits,
(c) a tax on advertisements,
(d) a duty on certain transfers of property in the shape of an additional stamp duty,
(e) a water rate or water-rates for water supplied by the Corporation which may be imposed in the form of a tax assessed on buildings and lands including water charges.

In addition to tax on buildings or lands, the Corporation can levy a water supply cess at the rate of twenty per cent of such tax for the maintenance and improvement of water supply schemes in urban areas. The cess so collected is credited to the government.

The municipal council may levy any one or more of the following taxes :

(a) a tax on buildings or lands or both situated within the municipal area,
(b) a toll on vehicles entering the municipal area,
(c) a tax on all or any vehicles, other than motor vehicles, boats used for riding, draught or burden kept within the municipal area for use,
(d) a water rate for water supplied by the council,

(e) a lighting tax,
(f) a duty on transfer of immovable property in the shape of an additional stamp duty,
(g) a tax on advertisements erected, exhibited, fixed or retained upon or over any land, building, wall, hoarding, frame, posts or structure or upon or in any vehicle or displayed to public view visible from a public street or public place.

Every municipal council can levy taxes on buildings or lands or both, the aggregate of which is not less than fifteen per cent of the annual rateable value, in the case of Town Municipal Council and, twenty per cent of the annual rateable value in the case of City Municipal Council. In addition, the council can levy a water supply cess at the rate of twenty per cent of such tax for the maintenance and improvement of water supply schemes in urban areas and the cess so collected is credited to the Government.

DEVOLUTION OF FINANCES

Section 267 of the Karnataka Panchayat Raj Act, 1993, which derives its powers from the 73rd Amendment to the Constitution provides for the appointment of the State Finance Commission. Similarly, Section 503C of the Karnataka Municipal Corporation Act (Amendment), 1994 and Section 302-B of the Karnataka Municipalities Act (Amendment), 1994 provide for a Finance Commission as per the 74th Amendment to the Constitution. The State Finance Commission was common to both Panchayat Raj institutions and Urban Local Bodies. The three-member Finance Commission was headed by an academician. In addition to common references as enshrined in the Constitution, the Commission was also entrusted :

1. to examine and make suggestions on the extent to which and the manner in which the resources available to the local bodies could best be utilised for meeting the expenditure of these bodies, and
2. to make a detailed analysis of the repayment of loans

> and advances extended by Government from time to time to the local bodies and make suitable recommendations for repayment of government dues and the possibility of adjusting these dues against future devolution of revenues from government to these bodies.

The Commission submitted its report in January 1996.

EXISTING REVENUE EFFORTS

Property Tax

Property tax is basically a benefit tax. Owners of properties derive tangible benefits. First, payment of property tax provides additional proof of ownership right. Secondly, the value of property goes on increasing as municipal bodies undertake development works in the area. Since property owners derive such tangible benefits from the developmental activities of municipal authorities, they have to pay some *quid-pro-quo* to the municipal authorities in return for enjoying such benefits. In this way, property tax becomes a benefit levy. Urban Local Bodies require funds for undertaking similar works and to make further improvement in the area. This is the logic behind levying property tax. The value goes on increasing as urban land becomes scarce, commercial activities develop and infrastructure facilities improve. This is the reason for justifying annual levy of property tax. Property tax has also come to be viewed as an ability to pay tax because the value of properties differs from property to property depending upon their location, quality of construction, plinth area and the purpose for which they are used. Therefore, urban local bodies have been levying progressive rates of property tax thereby converting what is basically a benefit levy into an ability to pay levy.

It has been observed that the Urban Local Bodies have not been utilising property tax, even to a modest extent. It constitutes about 20 per cent of total revenue receipts of City Corporations and 15 per cent of the total revenue receipts of City Municipal

Councils and Town Municipal Councils.

The first step in redesigning property tax is identification and listing of urban properties. The second step is determining of their rental value and periodic revision of that value. For undertaking these tasks, the State government should create Central Valuation Authority for conducting periodic survey of property and valuing the property both in urban and rural areas. This Authority could be attached to the Department of Urban Development and it should consist of structural and civil engineers and cost accountants. They should form the core group and this Central Valuation Authority should be a State level body headed by a Director. The main functions of the Authority should be to undertake regular survey of property in all urban as well as in rural areas. The survey should list property titles, nature, extent, quality and location of the property. On the basis of these factors, the Authority should divide cities into zones like residential zone, commercial zone, industrial zone and each of these zones should be further divided into different grades. Such zoning is necessary for the purpose of determining the true rental value of urban property. The Authority should determine the rental value of the properties located in different zones. For the purpose, the properties will have to be classified on the basis of age, plinth area, quality of materials used for construction and purpose for which property is used. The rental value may be determined by ascertaining the median market rent prevailing in the zone. The entire process should be completed within a period of five years. The list of properties, the purpose for which they are used and their median rental value is passed on to the respective urban local bodies. The concerned urban local bodies, in turn, should invite public objections to the criteria used for zoning, authenticity of the purpose and the median rental values. The objections should be processed by the Authority. Once the process is completed then the urban local bodies should be free to levy property tax.

The Commission recommends to levy tax on the properties of the Central Government's public undertakings. Besides, Urban Local Bodies can levy 75 per cent of the assessed property tax on properties of the Central Government's Departmental Undertakings like Railways. Similarly, all properties of the State government's public undertakings should be taxed on par with commercial properties located in various urban local bodies. The properties owned by the State Government's Departmental Undertakings may be taxed at 75 per cent of the assessed property tax as service charges.

The Commission feels that no exemption should be given to any property located in urban areas including educational institutions and philanthropic institutions. Probable exemptions may be the properties of orphanages, beggar homes, remand homes etc. They should be identified in each city and their names should be widely published inviting public opinion on the desirability of giving them complete exemption. For all other educational institutions including universities and colleges, 75 per cent of the property tax should be levied in the form of service charges. Furthermore, the Rent Control Act should be amended immediately to exclude from its purview all urban properties which carry a monthly rent of Rs. 250 for residential purpose and Rs. 500 for non-residential purpose. These exclusions will expand the tax base of property tax and increase the yield from property tax by one-third on an average.

In the next stage, the rate structure of property tax should be appropriately designed. The rates should be determined by the concerned urban local bodies. The State government should have no role in determining the rates. It should be the prerogative of the elected representatives of Urban Local Bodies to determine the rates of property tax.

The rates should be lowered and it is necessary to keep the rates of the property tax in line with the national Wealth Tax rates. It is necessary to make people to accept reasonable rates of tax. Urban property tax is fast becoming municipal wealth tax.

Licence Fees

People who want to undertake any economic activity like trading, business or provide services have to obtain a licence from municipal authorities. This is made compulsory even in villages. This licencing power provides legitimacy for economic activity. Therefore, it is a benefit tax. The licence fees have to be revised periodically in order to recover the cost of providing these services.

Parking Fee

The parking fee can be adopted for all roads particularly in the commercial areas. Further, breakdown of vehicles on roads has become another awful sight and the owners of such vehicles consider it their right to occupy that space without paying any penalty for running unfit vehicles on public roads. Therefore, all City Corporations should start towing service and charge for towing the vehicles which breakdown on roads. If the owners of vehicle do not move them within one hour, they should be towed out and levied a charge payable by the vehicle owner. This will compel the vehicle owners to keep their vehicle fit for plying on public roads and will help smooth flow of traffic in cities like Bangalore.

User's Charges

There are a number of services which are rendered to the urban dwellers for which adequate charges are not levied. The first and foremost is supply of safe drinking water. At present water is not charged at full cost. There is a great deal of hidden subsidy. The Commission, therefore, recommends that full cost should be determined and water charges should be recovered by the municipal bodies.

The Commission feels that the intervention of courts has reduced the income from properties. Therefore, it is necessary to incorporate appropriate provisions to minimise the impact of this problem on the rental income of urban local bodies. It would be necessary to bar lower courts from issuing any stay order on matters relating to the revenue of Urban Local Bodies. They may go to the higher courts. This will necessarily minimise the litigations. Second, in these cases where the problem cannot be resolved, Urban Local Bodies may sell the property in public auction.

Cess

Cesses like library cess, beggary cess, education cess, health cess etc. should be abolished.

DEVOLUTION SCHEME

In view of the financial position of the Urban Local Bodies, the Commission recommends that the State government should transfer 36 per cent of its non-loan gross own revenue receipts every year to the Panchayat Raj Institutions and Urban Local Bodies taken together. The divisible pool of the resources between State and local bodies would include gross yield from all taxes, duties and fees levied and collected by the State government and excludes Grants-in-aid and the State's share of Central revenues transferred on the recommendation of the National Finance Commission.

For the purpose of allocating the share between the urban and rural areas, the Commission has used five indicators. They are population (1991), area (1991), illiteracy rate (1991), number of persons per hospital bed (1991) and road length per sq. km. area (1991).

The Commission considers that population is an index of need for civic services hence an index of their financial need. Municipal area is also an index of need as most of the civic services have to be provided spatially in the urban areas. The other three indicators reflect the level of development or adequacy of some essential services, two of them being social indicators i.e. health and education and the other one economic infrastructure indicator (roads). All the three put together indicate some variant of relative backwardness. The Commission has given 33.33 per cent weight each to population and area and 11.11 per cent each to illiteracy rate and number of persons per bed in government hospitals and 11.12 per cent to road length per sq. km.

The Commission has reduced the weight hitherto given in the distribution of plan grants to the districts from 50 per cent to 33.33 per cent because there are a number of districts which have experienced decline in the decadal growth of population and as a result they have been experiencing declining share of plan funds.The share of urban local bodies in the total devolution is 15 per cent accounted as under :

Proportion of Urban Population	10.30 per cent
Proportion of Urban Area	0.74 per cent
Road Length per sq. km.	2.78 per cent
Illiteracy rate and no. of persons per hospital per bed	1.88 per cent
	15.70 per cent
Rounded off	15.00 per cent

The remaining 85 per cent of funds will go to Panchayat Raj Institutions.

The share of urban local bodies comes to 5.40 per cent out of 36 per cent of non-loan gross own revenue receipts of the State government. This amount is to be distributed among six Corporations, 21 City Municipal Councils, 135 Town Municipal Councils, 48 Town Panchayats, and a few non-municipal census towns including Notified Areas and Sanitary Boards. The City Corporations get a total of 19.89 per cent, City Municipal Councils get 15.27 per cent, Town Municipal Councils get 52.39 per cent and the Town Panchayats get 12.54 per cent.

Grants of Tenth Finance Commission

As regards distribution of grants sanctioned by the Tenth Finance Commission, the Commission recommends distribution on the basis of the same criteria as adopted for the share in the State government's revenue. The amount should be used only for reconstruction, improvement and repair of hospital buildings, school buildings, storm water drains and only after meeting these requirements, municipal roads may be attended to. They should also make an affordable matching contribution in order to receive this grant. Monitoring of the utilisation of these funds should be done by the Divisional Commissioners. Their reports may be sent to the State government for onward transmission to the Government of India.

Other Issues

In pursuance of the holistic approach for better municipal administration, the Commission has given recommendations on associated matters as well.

1. The Commission recommends to enact one common legislation entitled Karnataka Urban Local Bodies Act which should include provisions relating to City Corporations, City Municipal Councils, Town Municipal Councils and Town Panchayats. It is necessary to facilitate administrative coordination.
2. The Commission further recommends that the Karnataka Urban Water Supply and Drainage Board (KUWAS & DB) and Bangalore Water Supply and Sewerage Board may continue to be autonomous agencies outside the purview of the respective municipal bodies but confine themselves only to the construction of jack wells, laying of transporting pipes, construction of purification plants and distribution system. The responsibility of distribution of water within the municipal limits, maintenance of the distribution system and collection of water charges should be transferred to the respective municipal bodies immediately. The municipal bodies should be allowed to determine the structure of water rates providing cross subsidies within the rate structure.
3. The Commission recommends to set up a properly manned Finance Commission Cell on permanent basis.
4. The Commission recommends that the Directorate of Municipal Administration should be abolished as it is inconsistent with the philosophy of local self government. The State government can provide policy advice and coordinate the functioning of these bodies through the Department of Urban Development.

5. The Commission suggests that urban and rural water supply programmes should be merged into one and the Karnataka Urban Water Supply and Drainage Board should be entrusted with the integrated water supply programme. Accordingly, administration of Water Supply Programmes should be brought under the Urban Development Department and it may be called Urban Development and Water Supply Department. Housing may be separated and formed into a separate department encompassing urban as well as rural housing.
6. The Commission emphasises upon the provision of civic services. In case of water supply, the Commission has fixed 100 litres for City Corporations, 80 litres for City Municipal Councils and 70 litres for Town Municipal Councils and Town Panchayats as per capita per day as the desired normative levels.
7. The Commission recommends the normative standard for street lights prescribed by the Task Force on Housing and Urban Development namely twenty street lights per km. of road length.
8. The large City Corporations may explore the possibility of privatising garbage collection particularly in areas where intensity of garbage accumulation is very high. They should also try to involve NGOs in this scheme.
9. An Administrative Reforms Commission may be set up to suggest reorganisation of the State government's administrative structure including municipal administration.
10. The existing urban development authorities and Slum Improvement Board should be brought under the respective municipal bodies.
11. Town planning units may be transferred to municipalities.
12. A sum of Rs. 26.04 crore due to Karnataka Urban Water Supply and Drainage Board should be recovered from the funds devolved to Urban Local Bodies.

13. An amount of Rs. 102.95 crore outstanding against Urban Local Bodies to financial institutions be repaid by the State government.

The State government has accepted a good number of recommendations and a large number are under consideration.

4

KERALA

The ancient history of Kerala is largely shrouded in midsts of tradition. Legend apart, Kerala's culture has been an integral part of the mainstream of Indian culture. Its history is the story of synthesis, assimilation and fusion of old traditions and new values in every spheres of human thought and activity. In between the high western ghats on the east and the Arabian Sea on the west, the width of the State varies from 35 km. to 120 km.

Agriculture forms the main occupation of the people as about half of the population depends upon it for their livelihood. The State is featured with the pre-dominance of cash crops. Kerala is not self-sufficient in food production but rich in industrial potentialities and infrastructural facilities.

The length of roads in the State is 1.42 lakh km. and total railway network is 1198 km. There are three airports and about a dozen sea ports. The State is divided into 14 districts.

Urban Status

The State covers about 1.21 per cent of total area of the country, while in respect of population, it ranked twelfth in 1981 as well as in 1991. As regards urban population, the State accounts for about 3.54 per cent of country's urban population. The share in 1981 was 2.99. A little less than one-fourth (26.44 per cent) of the population of State live in urban areas. The proportion in 1981 was 18.74. Kerala witnessed a tremendous decennial growth of 60.98 in 1991 which was much more than that of 37.64 recorded in 1981. The level of urbanisation is spread over the State. Out of 14, only one district of Kannur having 7.7 per cent of total population witnessed highest urbanisation with 51.02 per cent of urban content. Ernakulam which has 9.7 per cent of total population has urban content of 48.79 per cent. Three districts accounting a little more than one-fourth population fall between 40-50 and five districts between 10-20 per cent and three districts less than ten per cent. Kannur, Kozhikode, Alappuzha, Thiruvananthapuram and Ernakulam are districts with urban content of more than 30 per cent. Ernakulam having 17.9 per cent of urban population is the most urbanised followed by Kannur (14.9%), Kozhikode (13.1%) and Thiruvananthapuram (13%) districts. All other districts could muster only single digit urban content. Idukki (0.7%) and Wayanad (0.3%) are least urbanised, preceded by Pathanamthitta (2%), Kasaragod (2.3%), Malappuram (3.7%), Kottayam (4.2%) and Palakkad (4.9%).

As regards urban centres, the State has witnessed a tremendous increase. There were only 85 towns in 1981 which rose to 109 in 1991. The number of class one towns increased from 8 in 1981 to 14 in 1991. There has been recorded an increase in urban content as well. The big towns contained about 53.14 per cent of urban population in 1981. The proportion increased to 66.34 per cent in 1991, thus showing an influx in major urban centres.

Prior to the Constitution (Seventy Fourth) Amendment Act, 1992, urban affairs in the State was being managed by the Kerala Municipalities Act, 1960, the Kerala Municipal Corporation Act, 1961 and the Guruvayur Township Act, 1961. All these Acts have been repealed and presently there is only the unified Municipality Act, 1994 to regulate the municipal affairs in the State.

Prior to the Panchayat Raj Legislation, 1994 Kerala had only Village Panchayats, Municipal Councils and Municipal Corporations. The Kerala Panchayat Raj Act, 1994 has created two new tiers of Panchayats viz. Block Panchayats and District Panchayats. These came into existence for the first time in the State on 2nd October, 1995.

The Urban Local Bodies in the State comprise 54 Municipal Councils and 3 Municipal Corporations — Thiruvananthapuram, Kochi and Kozhikode. The Municipalities are divided into three categories on the following basis :

(i)	Grade - I – Annual income of Rs. 70 lakh and above	25
(ii)	Grade - II – Annual income of Rs. 40 to 70 lakh	20
(iii)	Grade - III – All other Municipalities	9

The combined share of Corporations is 36 per cent of urban population and the Municipalities cater 64 per cent of the population spread over the State.

The average population of a Municipality in 1991 was 52,058, compared to 43,829 in 1981. The range of variation is considerable from 19,657 (Kannamkulam in Thrissur District) to 1,74,666 (Alappuzha in Alappuzha District). Among the three Corporations the most populous is Kochi (5.46 lakhs), followed by Thiruvananthapuram (5.24 lakhs) and Kozhikode (4.19 lakhs).

The average area of a Municipality is 22.63 sq. km. The biggest Municipality is Payyannoor in Kannur district (54.63 sq. km.) and the smallest is Kunnamkulam in Thrissur district (6.90 sq. km.).

FUNCTIONAL DOMAIN

The laws provide for lengthy schedule of mandatory, general and sector-wise distribution of functions and responsibilities to urban local bodies.

Mandatory Functions

1. Regulation of building construction.
2. Protection of public land from encroachment.
3. Protection of traditional drinking water sources.
4. Preservation of ponds and other water bodies.

5. Maintenance of waterways and canals.
6. Collection and disposal of solid waste and control of liquid waste disposal.
7. Storm water drainage.
8. Maintenance of environmental hygiene.
9. Management of markets.
10. Vector control.
11. Regulation of slaughtering of animals and sale of meat, fish and other perishable food items.
12. Regulation of eating establishments.
13. Prevention of food adulteration.
14. Maintenance of roads and other public assets.
15. Street lighting and their maintenance.
16. Immunisation.
17. Carrying into effect national and State level strategies and programmes for disease prevention and control.
18. Opening and maintenance of burial and burning grounds.
19. Licensing of dangerous and offensive trades and industries.
20. Registration of births and deaths.
21. Provide bathing and washing ghats.
22. Provision of ferries.
23. Provide parking space for vehicles.
24. Provide waiting-sheds for travellers.
25. Provide toilet facilities in public places.
26. Regulate conduct of fairs and festivals.
27. Licensing of pet dogs and destroying stray dogs.
28. Provision of basic minimum service in slums.
29. Amenities for pedestrians including footpath and road crossing facilities.
30. Preparation of detailed town plans and action plan for phased implementation.

General Functions

1. Collection and updating of essential statistics.
2. Organising voluntary labour and contribution for

community works.

3. Carrying out campaigns for thrift.
4. Awareness building on control of social evils like drinking, consumption of narcotics, dowry and abuse of women and children.
5. Ensuring maximum people's participation in all stages of development.
6. Organising relief during natural calamities.
7. Inculcating environmental awareness and motivating local action for environmental upgradation.
8. Promoting co-operatives.
9. Enhancing communal harmony.
10. Mobilising local resources in cash and in kind, including free surrender of land for development purposes.
11. Spreading legal awareness among the weaker sections.
12. Campaigning against economic crimes.
13. Organising neighbourhood groups and self-help groups with focus on the poor.
14. Awareness building on civic duties.

SECTOR-WISE DISTRIBUTION OF RESPONSIBILITIES

I. Agriculture

1. Bring into cultivation waste lands and marginal lands.
2. Bring about an optimum utilisation of land.
3. Soil conservation.
4. Production of organic manure.
5. Establishment of nurseries.
6. Promotion of co-operative and group farming.
7. Organising self-help groups among cultivators.
8. Promotion of horticulture and vegetable cultivation.
9. Fodder development.
10. Plan protection.
11. Seed production
12. Farm mechanisation.
13. Management of Krishi Bhavans.
14. Conduct of agricultural exhibitions.

II. Animal Husbandry and Dairy

1. Cattle improvement programmes.
2. Dairy farming.
3. Poultry farming, bee keeping, piggery development, goat rearing, rabbit rearing.
4. Running of veterinary dispensaries.
5. Running of ICDP sub-centres.
6. Preventive health programmes for animals.
7. Prevention of cruelty to animals.
8. Fertility improvement programmes.
9. Control of diseases of animal origin.
10. Running of veterinary poly clinics and Regional Artificial Insemination Centres.
11. Provide speciality service in animal husbandry.
12. Conduct cattle and poultry shows.

III. Minor Irrigation

1. All minor irrigation and lift schemes within the area of a municipality.
2. All micro-irrigation schemes.
3. Water conservation.
4. Development of ground water resources.

IV. Fisheries

1. Development of fisheries in ponds and fresh water and brackish water fish culture, mari culture.
2. Fish seed production and distribution.
3. Distribution of fishing implements.
4. Fish marketing assistance.
5. Provision of basic minimum services for the families of fishermen.
6. Welfare schemes for fishermen.
7. Development of traditional landing centres.
8. Management of fisheries schools.

V. Social Forestry

1. Raising of fodder, fuel and fruit trees.
2. Organising campaigns for tree planting and environmental awareness.
3. Afforestation of waste lands.

VI. Small Scale Industries

1. Promotion of cottage and village industries.
2. Promotion of handicrafts.
3. Promotion of traditional and mini industries.
4. Setting up of mini industrial estates.
5. Promotion of industries with investment limit of one-third of SSI.
6. Self employment schemes in industrial sector.
7. Promotion of small scale industries.
8. Entrepreneur development programmes.

VII. Housing

1. Identification of homeless people and poramboke dwellers and provide house sites and houses.
2. Implementation of rural housing programmes.
3. Implementation of shelter upgradation programmes.
4. Popularisation of low cost housing.
5. Promotion of housing co-operative societies.
6. Housing complex infrastructure development.
7. Mobilising housing finance.

VIII. Water Supply

1. Running of water supply schemes covering one Municipality.
2. Setting up of water supply schemes covering one Municipality.

IX. Electricity and Energy

1. Street lighting.
2. Promotion of bio-gas.
3. Promotion of non-conventional energy sources.

X. Education

1. Management of Government pre-primary schools, Government primary schools and Government High Schools.
2. Literacy programmes.
3. Management of Industrial Training Institutes in the Municipal area.
4. Management of Government higher secondary schools in municipal area.
5. Management of Government technical schools in municipal area.
6. Management of vocational training centres and polytechnics in the municipal area.
7. Management of vocational higher secondary schools in the municipal area.

XI. Public Works

1. Construction and maintenance of roads within the Municipality, other than National Highways, State Highways and Major District Roads.
2. Construction of building for institutions including those got transferred from Government.

XII. Public Health and Sanitation

1. Management of dispensaries and primary health centres and sub-centres (in all systems of medicine).
2. Management of child welfare centres and maternity homes.
3. Immunisation and other preventive measures.

4. Family welfare.
5. Sanitation.
6. Management of community health centres and taluk hospitals within the municipal area in all systems of medicine.

XIII. Social Welfare

1. Running of anganwadies.
2. Sanctioning and distribution of pensions of destitutes, widows, handicapped and agricultural labourers.
3. Sanctioning and distribution of unemployment assistance.
4. Sanctioning of assistance for marriage of daughters of widows.
5. Management of group insurance scheme for the poor.
6. Payment of grants to orphanages.
7. Starting of welfare institutions for disabled, destitutes etc.

XIV. Poverty Alleviation

1. Identification of the poor.
2. Self-employment and group employment schemes for the poor especially women.
3. Providing community assets of continuing benefit to the poor.
4. Skill upgradation of the poor for self-employment and wage employment for people below poverty line.
5. Providing infrastructure for self-employment programmes.

XV. Scheduled Castes and Scheduled Tribes Development

1. Beneficiary oriented schemes under SCP and TSP.
2. Management of nursery schools for Scheduled Castes and Scheduled Tribes.
3. Provision of basic amenities in Scheduled Castes and

Scheduled Tribes habitats.

4. Assistance to Scheduled Castes and Scheduled Tribes students.
5. Discretionary assistance to Scheduled Castes and Scheduled Tribes in need.
6. Management of pre-matric hostels in the municipal area.
7. Promoting Scheduled Castes and Scheduled Tribes co-operatives.
8. Management of post-matric hostels in the municipal area.
9. Management of vocational training centres for Scheduled Castes and Scheduled Tribes in the municipal area.

XVI. Sports and Cultural Affairs

Construction of play grounds and stadiums.

XVII. Public Distribution System

1. Examination of complaints against the public distribution system and taking of remedial measures.
2. Organisation of campaigns against weights and measures offences.
3. General supervision and guidance of ration shops and *maveli* stores and other public distribution centres and if necessary starting new public distribution centres.

XVIII. Natural Calamities Relief

1. Management of relief centres.
2. Organisation of relief works.
   (Repair works to assets will be divided and carried out by the municipality in charge of assets).

XIX. Co-Operatives

1. Organisation of co-operatives within the jurisdiction of the Municipality.
2. Payment of Government grants and subsidies within the jurisdiction.

TAXATION POWERS

Every municipality may levy :

(i) a property tax,
(ii) a profession tax,
(iii) a tax on animals and vessels,
(iv) a show tax,
(v) a tax on advertisement,
(vi) a tax on timber brought into the municipal area,
(vii) a duty on certain transfer of immovable property in the shape of an additional stamp duty.

The Municipality may for the purpose of providing any specific service or amenity levy a surcharge on any tax other than profession tax levied by the Municipality. The surcharge cannot exceed ten per cent of the amount of the tax. Municipality may levy a land conversion cess not exceeding rupees seventy five per acre from the landholder in respect of paddy field, marshy land, pond or watershed held by him which is converted into garden land or building site.

DEVOLUTION OF FINANCES

The three-member State Finance Commission was appointed by the State Government on 23rd April, 1994. An Interim Report was submitted to the Government on 30th September, 1995. The Commission was headed by a retired IAS officer. Other two members were also bureaucrat. The final report was submitted on 29th February, 1996. The recommendations of the Commission are intended to cover the period from 1996-97 to

2000-2001 or till the State government take decision on the recommendations of the Second State Finance Commission, whichever is later.

EXISTING SOURCES

Property Tax

Property Tax or Building Tax forms the single most important source of revenue and the Local Bodies should be prepared to realise its full potential. The entire area of building tax/property tax is afflicted by under-valuation and lack of uniformity in valuation. It is also characterised by a large number of exemptions and artificial restrictions on the permitted extent of revision etc. Keeping all the considerations in view, the Commission recommends that the present system of assessing rental value of residential buildings in Rural and Urban Local Bodies may be dispensed with and plinth area may be adopted as the basis for arriving at the rental value.

The *modus operandi* may be on the following basis. The entire area of the Local Body may be divided into territorial zones based upon the following factors :

1. Civic amenities like roads, surface drainage, street lighting etc.
2. Proximity to markets and shopping centres,
3. Proximity to public offices such as Post Offices, educational institutions, banks etc.,
4. Proximity to medical institutions,
5. Proximity to factories and industries.

As far as possible, the number of zones should be kept to a minimum and in rural areas need not be more than two.

The next step is to classify the different residential buildings which come under each territorial zone. They may be classified based on the nature of construction such as :

1. R.C.C. buildings with superior quality wood, mosaic or

marble flooring, sanitary fittings attached bath rooms etc.,

2. R.C.C. ordinary buildings with ordinary quality wood, ordinary flooring and sanitary fittings,
3. Tiled roof or asbestos or GI roof,
4. Huts,
5. Any other type of buildings not coming under the above categories.

The annual rental value currently being assessed in respect of the different types of buildings in a zone should be taken into consideration and an average monthly rent or yearly rent for each category of buildings expressed as a rate per sq. km. of plinth area should be arrived at. The average rental value thus arrived at should be the unit rate which will be the basis to determine the tax. The unit rate should be made available to the public in the form of a draft notification and after considering any suggestions or objections received, a final notification fixing the unit rate per sq. mt. for each zone and for each type of buildings should be published.

The rebate is granted on the basis of age of the buildings. For buildings which are 25 years and below in age, a rebate of 10 per cent of the annual rental value may be given and for buildings above 25 years, a rebate of 20 per cent may be given. For residential buildings which are rented out, a surcharge of 25 per cent may be levied. In the case of commercial properties, the higher rate be set. The rates as recommended by the Commission are as under :

Building Tax/Property Tax for Commercial Properties

	Corporations		*Municipalities*		*Panchayats*	
	Min.	*Max.*	*Min.*	*Max.*	*Min.*	*Max.*
Basic Charge (%)	12	—	10	—	9	12
Service Tax for Lighting (%)	2	—	2	—	—	—
Service Tax for Drainage (%)	2	—	—	—	—	—
Service Tax for Water (%)	1	—	—	—	—	—
Service Tax for Sanitation (%)	3	—	3	—	—	—
Total (%)	20	25	15	25	9	12

For owner occupied commercial properties, a rebate of 10 per cent may be allowed provided the owner and the occupier are identical. Where the occupier is a company, a partnership or any other judicial persons, the rebate will not apply.

For commercial properties where rental value is proposed for retention as the basis, rate payers whose annual rental value exceeds Rs. 12,000 may be statutorily required to file a return yearly at the end of the year showing the actual rental income earned and the tax on it on the prescribed rate.

The Commission recommends that the general revisions may take place every four years instead of five years.

All residential buildings with a plinth area of less than 20 sq. mt. in Panchayats and Municipalities with mud walls or thatched roofs may be exempted from building/property tax. All non-residential buildings irrespective of their area or type of construction should be made liable to pay the tax.

The Commission feels that there should be minimum property/building tax payable by a tax payer and this may be fixed at Rs. 15 per half year in a Panchayat, Rs. 20 in a Municipality and Rs. 25 in a Corporation.

In order to assist Local Bodies in collecting the amounts due to them, a provision may be introduced for charging interest at the rate of 2 per cent per month on arrears.

Entertainment Tax

Entertainment Tax and Additional Entertainment Tax are leviable on any exhibition, performance, amusements, game, race, sports or gambling and the single largest source is the cinema. The rate of tax is to be fixed between the minimum of 15 per cent and maximum of 30 per cent on the price of tickets and the Additional Entertainment Tax is fixed at 60 per cent of the tax. The method of assessment is by stamping the admission tickets with a seal or adhesive stamp on payment of tax. The tax is collected in advance either at the time of stamping the tickets or its sale to the customer. The Local Bodies in the State are entitled to get between a minimum of 24 paise and a maximum of 48 paise as Entertainment Tax and Additional Entertainment

Tax for every rupee collected as price of the admission ticket.

The Commission would not like to recommend a wholesale shift of gross collection capacity as the basis for Entertainment Tax for all cinema houses. The Commission feels that it is required under the circumstances that an option is given to Local Bodies to follow either the current system or a modified system based upon gross collection capacity as the basis for taxation. The objective criteria should be the actual Entertainment Tax that the exhibitor has been paying during the immediate preceding year and if the tax paid, considered along with the tax rate, the total seating capacity and price of tickets is consistent with an occupation ratio of less than 25 per cent of the gross seating capacity at a minimum of 25 per cent of the seating capacity. The Local Body should be free to fix the rate above the minimum. The Entertainment Tax remitted during the immediately preceding year should be the criterion and the Local Bodies should fix the tax on the basis of gross seating capacity within a period of two months from the date stipulated by Government after making necessary changes in the legal provisions.

The State Finance Commission recommends the merger of Entertainment Tax and Additional Entertainment Tax in a single item suitably refixing the rate of Entertainment Tax.

Show Tax

The Local Bodies are empowered to levy and collect a show tax on every exhibition performed in their territory as under :

(a) Regular cinematographic exhibitions in licenced theatres – Rs. 2 per show.

(b) Other cinematographic exhibitions – Rs. 10 per show.

(c) Regular Exhibitions other than cinema – Rs. 5 per show

(d) Other Exhibitions – Rs. 30 per show.

In addition to Show Tax, the local bodies are also empowered to levy and collect a surcharge on Show Tax at the rate of 25 per cent of Show Tax on every show.

The Commission recommends that the distinction between the Show Tax and Surcharge on Show Tax may be abolished and both merged into one. The regime of fixed rates may be replaced by one where the present rates are fixed as minimum with freedom given to local bodies to fix rates above them at intervals of not less than two years.

Profession Tax

Local bodies are levying Profession Tax on individuals and companies. All companies and individuals transacting business or engaged in a profession for not less than 60 days in a half year are liable to pay the tax. The Commission recommends that the rate of Profession Tax may be uniform in urban and rural local bodies and the number of slabs be reduced and rates rationalised as under :

Class	*Half Yearly Income*	*Maximum Half Yearly Tax*
I	Rs. 3,000 - 5,999	Rs. 30
II	Rs. 6,000 - 11,999	Rs. 60
III	Rs. 12,000 - 17,999	Rs. 120
IV	Rs. 18,000 - 29,999	Rs. 180
V	Rs. 30,000 - 44,999	Rs. 300
VI	Rs. 45,000 - 59,999	Rs. 450
VII	Rs. 60,000 - 74,999	Rs. 600
VIII	Rs. 75,000 - 99,999	Rs. 750
IX	Rs. 1,00,000 – 1,24,999	Rs. 1000
X	Rs. 1,25,000 and above	Rs. 1250

The allowances such as HRA and Travelling Allowances should be excluded as they are essentially in the nature of reimbursement of specific purposes. DA, Bonus etc. should be taken as part of taxable income.

Tax on Advertisement

The Municipal Act empowers the Municipalities to resolve the rate of Advertisement Tax but such rates require the approval of the Government. These areas of decision making should be vacated by the government and at best government may fix the minimum rates chargeable and leave it to local body to fix it above those rates. Afterall, public display of advertisements at a particular spot is not a fundamental right and if a prospective customer finds the rate too high, he will not use the site and the demand and supply equation will result in an appropriate rate without the intervention of government.

Non-Tax Revenue

Local bodies derive non-tax revenue principally through income from properties, licence fees, receipts under Special Acts and miscellaneous receipts. There is a good scope for increasing income from properties as well as licence fees. The property income is derived mainly from developed properties such as offices and shopping complexes. The Commission is of the view that construction of shopping complexes and office complexes should not be a high priority item. If local bodies have real estate suitable for development as complexes, they can invite private developers to develop on the basis of open competitive tenders with provision for payment of a share of the rent or for giving free a portion of the developed property.

As regards licence fees, the Commission recommends that instead of specifying a unique rate of each item, government may specify only the minimum rate and leave it to local bodies to fix rates above it, except in the case of births and deaths. It is not possible to notify an exhaustive list of trades which would need licence and fees. After enumerating various items, a residuary category may be added and a minimum licence fees prescribed for it.

STRENGTHENING OF RESOURCE BASE

The existing structure of devolution of finances to local bodies shows that local bodies in Kerala have a set of exclusive revenue sources such as Buildings/Property Tax, Profession Tax,

Entertainment Tax, Advertisement Tax etc. Almost all the tax instruments have been placed at the disposal of local bodies in the State with the exception of octroi even before the 1994 Act. This, alongwith the sharing of Motor Vehicle Tax and grants given by the State government, has imparted a measure of financial strength to local bodies.

Octroi

The Commission is of the view that while octroi may turn out to be a good source of income to the local bodies, arguments against its introduction are quite persuasive and strong. Octroi is basically a tax on goods and it should not be possible to levy a tax on such goods sold in the locality without resorting to the practice of stopping the transport vehicle carrying the goods for collecting the tax.

Building Tax

One of the taxes currently being levied and appropriated by Government which appear eminently suitable for assignment to local bodies is the Building Tax levied and collected by the government. This tax is levied under the Kerala Building Tax Act, 1975. Every building whose plinth area is more than 75 sq. mt. is subjected to Building Tax at specified rates on the basis of plinth area.

The Commission recommends that the Building Tax currently collected by the State government may be exclusively assigned to the Village Panchayats and Municipalities who may assess and appropriate the tax.

Tax on Sale of Properties

The Commission recommends that District Panchayats may be empowered to levy tax on the sale of price of all immovable properties within the District where the price is Rs. 25,000 or more at the rate of one per cent. Three per cent of collection may be retained by government as collection charges. The revenue realised from urban local areas in the District may be given to Urban Local Bodies as a statutory grant on the basis of collection from their respective areas. The revenue from the rural areas of the district may be divided in equal proportion between District Panchayat and Block Panchayats. The *inter se* distribution among Block Panchayats may be in proportion to the population of each Block Panchayat to the 1991 population of the district.

Tax on Operators of Cable TV

Proprietors of cable television, video parlours and video games derive income from providing the service besides providing amusement and entertainment to the public. This mode of entertainment may be subjected to Entertainment Tax to be levied and appropriated by local bodies on the following lines :

1. Cable television operators may be required to pay annual licence fees at a minimum of Rs. 500 or at the rate of Rs. 5 per connection whichever is higher.
2. In addition, cable TV operators and proprietors of video parlours and video games may be made liable to Entertainment Tax at the rate of 20 per cent of the payment made by a customer in Municipal Corporations, 15 per cent in Municipalities and 10 per cent in Panchayats.

Taxation of Government Properties

The Commission strongly recommends that Central Government properties should be liable for Building Tax/Property Tax by local bodies with a proviso that Central Government may exempt any specified class of building.

Sharing of Non-Tax Resources

Court Fee Stamps

Local bodies at all levels receive a number of applications for prescribed licences, permits etc. as well as a number of petitions on various statutory and non-statutory matters which are required to be affixed with Court Fee Stamps. The Commission finds justification for local bodies getting the benefit of Court Fee Stamps which are required to be affixed to documents filed before local bodies. For the purpose, it is assumed that 5 per cent of the total collection is the collection charge and the balance 95 per cent may be distributed equally between the Government and local bodies. Among the local bodies, the amount may be distributed on population basis.

Building Exemption Fees

Under the Kerala Building Rules, 1984 Government is the authority competent to give exemptions from the Rules to applicants. The Rules empower Government alone to give exemptions and a number of applications for exemptions are made and are given also. Government has also laid down a scale of fees ranging from Rs. 50 to Rs. 5000 to be paid by each applicant while applying for the exemption. The procedure for grant of exemption is that the application in the prescribed form is routed through the concerned local body. The local body has to inspect the site, attest the building plan and clearly identify the points which require relaxation of the Building Rules.

The Commission is of the view that it is only fair and just that a portion should go to the concerned local body. The Commission recommends that the local body should be made eligible for 50 per cent of the Building Exemption Fee. The applicant should remit it direct to the local body at the time of applying for exemption and the balance to government by challan into treasury. The Commission also recommends to increase the rate by 100 per cent.

Library Cess

The Kerala Public Libraries Act, 1985 prescribes levy of a library cess as a surcharge on the Building/Property Tax at the rate of 5 per cent of the tax. This is collection by local bodies and remitted to the State Library Council.

The Commission feels that the financial support to the State Library Council should be the responsibility of the State and the present arrangement seeks to devolve on local bodies a part of the responsibility of State government of financially supporting the libraries. Local taxes are meant to be used locally and the local government is accountable to the rate payers for the taxes levied from them. Since this tax has become a part of the tax scenario and therefore may continue to be collected by the local bodies and earmarked for improving the infrastructure of the educational institutions under their control.

FISCAL DEVOLUTION

Plan Funds

The Commission is of the view that the 1991 census data on socio-economic characteristics provide a workable basis for constructing criteria for devolution of plan funds. The chosen indicators with the suggested weights are as under :

	Indicators	*Urban Local Bodies*	*Rural Loca Bodies*
1.	Population in 1991 census	75	70
2.	Population of SC/ST in 1991 Census	10	10
3.	Total workers excluding workers in manufacturing, processing, servicing and repairs outside household industry	15	10
4.	Proportion of agricultural workers among workers	—	10

Non-Plan Grants

The Commission is of the view that the distinction between non-plan specific purpose and general purpose grants need not be maintained and the entire non-plan non-statutory grant may be given as a single general purpose grant. It should be left to the local bodies to decide on the application of the non-plan grants according to their own priority and perception of their needs. The Commission further recommends that the past non-plan specific purpose grants which may be lying unutilised or have been diverted for purpose other than those envisaged in the grant may also be treated as a general purpose grant.

Constitution of Urban Pool

Municipalities are not at present entitled to a share of the Land Tax. The surcharge on Stamp Duty collected from municipal areas is given to the concerned municipality in its entirety without keeping any part of it in a common pool. The Commission recommends that the urban local bodies may also be made eligible for the Land Tax estimated at about 3 per cent of the total collection and this may be put in a common pool. The Commission has also recommended that 25 per cent of the surcharge on stamp duty from the Municipal Council areas may be put in a State Pool to be distributed among the municipal councils. The surcharge collected from the corporations will not be subjected to this and the entire amount collected may be transferred to them on collection basis. Thus, the Urban Pool will consist of :

(a) Various non-statutory non-plan grants being given by State government consolidated into one general grant at one per cent of State Revenue. The share of Urban Pool will be in proportion to the population in Municipal Council areas to the State's population,

(b) 100 per cent of the Basic Tax collected from Urban areas,

(c) 25 per cent of surcharge on Stamp Duty collected from Municipal Council areas.

The non-plan grants which government will be paying to local bodies for the transferred responsibilities will not form part of pool.

Devolution of Pool Fund

The Commission has recommended that one per cent each of the Rural and Urban Pools may be credited to the proposed Fund for Local Development. The remaining 99 per cent of the annual accruals may be distributed on the basis of following composite criteria :

	Village Panchayats	*Municipal Councils*
1. Population in 1991 census	75	80
2. Population of SC/ST in 1991 census	5	5
3. Financial need of local bodies	15	10
4. Tax efforts of local bodies	5	5

The financial needs of local bodies are based on the classification of local bodies on the basis of income from all sources excluding Motor Vehicle Tax and loans. The following classification has been suggested by the Commission :

1. Group I — Annual Income of above Rs. 1 crore.
2. Group II — Annual Income of above Rs. 75 lakh and upto Rs. 1 crore.
3. Group III — Annual Income of above Rs. 50 lakh and upto Rs. 75 lakh.
4. Group IV — Annual Income of above Rs. 40 lakh and upto Rs. 50 lakh.
5. Group V — Annual Income of Rs. 40 lakh and above.

Of the 10 per cent set apart for financial needs, 50 per cent may be distributed among Group V, 30 per cent among Group IV, 20 per cent among Group III on the basis of the population in the total population in the same group.

The tax effort of local bodies may be judged by two indicators viz :

1. The percentage of collection to demand,
2. The rate at which Property Tax is levied.

The Commission feels that half of the 5 per cent may be distributed among those whose collection rate is 95 per cent or more during the preceding year and the remaining half may be distributed on population basis among Municipalities who are charging House Tax above the meridian rate i.e. about 18 per cent.

Maintenance Grants for Building and Roads

The Commission recommends that maintenance grant should be based on current cost of construction estimated at about Rs. 2,750 per sq. mt. for a school and about 4,200 per sq. mt. for a dispensary or health centre at 1995 prices. Two per cent of this should be the annual maintenance grant in respect of schools and three per cent for buildings, like hospitals and dispensaries. The cost of construction should be indexed for inflation. The rate recommended above may hold good for 1996-97 and for subsequent years, it may be reflexed as follows :

1. For 1997-98 — 96 rate + 7 per cent
2. For 1998-99 — 96 rate + 15 per cent
3. For 1999-2000 — 96 rate + 22 per cent
4. For 2000-01 — 96 rate + 28 per cent

As regards maintenance of roads, the Commission recommends that the Vehicle Tax compensation may be 25 per cent of the net collection of Motor Vehicle Tax and it may be distributed among various local bodies in charge of the network on the principles of appointment. As and when additional PWD roads are transferred to local bodies, additional fund may be transferred to them.

Tenth Finance Commission Grants

The Commission has recommended that 85 per cent of the Central Finance Commission grants may be earmarked for distribution among the Village Panchayats. The remaining 15 per cent may be distributed among Block and District Panchayats in proportion of 3 : 2 and on a per capita basis. The grant earmarked for urban local bodies may be distributed on per capita basis. From the total grant, one per cent is earmarked for the Fund for Local Development and only the balance 99 per cent will be distributed.

Budget and Accounts

The Commission has suggested that government may appoint a small expert group which will go into the whole question of the formula used for preparing budget and maintaining accounts and other related questions such as the need for a sinking fund, depreciation reserve etc. In the light of the recommendations of the Expert Group and in consultation with the representatives of the local bodies, a final decision can be taken.

The Commission also suggests to adopt the system of accounting in conformity with the commercial system of accounting and the audit function be performed by professionally qualified auditors.

Local Development Fund

The Commission is of the view that a fund should be built up which can be used for leveraging funds and for subsidising the interest rate in non-remunerative but desirable schemes to strengthen civic infrastructure. The Fund may be constituted from contribution from the following sources :

1. From the funds coming from the Tenth Finance Commission recommendation, one per cent may be set apart each year,
2. From the Urban Pool and Rural Pool, one per cent may be set apart for the Fund,
3. One per cent of the surcharge on Stamp Duty and one per cent of the non-statutory non-plan grants payable to the Municipal Corporations be credited to the Fund,
4. One per cent of the own income of all local bodies may be contributed to the Fund.

Initially, there will be no contribution from the District and Block Panchayats. In order to become eligible for benefits from the Fund, they will have to contribute annually to it.

The main purpose of the Fund are :

1. to leverage funds from market, and
2. to offer a scheme of interest subsidy on desirable but non-remunerative schemes.

Water Supply

The Kerala Water Supply Authority is a statutory body established under the Kerala Water Supply and Sewerage Act, 1986 for the development and regulation of water supply and waste water collection and disposal in the State. The responsibility of local bodies with regard to drinking water in the State is a limited one confined mainly to providing street taps which constitute 17 per cent of all connections. The Authority levies an annual charge of Rs. 1314 per street tap in Municipalities and Rs. 875 in Panchayats. The supply of water is assumed at a rate of 5 litres per minute for 12 hours in Municipalities and 8 hours in Panchayats and is billed at Re. one per kilo litre.

In this regard, the Commission makes the following recommendations :

1. the pre 1-4-1984 arrears may be written off,
2. the arrears accumulated during the period 1-4-84 to 31-3-1991 may be added to the arrears from 1-4-92 upto 31-3-96. The arrears should be recovered from the local bodies on a voluntary basis or by adjusting it from grants payable by the government over a period of 8 years but in no year should the arrear adjusted exceed 15 per cent of the grants due to local body during that year.

Miscellaneous Recommendations

(a) A special cell may be constituted in the Finance Department after the expiry of the term of the Commission to watch the implementation of the recommendations of the State Finance Commission and for other functions specified.

(b) Buildings constructed unauthorisedly in Panchayat areas may be brought under the tax net without conferring on them any right to regularisation or immunity from punitive action including demolition.

(c) Local bodies should be competent to execute civil works financed out of funds raised from public on the basis of estimates prepared by architects and without the intervention of any government agency in the award of supervision of the work.

(d) The arrears of 1996-97 should be adjusted against the grants payable to local bodies. It should not exceed 50 per cent of the grants payable to local bodies and in the case of consecutive defaults in two years, an additional 10 per cent of the grants may be adjusted.

(e) The repairs and maintenance function in respect of street taps may be looked after by the local bodies who are prepared to take it over and for such local bodies, 10 per cent rebate of the charges payable by a Panchayat and a 7 per cent rebate by a Municipality should be allowed by the Authority.

(f) 25 per cent of the various Centrally sponsored programmes for poverty alleviation should be at the disposal of local bodies to be spent on poverty alleviation programmes formulated by the local bodies and approved by the District Planning Committee.

(g) A Statutory Authority should give annual reports to the government showing the quantum of statutory and non-statutory grants due to local bodies and actually paid to them.

(h) Unique Premises Numbering — The Commission

recommends that all local bodies conduct a systematic tax mapping followed by assigning Unique Premises Number to each premise. The cost of tax mapping may be met by a Centrally sponsored scheme and computerisation of the data in urban local bodies may form part of the scheme. For Panchayats, it may be 100 per cent and for Corporations and Municipalities 50 per cent of the cost may be met by Centre and 50 per cent by the local bodies.

The State Government has accepted all the major recommendations and the necessary amendments in the laws are in the pipeline.

5

MADHYA PRADESH

Madhya Pradesh is centrally situated State of the country. The State is associated with some famous names in Indian history. Emperor Ashoka began his career from Ujjain. It formed part of Gupta empire and the Mughal empire and the empire of Emperor Harsha. However, the present enlarged State of Madhya Pradesh came into being on 1st November, 1956 by merging the erstwhile states of Madhya Bharat, Vindhya Pradesh and Bhopal. It is the second largest State in terms of area and ranks third in population.

The State is surrounded by seven States. It is bounded by Rajasthan on the north-west, by Uttar Pradesh on the north, by Bihar on the north-east, by Orissa and Chhatisgarh on the east, by Andhra Pradesh and Maharashtra on the south and Gujarat on the west.

The State is divided into 45 districts, out of which 13 districts have a significant share of scheduled tribes population. The scheduled castes and scheduled tribes population together contain a huge share of the total population of the State.

Agriculture is the mainstay of State's economy as about more than three-fourth of the population lives in rural areas. About 44 per cent area of the State is cultivable. The State has, however, entered the era of high-tech industries. Madhya Pradesh is the first State in the country producing optical fibre for tele-communication needs. The State is famous for its traditional handicrafts and handloom cloths. It has a distinct place in the sphere of mineral production. Total length of roads in the State was 97,343 km. in 1995-96 including 76,614 km. of metalled roads. The total length of rail routes in the State is 5761 km.

URBAN SCENARIO

The State recorded an urban population of 15.35 million in 1991, sharing 7 per cent of total urban population in the country. Madhya Pradesh has experienced rapid urban growth during the last three decades. From a small urban population of 4.63 million and 14 per cent of total population in 1961, urban population grew to 15.35 million or 23.3 per cent of total population in 1991, thus, registering an increase of 231 per cent. Out of 45 districts, seven districts have level of urbanisation below ten per cent and another 13 have urban content between 10 and 18 per cent. Thus, 20 districts are least urbanised whereas four districts of Jabalpur, Gwalior, Indore and Bhopal have level of urbanisation above 40 per cent. The huge urban population lives in 433 urban centres. The number of class one towns has increased from 14 in 1981 to 23 in 1991, sharing more than half of the total urban population. However, class two towns have grown faster than all size towns. The State has two metropolitan towns in Indore and Bhopal.

The beginning of local government in regions (Mahakoshal and Chhatisgarh sub-regions of former Madhya Pradesh, the erstwhile states of Madhya Bharat, Vindhya Pradesh, Bhopal and Sironj sub-region of Rajasthan) was simultaneous. In Mahakoshal, first municipality was set up in 1864 in Jabalpur. The Municipality Act of 1867 was enacted under which 18 mun icipalities were set up in the region. This Act was replaced in 1889 and 1903. The C.P. and Berar Municipality Act, 1922 repealed this Act with the object of giving more autonomy to urban local bodies. In 1950, City of Jabalpur Corporation Act, 1948 was enforced and in June 1950 Jabalpur Municipality was converted into Jabalpur Municipal Corporation.

Madhya Bharat was formed by merging a number of princely states. In most of the erstwhile states, municipalities were working under separate Acts. About 20 Municipalities Acts were in force in different parts. They were given more autonomy and were given enhanced powers and responsibilities. After the formation of Municipality in Indore, municipalities were set up in Neemuch and Lashkar (Gwalior) in 1887. With the enactment of Madhya Bharat Municipal Corporation Act, 1956, municipal corporations were established in Indore and Gwalior on 30th October, 1956.

In Vindhya Pradesh, first municipality was established in Datia in 1907. At the time of merger of Vindhya Pradesh, there were 6 municipalities in the region and Vindhya Pradesh Municipality Act was in operation.

In Bhopal, the Jamat Intizamia (Managing Body) of 1903 was converted into Municipality in 1916 with the enactment of Bhopal State Municipal Act. The second municipality under the Act was established in Sehore in 1940. The Bhopal State Municipalities Act was passed in 1955 which was later substituted by Madhya Pradesh Municipal Act, 1961.

In Sironj sub-division, Rajasthan Town Municipalities Act, 1951 was in force. After the formation of Madhya Pradesh, a Committee was constituted in July 1957 for bringing a uniformity in municipalities of the State. In compliance with the report, Madhya Pradesh Municipalities Act, 1961 was made applicable to all municipalities of the State and all other Municipal Acts were repealed. In the same manner, Madhya Pradesh Municipal Corporation Act, 1956 was made applicable to all municipal corporations with effect from May 20, 1961.

Presently, the 18 municipal corporations are governed under the Madhya Pradesh Municipal Corporation Act, 1961 and 92 Nagar Palika Parishads and 262 Nagar Panchayats are managed under the unified Act entitled as M.P. Municipalities Act, 1961. Both the Acts have been amended in consonance with the Constitution (74th Amendment) Act, 1992.

Madhya Pradesh has recently introduced a new system of urban governance on the pattern of West Bengal and Tripura. Under the new system of municipal governance, Mayor-in-Council and President-in-Council systems have been introduced. The new system envisages cabinet system in municipal administration, thus, making municipality more accountable to the people.

FUNCTIONAL DOMAIN

Municipal Corporation

The municipal corporations have to perform obligatory as well as discretionary functions :

Obligatory Duties

The Corporation has to make adequate provisions for the following matters :

1. lighting public streets and buildings;
2. cleaning public streets, places and sewers and all spaces;
3. disposing of nightsoil and rubbish;
4. the maintenance of the fire brigade;
5. regulating or abating dangerous or offensive trades or practices;
6. removing obstructions and projections in public streets and places;
7. establishing and managing cattle pounds;
8. securing or removing dangerous buildings or places;
9. acquiring and maintaining, changing and regulating places for the disposal of dead and disposing of unclaimed dead bodies and dead bodies of paupers;
10. constructing, altering and maintaining public streets, culverts and Corporation boundary marks, latrines, urinals, drains, sewers and providing public facilities for drinking water, watering public streets and places;
11. the management and maintenance of the Municipal Water Works and the constructions and maintenance of new work and means for providing a sufficient supply of suitable water for public and private purposes;
12. the erection in proper and convenient situations on municipal land of water closet, closet accommodation, urinals and other convenience for the public and maintenance and cleansing of the same;

13. the construction and maintenance of public market and slaughter houses and the regulation of all markets and slaughter houses;
14. the maintenance of an ambulance service;
15. naming streets and numbering houses;
16. registering births, marriages and deaths;
17. public vaccination;
18. establishing and maintaining primary schools;
19. taking measures to prevent the outbreak, spread or recurrence of infectious diseases;
20. the maintenance of municipal office and of all public monuments and other property vested in the Corporation;
21. provision of traffic sign;
22. printing and publishing Annual Reports and Returns of the administration of the Corporation;
23. the maintenance of public park, gardens, recreation grounds, public places and open spaces in existence and vested in the Corporation;
24. fulfilling any obligation imposed by this Act or any other law for the time being in force;
25. construction and maintenance of veterinary dispensaries.

Discretionary Functions

The municipal corporation may provide provisions for the following :

1. reclaiming healthy localities and laying out new street;
2. constructing, establishing or maintaining public parks or gardens, library, museum, halls, theatres, stadiums, offices, *sarais*, rest houses and other public buildings;
3. construction and maintaining residential quarters for Municipal officers and servants;
4. construction, maintenance and cleansing of washing and bathing places;
5. furthering educational objects other than the

establishment and maintenance of primary schools and making grants to educational institutions;

6. planting and maintaining roadside and other trees;
7. registration of vital statistics;
8. making a survey;
9. the destruction or the detention of ownerless dogs or stray pigs or detention of animals causing nuisance;
10. securing or assisting to secure suitable places for the carrying on of the offensive trades or practices;
11. supplying, constructing and maintaining pipe and other fittings for the supply of water to private premises from water-works maintained by the Corporation;
12. supplying, constructing and maintaining receptacles, fittings, pipes, and other appliances on or for the use of private premises for receiving and conducting the sewage thereof into sewers under the control of the Corporation;
13. fairs and exhibitions, or athletics or games, competitions or tournaments;
14. constructing and maintaining such roads and buildings and other government works as the government may transfer to the Corporation;
15. organisation and management of chemical or bacteriological laboratories for the examination or analysis of water, food or drugs;
16. the construction and maintenance in the public streets of drinking fountains for human beings and water-troughs for animals;
17. the prevention of cruelty to animals;
18. the playing music in squares, or gardens or other places of public resort;
19. the construction, purchase, organisation, maintenance or management of tramways or motor transport facilities for the conveyance of the public;
20. preparation and presentation of address to persons of distinction;
21. prevention of vagrancy; establishing and maintaining

poor houses;

22. establishing and maintaining a farm or factory for the disposal of sewage;
23. organisation and maintenance of maternity homes and infant welfare centres;
24. the organisation, maintenance or management of institutions for the care and training of blind, deaf, dumb or otherwise disabled persons;
25. swimming pools, public wash houses, bathing places, and other institution designed for the improvement of public health;
26. dairies of farms within or without the city for the supply, distribution and processing of milk or milk products, for the benefit of the residents of the city;
27. establishment and control of *gwala* colonies and cattle pens within or without the city;
28. the purchase of any undertaking for the supplying of electric energy or gas or starting or subsidising of any such undertakings;
29. the acquisition and maintenance of grazing grounds within or without the city;
30. granting rewards for information regarding the infringement of any provisions of this Act or any other Acts, the enforcement of which is entrusted to the Corporation by regulation or standing order thereunder;
31. the construction and maintenance of sanitary stables for animals or vehicles, or garages;
32. measures to meet any calamity affecting the public in city;
33. the regulation of lodging houses and boarding houses in the city;
34. the grant of loans for building purposes or for purchase of conveyance to municipal officers and servants,
35. any other measures for the welfare of municipal servants;
36. contribution towards any public fund raised for the relief of human sufferings within the city or for the

public welfare;
37. establishing and maintaining pre-primary schools;
38. establishing and maintaining public hospitals and dispensaries and carrying out other means necessary for public relief;
39. any other matter likely to promote the public health, safety or convenience of the public;
40. urban planning including town planning;
41. regulation of land-use and construction of buildings;
42. planning for economic and social development and promotion of ecological aspects;
43. safeguarding the interests of weaker sections of society, including the handicapped and mentally retarded;
44. urban poverty alleviation.

MUNICIPALITIES

Municipalities in the State are entrusted with obligatory as well as discretionary functions.

Obligatory Duties

The municipalities are obliged to perform following functions :

1. lighting public streets, places and buildings;
2. cleansing public streets, places and sewers, removing noxious vegetation, and abating all public nuisances;
3. disposing of night-soil and rubbish and preparation of compost manure from night-soil and rubbish;
4. extinguishing fire and protecting life and property when fire occurs;
5. regulating or abating offensive or dangerous trades or practices;
6. removing obstructions and projection in public streets or places;
7. acquiring, maintaining, changing and regulating places for the disposal of the dead;
8. taking special measures for disposal of dead bodies

during epidemics and other unforeseen emergencies;

9. securing or removing dangerous building or places, and reclaiming unhealthy localities;
10. constructing, altering and maintaining public streets, culverts, Municipal boundary marks, markets, *hats*, slaughter houses, latrines, privies, urinals, drains, sewers, drainage works, sewerage works, baths, washing places, drinking fountains, tanks, wells, dams and the like;
11. establishing and managing cattle pounds;
12. obtaining a supply or an additional supply of water, proper and sufficient;
13. naming streets and parks and numbering houses;
14. public vaccination;
15. providing suitable accommodation for any calves, cows or buffaloes for the supply of animal lymph;
16. registration of cattle and carrying out the census of agricultural cattle;
17. taking measures to prevent the outbreak or spread or recurrence of infectious diseases;
18. preparing annual reports on the Municipal administration;
19. erecting substantial boundary marks defining the limits or any alteration in the limits of the Municipality;
20. constructing and maintaining residential quarters for the conservancy staff of the Council;
21. establishing and maintaining primary schools.

Discretionary Duties

A Council may, at its discretion provide either wholly or partly out of the Municipal property and fund, for all or any of the following matters namely :

1. reclaiming unhealthy localities, laying out new public streets;
2. constructing, establishing or maintaining public parks, gardens, play grounds and open spaces, libraries,

museums, lunatic asylums, halls, offices, *dharamshalas*, rest houses and other public buildings;

3. furthering educational objects;
4. planting and maintaining roadside and other trees;
5. watering public streets and places;
6. playing of music in squares, gardens or other places of public resort;
7. registration of vital statistics;
8. making a survey;
9. paying salaries and allowances, rent and other charges incidental to maintenance of the Court of any stipendiary or honorary Magistrate;
10. destruction or the detention of dogs and pigs;
11. securing or assisting to secure suitable places for the carrying on of the dangerous and offensive trades;
12. supplying, constructing and maintaining receptacles, fittings, pipes and other appliances for the use of private premises for receiving and conducting the sewage thereof into sewers under control of the council;
13. establishing and maintaining a farm or factory for the disposal of sewage;
14. promoting the well-being of Municipal employees or class of employees and of their dependants;
15. providing housing accommodation for any class of employees of the Council other than the conservancy staff;
16. the construction of sanitary dwelling houses for the poorer classes;
17. making contribution towards the construction, establishment or maintenance of educational institutions including libraries and museums, hospitals, dispensaries or similar institutions providing public medical relief or engaged in social work or other institutions of a charitable nature;
18. the acquisition and maintenance of pasture lands or grazing grounds and the establishment and

maintenance of dairy farms and breeding stud;

19. the setting up of dairies or farms for the supply, distribution and processing of milk or milk products;
20. securing and distributing particularly for the use of expectant and nursing mothers, children and invalids, full-cream or skimmed milk, condensed milk, evaporated milk, milk powder and synthetic or soyabean milk;
21. establishing and running lodging and boarding houses;
22. establishing and running eating houses;
23. providing and maintaining public bathing places or swimming pools;
24. undertaking any commercial enterprises;
25. constructing and maintaining such roads, buildings and other government works other than irrigation works, as the State government may transfer to the Council;
26. providing for maintenance and treatment of lunatics and lepers at an asylum or hospital;
27. arranging for removal of lunatics, lepers and persons needing anti-rabic treatment to an asylum, hospital or house;
28. holding *melas* and fairs;
29. establishing *ashrams* for destitutes, blind, crippled, lame, disabled and old persons;
30. establishing and maintaining veterinary dispensaries;
31. any public reception, ceremony, entertainment or exhibition;
32. any matter likely to promote the public health, education, safety and convenience of the public;
33. establishing and maintaining hospitals and dispensaries;
34. establishing and maintaining poor houses;
35. urban planning including town planning;
36. regulation of land-use and construction of buildings;
37. planning for economic and social development;
38. urban forestry, protection of the environment and promotion of ecological aspects;

39. safeguarding the interests of weaker sections of society including the handicapped and mentally retarded;
40. urban poverty alleviation;
41. any other matter with the previous approval of the State Government.

TAXATION

Municipal Corporation

The municipal corporations in the State are liable to impose following taxes :

1. a tax by the owners of buildings or lands situated within the city with reference to the gross annual letting value of the buildings or lands, called the property tax;
2. a water tax, in respect of lands and buildings to which a water supply is furnished;
3. a general sanitary cess, for the construction and maintenance of public latrines and for removal and disposal of refuse and general cleanliness of the city;
4. a general lighting tax, where the lighting of public streets and places is undertaken by the corporation;
5. a general fire tax, for the conduct and management of fire service and for the protection of life and property in the case of fire;
6. a local body tax on the entry of such goods as may be declared by the State Government by notification in the Official Gazette into the municipal area for consumption, use or sale therein at a rate not exceeding four per cent of the value of goods.

Municipalities

The municipalities are empowered to levy compulsory as well as optional taxes.

Compulsory Taxes

1. a tax by the owners of buildings or lands situated within the city with reference to the gross annual letting value of the buildings or lands, called the property tax;
2. a water tax, in respect of lands and buildings to which a water supply is furnished;
3. a general sanitary cess, for the construction and maintenance of public latrines and for removal and disposal of refuse and general cleanliness of the city;
4. a general lighting tax, where the lighting of public streets and places is undertaken by the corporation;
5. a general fire tax, for the conduct and management of fire service and for the protection of life and property in the case of fire;
6. a local body tax on the entry of goods into the municipal area for consumption, use or sale therein at a rate not exceeding four per cent of the value of goods.

Optional Taxes

A municipality may impose any or all of the following taxes :

1. a latrine or conservancy tax payable by the occupier or owner upon private latrines, privies or cesspools or open premises or compounds cleansed by Council agency;
2. a drainage tax, where a system of drainage has been introduced;
3. a tax on persons exercising any profession or art or carrying on any trade or calling within the city;
4. a tax payable by the owners on all or any vehicles or animals used for riding, driving, draught or burden or on dogs;
5. a toll on vehicles and animals;
6. fees on the registration of cattle sold within the city;
7. market dues on persons exposing goods for sale;
8. a betterment tax on properties whose value may have

improved as a result of town planning scheme undertaken by the council;

9. a tax on pilgrims resorting periodically to a shrine within the limits of the Council;
10. a tax on persons occupying houses, buildings or lands within the limits of the council according to their circumstances and property;
11. a toll on new bridge constructed by the Council;
12. a tax on advertisements other than advertisements published in newspapers;
13. a tax on theatres, theatrical performances and other shows for public amusement;
14. a terminal tax on goods or animals exported from the limits of the Council; and
15. any other tax which the State Government has power to impose under the Constitution of India, with the prior approval of the State Government.

FISCAL DEVOLUTION

In compliance with the Madhya Pradesh Finance Commission Act, the Governor constituted the State Finance Commission in June 1994. The Commission was expected to recommend :

1. Distribution between State Government and urban local bodies, of the net proceeds of taxes leviable by the State and which may be shared between the two, and determination of such taxes, fees etc. which may be assigned to or appropriated by urban local bodies,
2. Grants-in-aid to urban local bodies;
3. Measures to improve financial position of urban local bodies;
4. Review of financial position of municipalities.

Later on, the State Government modified the earlier reference and expected that the Commission while making its recommendations would keep the following points in view besides other matters :

1. The objective of not only achieving balance between receipts and expenditure on revenue account of the State Government and municipalities but also yielding surplus for investment and reducing fiscal deficit;
2. The resources of the State and demands on them, particularly of civil administration, police and judicial administration, debt servicing and other committed expenditure and liabilities;
3. Maintenance expenditure on plan projects to be completed by 31-9-96 and the norms on the basis of which expenditure on maintenance of capital assets has been recommended and the procedure for monitoring such expenditure;
4. On the basis of taxation level of 1994-95, the source of revenue of the State Government on one hand and of municipalities on the other, for five years beginning April 1996, deployment of additional funds for plan and determination of targets and possibilities of additional taxation.
5. Possibility of either financial management through efficiency and economy in expenditure;
6. In compliance with the Constitution Amendment, transfer of responsibilities and services by the State Government to municipalities and corresponding to this transfer of services of employees engaged in such activities and responsibilities.

The notification further states that while making its recommendations the Commission :

1. will adopt normative approach in determining the receipts and expenditure on revenue account of the State Government as well as of Municipalities,
2. will keep in view the need for reasonable incentives for better mobilisation of resources and enforcing fiscal discipline and for linking clearly the decisions to increase expenditure and revenue,
3. will consider the need for speed, efficiency and

effectiveness in system of procedures relating to Government programmes.

The five-member Commission was headed by former Union Minister of State for Finance and consisted of academics and bureaucrats. The Commission submitted its report in June 1996.

Existing Tax Base

The Commission recommends that the base of every tax should be made practical and broad and its rate structure should be rationalised in such a manner that a minimum revenue of Rs. 400 crore could be mobilised through that tax during 1996-97.

Transfer of Funds

The Commission recommends that the present amount of transfer from the State government to urban local bodies which comes to 4.63 per cent of the State's net tax and non-tax revenue be increased to 8.67 per cent net revenue of the State government. The Commission further recommends to continue, apart from share of Entry Tax and Vehicle Tax, specific grants-in-aid in lieu of Passenger Tax which has been abolished, also fees, penalties and other receipts under different Acts.

District-wise inter se Distribution

For determining the share of different districts, the Commission has adopted following criteria :

1. 40 per cent on the basis of urban population as per 1991 census,
2. 35 per cent on the basis of contribution to actual receipt of Sales Tax during 1992-93 and 1993-94,
3. 15 per cent on the basis of urban SC/ST population as per 1991 census,
4. 10 per cent on the basis of inverse of per capita power consumption in urban areas during 1992-93 × urban

population in 1991.

In mathematical terms, the following formula can be used for working out inverse power consumption :

$$b_i = \frac{(N_i / C_i)}{E(N_i / C_i)}$$

where

b_i = Share of the *i*th District

N_i = Urban Population of *i*th District

C_i = Per Capita power consumption of *i*th district.

Grants-in-Aid

The Commission recommends that:

1. there should be no reduction in amount of the grants/financial assistance to be provided to the urban local bodies;
2. the payment to these bodies should be made in twelve equal monthly instalments. It should also be ensured that the amount of grant is deposited in the accounts of respective bodies as per schedule relating to district-wise allocations.

Incentive Grant

The Commission expects that the State Government at its own level or through some private institution, should make evaluation of taxable capacity of each and every urban local body on the basis of some scientific methodology and also the efforts made in this direction of revenue mobilisation and devise a mechanism of incentive grants. The norms, criteria, magnitude and *modus operandi* of such grants may be determined in such a manner by the State Government that local bodies exceeding their targets of revenue mobilisation may receive adequate incentive.

Tenth Finance Commission Award

In regard to the grants allocated by the Central Finance Commission, the State Finance Commission recommends to establish an Urban Development Finance Corporation with an authorised share capital of Rs. 250 crore. This corporation will arrange adequate assistance for financial capital projects of urban local bodies. The Commission further recommends that the amount of Rs. 61.74 crore to be received from the Government of India as per recommendations of the Central Finance Commission, may be used as a part of the authorised share capital of the Corporation.

Miscellaneous

1. Urban Infrastructure Development Fund

The Commission recommends the setting up of an Urban Infrastructure Development Fund at the State level for facilitating the flow of additional funds to local bodies and for proper allocation of funds for the purpose of financing urban infrastructure projects. The following items can be included in the resources of the Fund :

(a) The loan fund from the Central and State Governments which could be utilised as revolving fund and which may be linked with government budget and may, always be replenished with the assistance of bilateral and multilateral funding agencies.

(b) The State controlled institutions which manage pensions and insurance funds may provide grants and loans for the creation of fund for infrastructure which may serve as a single window for financial assistance.

2. Audit

The Commission recommends that with a view to giving

effective shape to internal audit in all urban local bodies, all serious issues in the audit reports should be referred to a local self government Audit Committee, which should be formed at government level on the pattern of Public Accounts Committee of the State Legislature. This Committee would consider all serious matters in audit reports and take appropriate action on them so that the urban local bodies may ultimately be made accountable to the government and the general public in conformity with the spirit of the Constitution.

3. Monitoring Cell

The Commission recommends that after the expiry of working period of the Commission, a small secretariat with skeleton staff should be maintained on a continuous basis in the form of monitoring cell. The cell can be entrusted with the task of monitoring of the implementation of different recommendations of the Finance Commission on a continuous basis.

The Commission further recommends the confirmation of the persons currently working. This cell may work under the Finance Department and be fully responsible to this department.

4. With the objective of balancing revenue and expenditure of urban local bodies, the cost of public utility services should be recovered by charging appropriate fees from the users of services.

5. The Commission recommended that in order to enable the urban local bodies to render basic services, the State Government should release to the urban local bodies Rs. 407 crore in 1996-97 from its Consolidated Fund in terms of Art. 243Y(a)(i) of the Constitution.

6. For affecting economy in the cost of collection and disposal of waste material, the urban local bodies should get municipal waste and industrial waste disposal arranged through private agencies on the principle of energy management.

6

MANIPUR

The recorded history of Manipur is not available though it has been in existence since long. According to historians, Pakhangba founded a dynasty which ruled Manipur till it came under the British rule in 1891. On October 15, 1949, Manipur merged in the Indian Union as Part 'C' State. In 1950-51, an advisory form of the government was introduced. In 1957, it was replaced by a Territorial Council of 32 elected and two nominated members. Later in 1963, a Legislative Assembly of 30 elected and three nominated members was established under the Union Territories Act, 1963. Manipur attained full fledged statehood on 21st January, 1972.

Geographically, the State is divided into two tracts—the hills comprising of five districts and the plains with three districts. Manipur is bounded by Upper (Burma) Myanmar on the east, the Chin Hill of (Burma) Myanmar on the south-east, Nagaland on the north, Assam on west and Mizoram on south and south-west.

Manipur is industrially backward, primarily due to its locational disadvantages. However, small scale industries have started coming up. Agriculture and allied activities is the single largest source of livelihood of the majority of the rural masses. The State has 5,816 km. of road. It is now included in the railway map of India with the opening of the rail head at Jiribam in May 1990. Imphal is the only airport which is linked with other parts of the country.

Characterised by its economic backwardness, Manipur is a small State having a total geographical area of only 22,327 sq. km. of which 90 per cent is covered by hills. The physiographical feature of the State presents notably two distinct areas viz. the valley area and the hilly area which are conspicuous by the absence of uniform development strategies for many decades whereby the valley has been placed a favourable position with higher concentration of population (about 70 per cent of the total population of the State).

In terms of rate of growth of urbanisation in Manipur especially during 1951-81, it registered 37.22 per cent for the decade 1951-61. This declined to 7.65 per cent during 1961-71 as against 10.25 per cent during 1971-81 but increased to 15.30 per cent in 1981-91 decade. Thus the population living in urban areas has multiplied about one hundred thirty four times during the period 1951-81, and further to one hundred and forty eight times in 1991. An important characteristic is that about 88 per cent of the total urban population of the State is still in valley area. In other words, the process of urbanisation in Manipur is by and large a process of urban agglomeration mainly in the valley area accompanied by industrialisation and expansion of urban amenities leaving the hill area still predominantly rural.

The hill area of Manipur for which District Councils exist, have been excluded from the purview of Part IX, however, there is no such exemption vide Article 243 ZC in relation to municipalities. Moreover, confusion is likely to be created when Part IX has been extended to the valley and Part IX A to the entire State with the hill areas left without any guidelines.

The State has more than one-fourth of its population inhabiting in 30 towns, comprising one class one town accounting about 40 per cent of total urban population. The State has enacted the Manipur Municipalities Act, 1994 providing administrative provisions for all three types of urban local bodies, although there is no municipal corporation in the State. The Act has been enacted in view of the Constitution (74th Amendment) Act 1992.

FUNCTIONAL JURISDICTION

As per the provisions of the Act, the State government may entrust the municipalities with the functions of the preparation of plans for economic development and social justice and the performance of functions and the implementation of schemes as may be entrusted to including those listed in the Twelfth Schedule. In addition, the Act provides for following categories of functions to be performed by municipalities.

Obligatory Functions

The municipalities are obliged to make reasonable provision for the following matters :

1. lighting public roads and places;
2. watering public roads and places;
3. cleaning public roads, places and sewers and all spaces which are open to the enjoyment of the public; removing noxious vegetation and abating all public nuisance;
4. removing filth, rubbish, night-soil, odour or any other noxious or offensive matter from privies, latrines, cess-pools or other common receptacles for such matter in or pertaining to a building or buildings;
5. extinguishing fires and protecting life and property when fire occurs;
6. regulating offensive or dangerous trades or practices;
7. removing obstructions and projections in public roads or places;
8. securing or removing dangerous buildings or places and reclaiming unhealthy localities;
9. acquiring, maintaining, changing and regulating places for the disposal of dead bodies and of the carcasses of dead animals;
10. constructing, altering and maintaining public roads, culverts, municipal boundary marks, markets, slaughter houses, drains, sewers, drainage-works, sewerage-works, baths, washing places, drinking fountains, tanks, wells, dams and the like;
11. constructing public latrines, privies and urinals;
12. obtaining a supply or an additional supply of water,

13. naming streets and numbering houses;
14. registering births and deaths;
15. suitable accommodation for any calves, cows or buffaloes required within the municipality for the supply of animal lymph;
16. printing annual reports on the administration of the municipality;
17. making arrangements for preparation of compost manure from night-soil and rubbish; and
18. establishing and maintaining cattle pounds.

Special Duties

Every municipality has to make reasonable provisions for the following special duties :

1. providing special medical aid and accommodation for the sick in times of dangerous disease and taking such measures as may be required to prevent the outbreak or suppress and prevent the recurrence of the disease; and
2. giving relief and establishing and maintaining relief works, in times of famine or scarcity, to or for destitute persons within the limits of the municipality.

Discretionary Functions

A municipality may, at its discretion, provide out of the municipal property and fund, either wholly or partly for :

1. laying out new public roads and acquiring land for the purpose,
2. constructing, establishing, maintaining or contributing to the maintenance of public parks, gardens, libraries, museums, reading rooms, halls, offices, *dharamshalas*, rest-houses, encamping grounds and other public buildings and places;
3. constructions and maintaining, where necessary suitable sanitary houses for the habitation of the poor

and granting loans for the construction of such houses or for effecting necessary improvements connected therewith;

4. providing accommodation for any class of servants employed by the municipality or granting loans to such servants for construction of houses;
5. planting and maintaining trees on the roadside;
6. securing or assisting to secure suitable places for carrying on the offensive trades;
7. supplying, constructing and maintaining receptacles, fittings, pipes and other appliances for receiving and conducting the sewage thereof into sewers under the control of the municipality;
8. public health and infant welfare;
9. contribution towards any public fund raised for the relief of human suffering within or without the municipality;
10. any public reception, ceremony, entertainment or exhibition;
11. the organisation or maintenance of shops or stalls for the sale of necessities of life;
12. holding fairs and exhibitions;
13. supply of milk;
14. establishing labour welfare centres for its employees and subsidising the activities of any association, union or club of such employees by grant of loan for its general advancement;
15. maintenance of ambulance service;
16. establishing and maintaining public hospitals and dispensaries and providing public medical service;
17. providing facilities for antirabic treatment and meeting the expenses of indigent person undergoing antirabic treatment;
18. housing and maintaining destitute, orphans and cripples and maintaining maternity centre and child welfare clinics;
19. establishing rescue homes;

20. any other matter which is likely to promote education or the public health, safety or convenience or the advancement of economic condition of the inhabitants of the municipality.

For the successful performance of these functions, the municipalities are empowered to impose certain taxes.

TAXATION

With the previous approval of the State Government, municipality may impose in the whole or in any part of the municipality any of the following taxes and tolls :

1. a tax on holding situated within the municipality assessed on their annual value,
2. a tax on vehicles or animals used for riding, driving, draught or burden and used within the limits of the municipality;
3. an octroi on goods brought within the limits of the municipality for sale, consumption or use within such limits;
4. a latrine tax payable by the owners or occupiers for collections, removal and disposal of excrement or offensive matter from latrine, privies, urinals, cess-pools or compounds;
5. a scavenging tax;
6. lighting tax where the lighting arrangement is made by the municipality;
7. a drainage tax where the system of drainage has been introduced by the municipality;
8. a tax on deeds of transfer of immovable property situated within the limits of the municipality;
9. a tax on advertisements made within the limit of the municipality other than non-commercial undertaking advertisements published in newspapers;
10. a water-tax where water is supplied by the municipality;

11. market fees on person exposing goods for sale;
12. a betterment charge on properties the value of which may be increased as a result of town planning scheme implemented by the municipality; and
13. any other tax, toll, rate or charge or fee.

FINANCIAL DEVOLUTION

In pursuance of the provisions contained in the Constitution (74th Amendment) Act, 1992, the Governor of Manipur constituted the Finance Commission on 22nd April, 1994. The one-man Commission headed by the former Speaker of the State Assembly started functioning with effect from 9th June, 1995. The Commission was in the process of drafting the report when the Chairman resigned in February 1996. Subsequently, the Manipur State Finance Commission Act, 1996 was passed in May 1996. The Commission was directed to :

(i) recommend distribution of net proceeds of taxes, duties etc. leviable by the State, between the State Government and the rural and urban local bodies,
(ii) determine taxes, duties etc. to be assigned to the local bodies,
(iii) recommend grants-in-aid from the Consolidated Fund of the State for the local bodies.

The new three-member Commission was chaired by an IAS officer. The other members were a bureaucrat and an academician. The Commission submitted its report in September 1996.

Existing Taxation

Overviewing the present tax jurisdiction, the Commission finds that at present there is a multiplicity of petty bye-laws in operation and under scrutiny of the government. There are proposals for imposing holdings tax and separately charge fee for drainage, scavenging, street lighting etc. There are some absolute taxes/fees on cattle etc. and there where cost of collection makes the tax effort infructuous, it is necessary to streamline the taxes/fees structure for the urban local bodies.

The Commission has noted the indifferent performance of Imphal Municipal Council in the matter of collection of octroi. It is understood that some more urban local bodies have sought the approval of the State Government to levy octroi. The Commission feels that imposition and collection of octroi in too many urban areas within such a small State with only two main trade routes may impose a heavy burden on the public. The Commission therefore recommends that in the long run octroi should be abolished and replaced by a surcharge on sales tax and the proceeds can be distributed as maintenance grant.

The Commission is of the view that there is one severe hindrance in the way of urban local bodies raising revenue through taxes and fees. The bye-laws have to be approved by the State government. The Commission feels that it will be appropriate if the State government approves a range of rates for each type of tax/fee so that a local body staying within the range need not take approval of the government in each case. In the alternative, an amendment of the relevant law may be carried out so that a proposal for imposition of fees/taxes could be deemed to be approved by the government if the objections thereto are not conveyed within one month. A third alternative may be to allow local bodies to impose taxes/fees subject to the right of the State government to issue directions in this matter from time to time.

Grants-in-Aid

The Commission recommends a number of grants-in-aid to local bodies :

Maintenance Grant

Since Imphal Municipality is the only local body to have levied both octroi and holdings tax, the Commission does not recommend any maintenance grant to this body. If the local body insists on maintenance grants, it has to surrender octroi and may be given Rs. 50 lakh per year for the five-year period. Existing collection staff may be diverted for doing justice to the holdings tax.

For the six municipal councils, maintenance grants may be retained at the 1995-96 level of Rs. 26.33 lakh for the year 1996-97. The Commission proposes a 10 per cent annual increase on this gross amount for the remaining years to take care of inflation.

Maintenance grants will be worked out on the basis of internal resource generation target of each municipality on the basis of its population and deduct the same from approved annual expenses with annual increase higher than 5 per cent. A small margin is kept to take care of genuine cases of difficulty at the discretion of the State government.

Development Grant

The Commission recommends that the entire TFC funds for the urban local bodies may be passed on to the municipal councils and Nagar panchayats as development grant at the rate of Rs. 12.50 per capita per year.

The Commission further recommends that a per capita grant of Rs. 7 and Rs. 10 may be allocated for the Nagar panchayats and municipal councils respectively per year till March 2001 to share the burden of development works in their respective jurisdiction.

Bonus Grant

The Commission recommends that bonus grants be allocated to all urban local bodies except Imphal on a 100 per cent matching basis for revenue generation beyond above.

Half of the development grant be paid automatically on the basis of population and the balance alongwith the plan funds on sanction of specific schemes and on receipts of utilisation certificates for the previous release of funds. Funds should be released quarterly. Entire amount has to be spent on schemes only.

Special Grant

The Commission recommends a grant of Rs. one lakh per year to Mao to upgrade the township to a respectable level as Mao takes care of the bulk of the passenger and freight traffic into or out of the State. It further recommends a grant of Rs. two lakh per year for More which has a small Town Committee and is gaining importance because of the opening of border trade lately. The allocation to these townships are over and above the existing grants.

Generate Internal Revenue

The Commission prescribes that five other municipal councils (excluding Imphal) should generate internal revenue at the rate of Rs. 28 per head of urban population by the year 2000-01. For the Nagar panchayats, target for internal revenue generation may be fixed at double the rate for Gram panchayats i.e. Rs. 10 per head of their respective population.

Miscellaneous

(a) The Commission recommends that assets created by government departments—roads and paths, street lighting, drainage/sewerage facilities, community services etc. should be handed over to the urban local bodies free of cost and expect them to maintain the same by raising resources for the same locality. It is for the inhabitants of the urban local bodies to pay for the upkeep of these assets.

(b) The Commission feels that the preparation of the budget in municipalities leaves much to be desired. It therefore recommends that a comprehensive budget formats should be prepared and circulated immediately.

(c) The Commission further recommends to strengthen the

Directorate of Local Fund Audit so that important issues like revision of old rates of taxes and fees, collection of arrears, budget making, deviations from budget projections and reasons thereof and so on receive their attention.

(d) The Commission recommends appointment of one full time Executive Officer in each of the Nagar panchayats. The other staff should be given the minimum wages prescribed by the State government. Training of municipal personnel should receive priority.

7

ORISSA

Orissa is a land of agriculture. Nearly 80 per cent of its work-force depends on this sector and half of the State Domestic Product comes from agriculture. The spatial and economic improvement of the State is closely interlinked with intensive agricultural improvement. Majority of urban settlements in the State have their origin in the agriculture base, specifically as market towns of agro-products. Simultaneously, the process of urbanisation has exerted its impact on agricultural performance and created localised employment opportunities. Both these factors are interwoven and interrelated.

If we take into account the history of Orissa, some of the present urban centres had achieved the local importance for which development and construction activities were taken up during different dynasties. During the 16th century Mughals ruled Orissa, and made a separate province keeping Cuttack as capital. The Mughal administration permitted the Europeans for their commercial enterprise and activities. As a result, sea ports of Baleshwar and Pipli developed and flourished. During the Maratha rule from 1757, pilgrimage to Orissa from other parts of the country was encouraged and attention was paid to uphold the sanctity of religious places and shrines. Orissa's economic vitality declined rapidly during the British rule and the government paid scant attention to the condition of people. The people of the princely states were left to themselves to suffer in their separate existence. The awakening towards freedom movement made Orissa into a substantial territorial and administrative entity in the Indian body politic. On 1st April,

1936 the new province of Orissa came into existence. It is, however, with the independence of India that the princely states were amalgamated with the exception of Sareikala and Kharasawan and from 1st January, 1949 the reorganised Orissa came under the control of Government of Orissa. Except the coastal belt, the urban centres were scattered here and there without proper communication linkages resulting in lower state of economy in urban sector.

Urban Scenario

Urbanisation of Orissa started after generation of post-war reconstruction schemes like Mahanadi Valley Project and Machhkund Duduma Hydro-Electric Project. Economic development as well as urbanisation gained momentum during the Five-Year Plan periods.

The population of Orissa has increased from 146.45 lakhs to 316.60 lakhs during 1951 to 1991. The urban population has increased from 5.94 lakhs to 42.35 lakhs in the corresponding period. The decadal growth rate of urban population during 1981-91 was 36.16 per cent as compared to the State's overall growth rate of 20.66 per cent and was less than that of national average of urban population which was 36.47 per cent. This decadal growth however, decelerated from 86.79 per cent in 1951-61. The level of urbanisation, though much below the national level, has shown an increasing trend over the decades i.e., increasing from 4.06 per cent in 1951 to 6.32 per cent, 8.41 per cent, 11.79 per cent and 13.38 per cent respectively in subsequent decades.

As regards urban settlements from 1901 to 1991 their number is found steadily increasing. There were only 14 towns in 1901 which increased nearly three folds i.e., 39 towns after a lapse of 50 years. A total of 85 urban centres have been added from 1951 to 1991. As per 1971 census there were 81 towns which became 108 in 1981 and increased further to 124 in 1991. The maximum increase in number of towns i.e., 27 was experienced during 1971-81 followed by 23 towns during 1951-61.

The percentage of urban population of Class I towns to the total population during 1981 was 35.53 per cent which increased to 41.86 per cent in 1991, whereas the percentage of population of smaller towns almost decreased during the period.

The State of Orissa has been divided into 27 districts. Ganjam is the most populous district followed by Cuttack and Mayurbhanj. Malkangiri is the least populous district. Sundargarh has the largest urban population followed by Khurda and Cuttack. Out of 27 districts only six districts i.e., Khurda (34.61 per cent), Sundargarh (33.47 per cent), Sambalpur (25.73 per cent), Cuttack (23.78 per cent), Koraput (16.26 per cent) and Ganjam (15.79 per cent) had more than State level urbanisation of 13.38 per cent in 1991. The largest number of towns are in Ganjam district.

MUNICIPAL ADMINISTRATION

Municipal administration in the State is managed by the Orissa Municipal Act, 1950. A new enactment concerning the Municipal Corporation is in offing. There are 2 Corporations, 30 Municipalities and 70 Notified Area Councils in the State.

Functions

The Municipal Act empowers the Municipalities to enjoy mandatory as well as discretionary powers :

Mandatory Functions

Every municipality in the State has to :

1. provide a sufficient supply of water for the domestic use of the inhabitants,
2. provide and maintain a sufficient system of drainage and conservancy,
3. cause the public roads to be sufficiently lighted.

Discretionary Functions

The Act in the State empowers every municipality with respect to :

1. preparation of plans for economic development and social justice, and
2. the performance of functions and implementation of schemes in relation to :
   (a) urban planning including town planning,
   (b) planning for economic and social development,
   (c) urban forestry, protection of the environment and promotion of ecological aspects,
   (d) safeguarding the interest of weaker sections of society including handicapped and mentally retarded,
   (e) slum improvement and upgradation,
   (f) urban poverty alleviation,
   (g) promotion of cultural, ecological and aesthetic aspects, and
   (h) vital statistics including registration of births and deaths.

TAXATION POWERS

The municipality may impose following taxes and fees :

1. a tax on holdings situated within the municipality assessed on their value,
2. a latrine tax on the annual value of buildings,
3. a water tax on the annual value of holdings,
4. lighting tax on the annual value of holdings,
5. a drainage tax on the annual value of holdings,
6. a tax on carriages, carts, horses and other animals,
7. a tax on profession, art and callings,
8. a poll tax, subject to maximum and minimum rates, on animals, carts and carriages,
9. a fee on registration of dogs,

10. a fee on vessels moored within the municipal area,
11. an octroi on goods brought within the municipal area for consumption, use or sale,
12. any other fee for services rendered by the municipality, and
13. any other tax which the municipality is empowered to impose.

FINANCIAL DEVOLUTION

The State Government constituted a five-member State Finance Commission by their order on 21st November, 1996 in pursuance of the provisions of the Constitution. For the purpose, the government enacted the Orissa Panchayati Raj Finance Commission (Miscellaneous Provisions) Amendment Act, 1996. Subsequently, the government reconstituted the Commission by their order of August, 24, 1998. The Chairman and the Member-Secretary were changed. Except them, the other three members were to render part time service. The Commission was asked to have regard among other considerations while making its recommendations to :

(a) the revenue resources of the State Government and the demands thereon on account of expenditure on civil administration, police and judicial administration, education, maintenance of capital assets, social welfare, debt servicing and other committed expenditure or liabilities,

(b) the functions and liabilities of local bodies in respect of discharging and implementing the schemes entrusted to them under Articles 243 G and 243 W,

(c) the revenue resources of local bodies at all levels for five years commencing on the 1st day of April, 1998 on the basis of levels of taxation reached in 1997-98 targets set for additional resources mobilisation and potential for mobilising additional revenues,

(d) the scope for better fiscal management consistent with the need for speedy efficiency and cost effectiveness of delivery of services, and

(e) the need for providing adequate incentive for better resources mobilisation as well as closely linked expenditure and revenue raising decision.

The Commission submitted its report on December 19, 1998 for a period of five years from April 1, 1998.

The Commission while making recommendations feels that with the available access to resources revenue, it may be beyond the capacity of local bodies to find the required additional resources for meeting the capital and revenue expenditure. The Commission thus taking into these factors suggests for resource augmentation of local bodies by various measures i.e., (i) by increasing the efforts to exploit the existing tax and non-tax potential and, (ii) by supplementing additional grants by Government through new tax measures, assignment and sharing revenue.

EXISTING SOURCES

Octroi

The Commission finds that despite many drawbacks imposition of octroi in urban local bodies is recognised as the mainstay of their income. However, the replacement of octroi in Orissa by introduction of entry tax would be a welcome measure provided the urban local bodies should not be deprived of getting the compensation from this flexible and buoyant source of revenue. Firstly, the apprehension of the urban local bodies not to get this compensation timely should be cleared. If government can assure to release the compensation in the first week of each month with automatic increase of 10 per cent in subsequent years, abolition of system of octroi has some justification. Otherwise, the present system of octroi should continue and some special drive should be made to check corruption and harassment in order to boost the income from this source and prevent the delay in movement of vehicles.

Holding Tax

It is unfortunate to note that most of the urban local bodies are not very serious about revision in every five years. Of course, making periodical revaluation and effecting the revision require greater degree of political will coupled with the efficient and honest official machinery. But since these are lacking, so the Commission has come to the conclusion that the periodical revaluation should be mandatory and if due to some unavoidable reasons valuation is not possible there should be 3 to 5 per cent hike in the existing holding tax as an interim measure.

SHARING OF SOURCES

Surcharge on Entertainment Tax

The proceeds of basic entertainment tax, additional entertainment tax, show tax and exhibition tax on advertisement are retained in full by the State government. The State government retains at the rate of 15 paise on every payment for admission in urban areas and entire 25 paise surcharge for admission in rural areas. The government is not releasing the share to local bodies on the pretext of lacking any decision of apportioning the surcharge under compounding system. The amount of surcharge is linked to the number of tickets of every denomination sold to the spectators. Under the compounding system the number of tickets sold has been taken to be 20 per cent of the number of seats specified in the licence issued to the cinema house. On this basis, there should be no difficulty in ascertaining the amount of surcharge collected from a cinema house. The Commission recommends that the amount of surcharge payable to the Municipal Councils be determined without further delay.

Keeping in view the collection and release of surcharge amount for urban local bodies at 1994-95 level, the urban local bodies excepting Cuttack, Bhubaneshwar, Berhampur, Rourkela, Puri and Sambalpur are entitled to get Rs. 44.85 lakh each year within the period 1998-99 to 2002-2003. The amount collected on account of compounding the surcharge on entertainment tax should be assessed immediately and the dues be given to the above six urban local bodies with arrears within this five years period.

The Commission further recommends to suitably amend the Orissa Entertainment Tax Act, 1946 entitling the urban local bodies to the whole of surcharge on payments for admission to entertainment.

Surcharge on Stamp Duty

The surcharge on Stamp Duty on transfer of immovable property is leviable in the areas covered by Development Authorities, Special Planning Authorities and Improvement Trusts. The urban local bodies are not covered and the rural local bodies are denied the benefit of income from this source. In view of the system prevailing in other States, the Commission recommends that surcharge on Stamp Duty be leviable in all the areas. It further recommends that a uniform rate of 3 per cent be prescribed for all local bodies including Gram Panchayats. The incidental expenses be fixed at 2 per cent of the amount collected.

Profession Tax

Despite the provision in the Municipal Act, no urban local bodies are venturing to exploit this source since this is considered to be an unpopular measure. The Commission therefore recommends that since the urban local bodies will not be in a position to make a break through in this tax collection efforts due to popular resistance, the government should assume this responsibility both for taxation and assignment of 50 per cent of gross collection of revenue from this source.

Motor Vehicle Tax

The Commission suggests that 10 per cent of gross collection of Motor Vehicle Tax be given to urban local bodies for maintenance of roads. The amount is divisible among municipalities and notified area councils in the ratio of 60:40.

GRANTS

The Commission is of the view that the local bodies have recklessly increased the staff strength ignoring their own source of income and the future liability on account of such decisions. In such a situation, the Commission does not feel it appropriate to pass on the entire salary and other terminal benefit liability to government except the claim of the approved staff appointed prior to 1-1-1974 and 1-11-1976 in an agreed percentage. It is now left to government to consider further claim of the urban local bodies towards salary and other liability to a reasonable level according to the economic capacity of the government, since 22 urban local bodies newly emerged after the cut off date of 1-1-1974 and 1-11-1976.

MISCELLANEOUS

1. *No Dues Certificate* — The Commission suggests that in order to collect arrears the Gram Panchayats and Urban Local Bodies should be empowered to issue no dues certificate to aspirant loanees on collection of certain fees. Government, semi-government and other financial institutions should also be advised to insist on such certificates before sanctioning any loan of any nature. Such no dues certificate may help to augment resources of local bodies.
2. *Maintenance of Roads* — The Commission recommends that in the first phase, government should transfer the roads owned by the various departments alongwith maintenance grant in proportion now available with such line departments. The officers in charge of such work should also be transferred to the urban local bodies so that they do not appoint additional staff to increase their liability.
3. *Drinking Water* — Providing drinking water is one of the basic services to be done by the urban local bodies. The Commission suggests that the construction work may be retained by government. But the maintenance

aspect of both tubewells and stand posts should be transferred to urban local bodies alongwith proportionate maintenance grant and staff component.

4. *Health* — In big municipalities, public health staff have been deployed by government. But the said urban local bodies do not have administrative control over these staff. So the Commission recommends that initially, the public health staff be placed at the disposal of the municipalities on internal deputation alongwith the allocation of proportionate salary, non-salary and other recurring grants to the municipalities to meet the expenses.

5. *Electricity* — In respect of street lights, there is now a dual control. Line construction and creation of poles are done by the GRIDCO whereas the maintenance is done by the municipalities. This dual control creates a great deal of difficulties for town dwellers. Hence, the Commission suggests that some bigger municipalities may be given some skeleton staff alongwith funds at their disposal for doing both types of work.

6. *Sewerage* — There is a separate agency to maintain sewerage line in the towns. The Commission suggests that the management of such lines should be entrusted to the municipalities along with maintenance. Funds alongwith staff which are under the control of PHED to manage and maintain sewerage line should be transferred to the municipalities.

7. *Sanitation* — Since the municipalities are not in a position to improve sanitation, the Commission suggests that an attempt should be made to privatise the service to control unhealthy environment in the urban areas.

8. *Training* — The Commission feels that to broaden the outlook and to develop expertise, regular training to staff and elected officials is essential.

9. *Data Bank* — Since the local self-governments have been constitutionally recognised, storage of

information is very much essential. So a Data Bank in each district under the disposal of the Collector and one at the State level should be developed for effective implementation of programmes of activities. A sum of Rs. 5 lakh is to be provided to each district to collect necessary data to establish a Data Bank.

At the State headquarters, the government may establish a Data Bank in collaboration with the Directorate of Economics and Statistics.

The Commission feels that unless massive external assistance is provided to urban local bodies to upgrade their basic services they cannot discharge their assigned functions.

8

PUNJAB

Ancient Punjab formed a part of the Persian Empire. Medieval Punjab saw a supremacy of the Muslims. After two abortive Anglo-Sikh wars, Punjab was finally annexed to the British empire in 1849. With Independence Punjab had to face the holocaust of partition. Eight princely states of east Punjab were grouped together to form one single State called PEPSU—Patiala and East Punjab States Union, with Patiala as its capital. PEPSU State was merged with Punjab in 1956. Punjab is situated in north-western corner of the country. It is bounded on west by Pakistan, on north by Jammu & Kashmir, on north-east by Himachal Pradesh and on south by Haryana and Rajasthan.

Agriculture is the mainstay of Punjab's economy, nearly 84 per cent of the total geographical area is under cultivation. Punjab's contribution to the industrial development of the country is mainly through its small scale units. The road length in Punjab is 39,950 km. of which provincial roads are 38,962 km. and national highways are 988 km. All villages of the State have been linked with metalled roads. The length of the rail routes passing through the State is around 3678 km.

With the total population of 202.82 lakhs in 1991, Punjab ranked fifth in the country. The rank in 1981 was ninth. The State covers an area of 50,362 sq. km. accounting about 1.57 per cent of the country's area. Although, percentage of urban content in total population of the State decreased from 27.68 per cent in 1981 to 29.72 per cent in 1991 (continuing to hold fifth rank in the country). The decadal growth in urban population fell down from 44.51 per cent in 1981 to 29.11 per cent in 1991.

Surprisingly, the number of towns also recorded a reduction from 134 in 1981 to 120 in 1991. The number of class one towns, however increased from 7 in 1981 to 10 in 1991. The population content in these big towns also increased from 46.38 per cent in 1981 to 54.36 per cent in 1991.

URBAN GOVERNANCE

The evolution of local government in Punjab dates back to the forties in the 19th century after Punjab came under the British rule. The local government at the time was totally under bureaucratic control. The administration of local services and other local affairs was entrusted to the district administration. Later on, a process of gradual decentralisation was initiated by the British Government in 1860 when the first law relating to the Municipal Bodies in Punjab was passed, followed by another law in the year 1873. These laws marked the beginning of Municipal Government with partially elected Municipal Bodies endowed with a few specified functions and powers. As a sequel to the recommendations of the Royal Commission, the functions and powers of the Municipal Governments were considerably exhausted by the passage of the Punjab Municipal Act, 1911. Three Municipal Corporations, for the cities of Amritsar, Ludhiana and Jalandhar, were set up under the Punjab Municipal Corporation Act, 1976.

Because of the constraints on their financial powers and the absence of systematic principles for the devolution of funds from the State, the Municipalities have always been suffering from financial inadequacies in relation to their expenditure responsibilities. This has affected, in many cases, the level and quality of the municipal services, such as water supply, street lighting, sewerage, sanitation and road maintenance.

Prior to the enactment of the 74th CAA, the Municipal Government in Punjab comprised three tiers of local bodies, namely the Municipal Corporation for three larger urban areas e.g. Ludhiana, Jalandhar and Amritsar, 92 Municipal Committees of class I, II and III status of the small urban areas, and 31 Notified Area Committees for the transitional areas.

While the Municipal Corporations and the Municipal Committees were by and large, representative bodies, the Notified Area Committees were nominated bodies in respect of a specified area.

The amended legislations brought about certain changes in the existing State laws to bring them in conformity with the provisions of the Constitution (74th Amendment) Act, 1992. The nomenclature of the Municipal Committees was changed to Municipal Councils and of Notified Area Committees was changed to Nagar Panchayats. Presently, there is one law entitled as the Punjab Municipal Corporation Act, 1976 to manage the affairs in larger urban area and also in the Chandigarh region. The smaller and transitional urban areas are managed under the Punjab Municipal Act.

FUNCTIONAL JURISDICTION

The laws authorise the Municipal Corporations to discharge obligatory as well as discretionary functions but only discretionary functions to the municipalities.

MUNICIPAL CORPORATIONS

Obligatory Functions

It is incumbent on the Corporations to make adequate provisions for :

1. the construction, maintenance and cleaning of drains and drainage works and the public latrines, urinals and similar conveniences,
2. the construction and maintenance of works and means for providing supply of water for private and public purposes,
3. the scavenging, removal and disposal of filth, rubbish and other obnoxious or polluted matters,
4. the reclamation of unhealthy localities, the removal of noxious vegetation and generally the abatement of all

nuisances,

5. the regulation of places for the disposal of dead and the provision and maintenance of places for the said purpose,
6. the registration of births and deaths,
7. public vaccination and inoculation,
8. measures for preventing and checking the spread of dangerous diseases,
9. the construction and maintenance of municipal markets and slaughter-houses and the regulation of all markets and slaughter-houses,
10. the regulation and abatement of offensive or dangerous trades or practices,
11. the securing or removal of dangerous buildings and places,
12. the construction, maintenance, alteration and improvements of public streets, bridges, culverts, causeways and the like,
13. the lighting, watering and cleaning of public streets and other public places,
14. the removal of obstructions and projections in or upon streets, bridges and other public places,
15. the naming and numbering of streets and premises,
16. the maintenance of municipal offices,
17. the laying out or the maintenance of public parks, gardens or recreation grounds,
18. the maintenance of fire brigade and the protection of life and property in the case of fire,
19. the maintenance and development of the value of all properties vested in or entrusted to the management of the Corporation,
20. the preparation of plan for economic development and social justice,
21. the fulfilment of any other obligation imposed on or under the Act,
22. the maintenance of monuments and memorials vested in a local authority.

Discretionary Functions

The Corporation may in its discretion provide either wholly or in part, for all or any of the following :

1. the furtherance of education including cultural and physical education,
2. the establishment and maintenance of and aid to libraries, museums, art galleries, botanical or zoological collections,
3. the establishment and maintenance of, and aid to, stadia, gymnasia, *akharas* and places for sports and games,
4. the planting and care of trees on road sides and elsewhere,
5. the surveys of buildings and lands,
6. the registration of marriages,
7. the taking of census of population,
8. the civic reception to persons of distinction,
9. the providing of music or other entertainments in public place and the establishment of theatres and cinemas,
10. the organisation and management of fairs and exhibitions,
11. the acquisition of movable or immovable property for the construction or adaptation of buildings,
12. the construction and maintenance of rest-houses, poor-houses, infirmaries, children's houses, houses for the deaf and dumb and for disabled and handicapped children, shelters for destitutes and disabled persons and asylums for persons of unsound mind,
13. the construction and maintenance of cattle pounds,
14. the building or purchase and maintenance of dwelling houses for Corporation officers and employees,
15. any measures for the welfare of the Corporation officers and employees,
16. the organisation or management of chemical or biological laboratories for the examination of water,

food and drugs,

17. the provision for relief to destitute and disabled persons,
18. the establishment and maintenance of veterinary hospitals,
19. the organisation, construction, maintenance and management of swimming pools, public wash houses, bathing places and other institutions designed for the improvement of public health,
20. the organisation and maintenance of farms and dairies within or without the city for the supply, distribution and processing of milk and milk products for the benefit of the residents of the city,
21. the organisation and management of cottage industries, handicrafts centres and sales emporia,
22. the construction and maintenance of warehouses and godowns,
23. the construction and maintenance of garages, sheds and stands for vehicles and cattle biers,
24. the provision for unfiltered water supply,
25. the improvement of the city in accordance with the improvement schemes,
26. the provisions of housing accommodation for the inhabitants of any area for any class of inhabitants,
27. the establishment and maintenance of hospitals, dispensaries and maternity and child welfare centres,
28. supply and distribution of electricity to the public, and
29. any measures likely to promote public safety, health, conveniences or general welfare.

MUNICIPALITIES

Powers and Authorities

The State Government may by notification endow the Municipalities with powers and authorities in regard to :

(i) the preparation of plans for economic development and

social justice,

(ii) the performance of functions and implementation of the schemes which may be entrusted to them including :

(a) urban planning including town planning,

(b) regulation of land-use and construction of buildings,

(c) planning for economic and social development,

(d) roads and bridges,

(e) water supply for domestic, industrial and solid waste management,

(f) public health, sanitation, conservancy and solid waste management,

(g) fire service,

(h) urban forestry, protection of the environment and promotion of ecological aspects,

(i) safeguarding the interests of weaker sections of society, including the handicapped and mentally retarded,

(j) slum improvement and upgradation,

(k) urban poverty alleviation,

(l) provisions of urban amenities and facilities such as parks, gardens and playgrounds,

(m) promotion of cultural, educational and aesthetic aspects,

(n) burials and burial grounds, cremations, cremation grounds and electric crematoriums,

(o) cattle ponds and prevention of cruelty to animals,

(p) vital statistics including registration of births and deaths,

(q) public amenities including street lighting, parking lots, bus stops and public conveniences,

(r) regulation of slaughter houses and tanneries.

The State Finance Commission has recommended the devolution of following functions to Urban Local Bodies :

Obligatory Functions

1. Regulation of land-use and building plans,
2. Roads and bridges,
3. Water supply for domestic, industrial and commercial purposes,
4. Public health, sanitation, conservancy and solid waste management,
5. Fire services,
6. Urban forestry, protection of the environment and promotion of ecological aspects,
7. Slum improvement and upgradation,
8. Provisions of urban amenities and facilities such as parks, gardens and playgrounds,
9. Burial and Burial grounds, cremations, cremation grounds and electric crematoriums,
10. Cattle pounds and prevention of cruelty to animals,
11. Vital statistics including registration of births and deaths,
12. Public amenities including street lighting, parking lots, bus stops and public conveniences,
13. Regulation of slaughter houses and tanneries,
14. Urban renewal and town planning schemes,
15. Traffic engineering and traffic infrastructure.

Agency Functions

1. Safeguarding the interests of weaker sections of the society, including the handicapped and the mentally retarded,
2. Urban poverty alleviation,
3. Promotion of cultural, educational and aesthetic aspects.

Discretionary Functions

1. Primary education,
2. Health facilities,

3. public transportation,
4. Electric supply.

TAXATION POWERS

The Municipal Corporations in the State enjoy mandatory as well as discretionary taxation powers while the municipalities have only optional taxes.

MUNICIPAL CORPORATION

Obligatory Taxes

The Corporation can levy the following taxes :

1. Taxes on lands and buildings—consisting of
   (a) water tax
   (b) fire tax
   (c) general tax not more than fifteen per cent of the annual rateable value,
2. a tax on advertisements,
3. a tax on buildings payable alongwith the application for sanction of the building plans,
4. a development tax on the increase in urban land values caused by the execution of improvement works.

Optional Taxes

Subject to prior approval of the State Government, the Corporation may levy :

1. a tax on professions, trades, callings and employments,
2. any other tax which the State Legislature has power to impose.

In addition to these taxes, after the close of each year, the government may pay to the Corporation the whole or such part as it may determine of the tax collected by it :

1. under the Indian Stamp Act, 1899 on account of stamp duty on transfer of property situated within the local areas of the city,
2. under the Punjab Motor Vehicle Taxation Act, 1924, from every person keeping a motor vehicle within the local area of the city,
3. under the Punjab Electricity (Duty) Act, 1958, on the energy supplied within the local area of the city,
4. under the Punjab Entertainment Duty Act, 1955, from every person admitted to an entertainment within the local area of the city,
5. under the Punjab Entertainment Tax (Cinematograph Shows) Act, 1954, from the proprietor of the premises where a public cinematograph exhibition is held within the local area of the city.

MUNICIPALITY

Optional Taxes

The Municipal Committee in the State may impose any of the following taxes :

1. a tax on buildings and lands not exceeding fifteen per cent of the annual value,
   (a) not exceeding one anna, per square foot of the ground area or
   (b) not exceeding three rupees, per running foot of frontage in streets or bazars.

   In case of buildings and lands occupied by tenants in perpetuity, the tax is payable by tenants,
2. a tax on persons practicing any profession or art or carrying on any trade or calling in the municipality,
3. a tax payable by owner on all or any vehicles, other than motor vehicles, animals used for riding, draught or burden and dogs, when such vehicles, animals and dogs are kept within the municipality,
4. a tax payable by the employer on municipal domestic

servants,

5. a tax payable by the occupier of any building which is undertaken by the committee for house scavenging,
6. scavenging tax payable by the occupier,
7. a tax payable by persons presenting building applications to the committee.

A committee will not impose any tax without the previous sanction of the State Government when it consists of members less than three-fourths of whom have been elected or its cash balances have, at any time within the three months preceding the date of the passing of the resolution imposing the tax, fallen below Rs. 20,000 or one-tenth of the income accrued in the previous financial year which is less.

FINANCIAL JURISDICTION

The State Finance Commission in Punjab was constituted under Articles 243-I and 243-Y of the Constitution of India to recommend principles for assigning the taxes, sharing of taxes and assignment of grants-in-aid to Municipalities and Panchayats. The five-member Commission was headed by a retired I.A.S. officer. Two other members were I.A.S. officers and an academician besides a member-secretary. The Commission submitted its report in December 1996.

Management of Revenue Income

Tax Sources

The current tax domain of the local bodies is found to be narrow and relatively inelastic. They have little flexibility in the matter of adjusting tax rates and charges. The rates and charges are fixed by the State and local bodies have little authority in the fixation of rates and charges. Besides the State constraints on the rates of taxes and charges, a large number of exemptions from Property Tax and Octroi to various groups of individuals, substantially depletes the revenue resources of the local bodies.

The private sector particularly in the matter of provision of service has also not been fixed by the Local Bodies on any significant role. Except in the collection of octroi, which has been recently tried in the State, there is not enough participation by the private sector in the provision and maintenance of services.

The Commission, having taken cognisance of the prevailing situation regarding the tax base of the local bodies and the inadequacy in the internal revenue effort is of the opinion that the tax powers of the local bodies need to be strengthened through widening of the tax base, enhancing the tax powers and assigning of the elastic and buoyant sources of income. For this purpose, not only the existing taxes which are assigned to them need rationalisation for making them buoyant and elastic, but the internal revenue effort of the local bodies also needs considerable improvement.

The Commission is of the opinion that the tax domain of the Municipalities should be clearly identified and its enforcement made obligatory upon this body. The exemption from Property Tax and Octroi should be drastically reduced by the government. No incentives to the industries or individuals should be granted by way of reducing or waving of Octroi or House Tax, at the cost of municipalities. Where such benefits are required to be given, the concerned municipalities should receive equivalent compensation from the States. The fixation or approval of the rate and schedules of various taxes by the State Government deprives the municipalities of the flexibility that they need in order to adjust the schedule of rates to meet their obligatory and functional expenditure responsibilities. The Commission recommends that the municipalities should have flexibility in the fixation of tax rates. In addition, they must take a minimum tax effort to claim incentive grants.

Octroi

The Commission suggests that agreements with the adjoining Gram Panchayats/Panchayat Samitis for the purpose of inspection of warehouses or storage space in the jurisdiction of the said Gram Panchayat or Panchayat Samiti be entered to evade octroi. To avoid unnecessary obstructions to the free flow of traffic, a system of Composite Permit be introduced. This growth oriented tax be allowed to continue in Municipal areas. Cost of collection should not exceed five per cent of the total collection.

Property Tax

The Commission feels that Property Tax be delinked from rentals to increase yield and reduce litigation. Vacant lands and lands used for marriage parties and for entertainment purposes be taxed at higher rates. Surcharge at the rate of 50 to 100 per cent be levied on commercial, industrial and other non-residential establishments and polluting industries involving hazardous processes. Exemptions be drastically reduced. Municipalities be entitled to compensation for loss of revenue due to exemptions granted by the State Government. Voluntary filing of statements by persons liable to assessment be made obligatory. Failure to file return be made punishable. Municipal Valuation Committees to hear objections be constituted. All records relating to assessment be made available to public on payment of a fee.

Water Supply and Sewerage Tax

The Commission recommends that stand posts be abolished unless water bills are paid by the community/consumers collectively. Water rates be linked with power tariff in addition to annual hike of 10 per cent to offset the cost of escalation. Sewerage charges be made equal to water rates. Different rates for water be fixed. Commercial and industrial connection be charged at higher rates. Entire water supply be metered. Maintenance of water supply, billing and collection of revenue be progressively privatised. Municipalities should improve water management and billing system to recover full expenditure on provision and maintenance.

Since electricity charges constitute 70 per cent of the total cost of maintenance of water supply and sewerage, water supply rates should be linked with the power tariff. Apart from the hike on account of linkage with power rates, 10 per cent should be added to the tariff per year to offset the escalation in the cost of operations and maintenance. Sewerage charges should be equal to water charges.

Non-Tax Sources

Non-tax sources constitute a sizable portion of the income of the Municipalities. It is recommended that where revision of levy has not taken place in the last five years, there should be substantial increase in rates to compensate the Municipalities for the cost excalation and for improving the level of service. Municipalities may collect a particular charge on 'one time payment' basis. This should be confined to such charges where the cost of collection is disproportionate to the return.

Additional Excise Duty on Liquor

Additional Excise Duty be enhanced from 7 per cent to 10 per cent on country liquor and from 16 to 20 per cent on Indian made foreign liquor.

User Charges

The Commission has directed that the principle of user charges should be extended to water supply and sewerage which implies that Municipalities should recover full cost of operations and maintenance, billing and collection and also the capital cost. This would enable the Municipalities to achieve an efficient and desirable level of service and greater transparency in the fixing of user charges. The Commission recommends that recovery of user charges be made as under :

1. full maintenance and operation expenses on upgraded water supply schemes,
2. 10 per cent of repayment of loans,

3. 5 per cent of the contribution of Municipalities,

4. separate accounts in respect of water and sewerage, both for expenditure and income, should be maintained to ensure transparency.

New Sources

The Commission suggests to explore the possibilities of levying a fee of Rs. 50 per annum per telephone by the local body.

NEW TAXES

The Commission recommends that the urban local bodies should tap other sources as well as the State Government should allow them to impose taxes in new areas. The Commission suggests new areas for taxation as under :

1. *Taxes on Profession, Trades, Callings and Employment* — Profession Tax should be levied and collected by the concerned Municipalities. This will include tax on individuals, traders, commission agents, shopkeepers etc. depending on their income.
2. *Tax on Advertisements and Hoardings* — Major portion of advertisement budget of national and multi-national companies are being earmarked for hoardings. The business of hoardings is fast increasing in volume. Therefore, municipalities should cash upon this emerging source of income.
3. *Licencing of Tubewells* — The tubewells installed by the rich households, industries and similarly placed individuals or bodies should be licenced and adequate fee charged according to the capacity of the tubewell installed. In addition, a surcharge on water pumped out, which ultimately is discharged in sewerage system, should be levied.

DEVOLUTION OF STATE REVENUE

Revenue devolution, covering the assignment and sharing of the State revenue with the Municipalities, is the fiscal instrumentality for reducing vertical gap, arising out of insufficient domestic revenue services, to meet their functional obligations.

Assigned Revenue

Assigned revenue includes revenue sources that are presently with the State Government but need to be assigned to the municipalities for the reason that these services are local in nature. The Commission is of the opinion that the Local Bodies should be assigned taxes on the basis of following principles:

1. Taxes based on immobile factors, such as land and its use, should be assigned to the Local Bodies. Taxes whose benefits extend to the residents of a particular jurisdiction without any spillover effects, would be local in nature and are best assigned to the local government. A tax whose benefits are spread over to larger areas, should stay with the higher level of the government. Thus, the taxes based on the goods for local consumption, local services and business should be allocated to the local government.
2. The tax instruments selected should meet the criteria of equity, cost effectiveness and buoyancy so as to ensure adequate flow of income to the local bodies. Taxes whose cost of collection is disproportionately high, as compared to its yield, should not be allocated to the local bodies.

The Commission is of the opinion that except for the yield from taxes, the tax power with the municipalities are adequate. All municipal taxes except octroi, suffer from low yield and inelasticity due to erosion of the tax base and inadequate revenue efforts by the local bodies. Apart from increasing the revenue from the existing tax resources through appropriate efforts by restructuring the tax base and tax rates, not further assignment of tax to the municipalities is recommended.

Revenue Sharing

The sharing of certain elastic sources of the State tax revenue with the local bodies is an important additional source of revenue for these bodies. It is important that such transfers should be so designed as to meet the avowed objective of removing the vertical and the horizontal imbalance, providing for upgradation in the existing levels of civic services and for the additional services to be performed by the local bodies. The Commission has determined following principles for the purpose :

1. The taxes identified for sharing between the State and the local bodies should be those which fall within the fiscal domain of the local government and the proceeds of which, the local bodies have a legitimate right.
2. The taxes identified should be elastic and buoyant in nature so as to provide a proportionately enhanced flow of income to the local bodies.
3. The proportion of the share to the local bodies should be fixed taking in view the fiscal needs of the local bodies. The share of the local bodies should be enough to reduce their dependence on the grants.
4. The distribution of the shared taxes between the State and the local bodies should be determined on a percentage basis of the selected taxes rather than on fixed amount basis. This will ensure that the quantum and frequency of the transfers is transparent and predictable.
5. To enhance the autonomy of the local bodies, no conditions should be attached to the transfers. However, the transfers must have in-built incentives for promoting local resources mobilisation and good performance.

After considering various alternatives and the diverse practices prevailing in other States, the Commission was of the opinion that the objectives of the local fiscal autonomy and financial self-sufficient would be well met by transferring to the local bodies a share of a few elastic and buoyant individual State tax resources. The Commission has recommended that 20 per cent of the net proceeds of following taxes, at present levied and collected by the State be shared with the Municipalities and Panchayat Raj Institutions :

1. *Stamp Duty* — The share of proceeds from Stamp Duty should be distributed between the Municipalities and the Panchayati Raj Institutions on the basis of derivative principle. The Stamp Duty collected from the urban areas should form the share of Municipalities and that from rural areas should be transferred to the Panchayat Raj Institutions. It is also recommended that separate records for the transactions relating to urban and rural areas should be maintained by the registering authority.

2. *Punjab Motor Vehicle Tax* — The sharing of the Punjab Motor Vehicle Tax be on the basis of proportionate length of roads maintained by the Municipalities and the Panchayat Raj Institutions. Keeping in view the intensity of usage of roads in urban and rural areas, the proportion of urban and rural roads should be worked out applying a multiplier of 10 to the actual length of municipal roads.

3. *Electricity Duty* — The sharing of Electricity Duty between the Municipalities and Panchayat Raj Institutions should be on the basis of collection.

4. *Entertainment Tax and Entertainment Tax (Cinematograph Shows)* — The sharing of these taxes should be on the following criterion :

Municipalities	80 per cent
Panchayat Raj Institutions	20 per cent

STATE GRANTS TO LOCAL BODIES

Most of the municipalities suffer from resource crunch and their inability to provide desirable level of civic services. There are also wide irregularities amongst the municipalities, not only of different classes but within the same class. Thus, the local bodies suffer both from the horizontal as well as vertical imbalances in their finances. There is no well-developed system of grants-in-aid to the local bodies. The grant-in-aid is given by the State government to the local bodies to meet their revenue deficit. The grants are given for specific developmental projects approved by the State or the District Planning Boards. Thus, it is clear that neither does it meet the requirement of the vertical imbalances. These problems make it necessary that grants-in-aid to local bodies should meet the following objectives :

(a) Reduction of their horizontal revenue gap,
(b) Provision of a desirable level of civic services,
(c) Meeting the expenses of undertaking State assigned responsibilities and tasks.

The Commission was of the considered opinion that the system of giving grants should be equitable. It should take into account the fiscal needs as well as the fiscal capacity of the recipient local bodies. The system should be so designed that the local bodies with weak fiscal capacities, are able to provide a level of civic services to the community which is not below the average level within the same class. In brief, the grants-in-aid policy should be based on following principles :

(a) The system of grants should be transparent, predictable and should be so designed that the various local bodies are able to predict their share of allocation for each year. In other words, it should be based on objective measurable factors.
(b) For considerations such as equity and justice, the grants should be related to the fiscal needs and the taxable capacities of the local bodies.

(c) The grant-in-aid from the State should provide the local bodies, sufficient autonomy and flexibility in planning their priorities as per the needs of the community. Stress should be on untied grants than on those which are tied to any specific government policy.

(d) There should be a system of incentive grants to encourage the local bodies to undertake better use of their own resources and sound management of their finances.

(e) The grants should be granted only for the improvement and upgradation of essential services and only a part should be utilised for salaries and wages.

(f) There should be some mechanism for the monitoring of the grants as regards their usage.

Specific Purpose Grants

The Commission has recommended three types of grants. The general purpose grants should be simple and directed to achieve the basic objective of removing the horizontal fiscal imbalance amongst the local bodies. The specific purpose grants should be designed to achieve the following objectives :

(a) To stimulate specific local functions, and

(b) to share local expenditure for providing essential services having Statewide priorities.

The Commission has recommended that the following guiding principles be kept in view while transferring specific purpose grants to the local bodies :

(a) The grants should be conditional and matching, given for improvement or to support a desirable level of essential civic services,

(b) The condition of the matching grant by the local bodies should be insisted upon to ensure local bodies' own commitment for the functions for which the grant has been received.

(c) The local bodies should be accountable to the higher levels of government for proper utilisation of these grants.

(d) Provision should be made so that the grants cover the emergency expenditure incurred by the local bodies.

(e) Full cost of performance of the State functions entrusted to the local bodies, such as elections, census, should be reimbursed to the local bodies by the State government.

Based on these principles the Commission has recommended that per capita grant-in-aid should be given to weak municipalities to bring them to a level of the average per capita income of the size class to which they belong. The grant-in-aid should be worked out by multiplying for each class, the difference between the average per capita income and the actual per capita income with the population. The actual transfer of this grant-in-aid should be worked out each year by the local government department before transferring it to the respective municipalities on the above principle. For this purpose, the Commission has recommended a lump sum grant of Rs. 30 crore in each of the next five years and no part of it should be utilised for salaries and wages.

Incentive Grants

The municipalities which put in a desirable amount of effort to make the optimal use of their own fiscal domain, augment their resources and improve upon their fiscal administration should be suitably rewarded with additional grants to be known as incentive grants. This system of incentive grants should be introduced in the mechanism of devolution of funds to be made upon the local bodies as this would activate and inspire them to manage their fiscal affairs more efficiently. The Commission has recommended norms for a working system adjudging the performance of individual local bodies, which require :

(a) that a municipality has utilised all tax/non-tax

measures, for raising resources, which fall within its fiscal jurisdiction,

(b) that a periodical revision in the rates of fees, levies and non-tax rates is effected,

(c) that the municipality has effected as minimum of 80 per cent recovery of assessed demand of taxes, non-taxes and user charges, including arrears upto the preceding year,

(d) that the cost of collection does not exceed five per cent of the total collection of taxes,

(e) that the municipal institutions have adopted the principle of user charges, which requires that the price of services should be so fixed as to recover the cost of provision and maintenance of the service. However, the water and sewerage rates should be linked with power tariff in addition to annual hike of 10 per cent to offset the cost escalation,

(f) that the expenditure on salaries, wages and contingencies is as per the norms fixed by the State government, from time to time, and

(g) that all the previous grants, devolutions and transfers have been properly utilised.

The municipalities which put in the effort, as per the parameters, should be entitled to incentive grants over and above their entitlement according to the principles of devolution adopted by the government at the following rates. The incentive grant as recommended in the maximum and the actual disbursement should be according to the proportionate performance of each body.

Nagar Panchayats	Rs. 10 lakh
Class III Municipal Council	Rs. 15 lakh
Class II Municipal Council	Rs. 20 lakh
Class I Municipal Council	Rs. 25 lakh
Municipal Corporation	Rs. 50 lakh

Expenditure on Development

The Department of Local Government has worked out the requirement of funds based on the following physical targets achievable for the years 1996-2001 in respect of the core services :

Roads — 75 to 100 per cent coverage by all-weather roads.
Street Lighting — 100 per cent coverage with an average distance of 30 metres between the lighting poles.
Solid Waste Management — 100 per cent disposal.
Water Supply — 90 per cent population coverage with per capita supply of 150-200 litres water per day.
Sewerage and Surface Drainage — 75 per cent underground sewerage and 25 per cent surface drainage.
Storm water drainage —Three municipal corporations and 27 Class I Municipal Council.

In addition, slum improvement, upgradation and augmentation of fire services has been included for assessing the requirement of the funds.

The Commission has provided for a contribution of 30 per cent share by the municipalities as seed money for raising 70 per cent of the required amount through loans from the financial institutions for providing core services. The 30 per cent contribution by the municipalities will be out of the income accruing from their own resources, transfers on account of shared taxes and the grants-in-aid.

Audit of Accounts of Municipalities

The Commission recommends that system of pre-audit be streamlined and applied on a selective basis. Municipal Accounts Committees in each Municipalities and a State Level Public Accounts Committee be set up.

Every Municipal Council should constitute its Municipal Accounts Committee from amongst its members, which may have the power to examine the accounts of the Municipal Council, examine and scrutinize the audit reports and also the report of physical verification of stocks and works executed and make report with suitable suggestions to the Municipal Council regarding any irregularity committed and the measures as to how the finances and maintenance of accounts of the municipalities could be improved.

A State level Public Accounts Committee for municipal finances should be constituted every year, from amongst the elected representatives of the public. The Committee will have powers to call for and scrutinize the accounts of any municipality, as also to examine and scrutinize the audit reports and make suitable recommendations. The report of the Committee shall be submitted to the government for final disposal.

The Public Accounts Committee to be constituted by the State government, should have not less than 11 and not more than 15 members. Due representation in the Committee be given to all groups, including opposition, women and scheduled castes. The Examiner, Local Fund Accounts should act as the Secretary and one of its members be elected as Chairman of the Committee. The tenure should be one year. The Committee cannot include any member who is holding an office in a Municipal Council/Corporation as Mayor, Deputy Mayor, President, Vice-President or Executive Officer.

Private Sector Participation

Pending transfer of assets, civic services be provided through private agencies. No liabilities on account of staff be transferred by the Urban Planning and Development Authority. Assets/ infrastructure be transferred immediately, after they become operational. Improvement Trust be abolished on account of transfer of functional domain to Punjab Planning and Development Authority.

For improving core services and reducing expenditure progressively, work should be off loaded to private agencies.

9

RAJASTHAN

Rajasthan, the largest State in India area-wise, prior to Independence was known as Rajputana. History of Rajasthan dates back to the pre-historical times. It was a territory of princely states. The process of uniting scattered states commenced from 1948 to 1956. First came Matsya Union (1948) consisting of a fraction of the states. Slowly and gradually other states merged with it. By 1949, major states like Bikaner, Jaipur, Jodhpur and Jaisalmer joining the Union making it United States of Greater Rajasthan. Ultimately in 1956, present State of Rajasthan formally came into being with Ajmer State, Abu Road Taluka and Sunel Tappa joining it. Rajasthan is surrounded by Punjab, Uttar Pradesh and Madhya Pradesh in north, north-east and south-east and by Gujarat in south-west.

Endowed with a rich culture Rajasthan is also mineral rich and is fast emerging on the industrial scenario of the country. Total length of roads was 63,078 km. as on March 1996. The State is well connected with rail and air networks. The State is divided into 31 districts.

URBAN DEMOGRAPHY

According to 1951 census, the urban population in the State was 29.55 lakhs constituting 18.50 per cent of total population. In 1961 though the population went up to 32.81 lakhs, the population of urban population fell to 16.28 per cent. In 1971 the number of people living in towns rose to 45.44 lakhs constituting 17.63 per cent of the total population. This trend in growth continued unabatedly and according to 1991 census, 100.67 lakhs people live in towns and they constitute 22.88 per cent of the State's total population.

The State witnessed a tremendous growth in its urban population over the decades. The decadal growth in 1951-61 was recorded merely as 11.03 per cent but it increased to 38.49 per cent in 1961-71 and further to 58.67 per cent in 1971-81. Although the number of inhabitants in urban areas increased, the decadal growth fell down to 39.63 per cent during 1981-91. The growth in urban population has been recorded more than that of the total population of the State. Surprisingly, the number of towns remained static as 141 in 1951 and 1961. The number increased to 151 in 1971 and stepped up to 201 in 1981 and further to 215 in 1991. The class one towns 11 in 1981 increased to 14 in 1991. The population content in class one towns in 1981 was measured as 46.82 per cent but increased to 50.09 per cent in 1991.

MUNICIPAL GOVERNANCE

The first municipality in Rajasthan was set up in Ajmer—Mewar in 1866. By the end of the 19th century, there were 16 municipalities in Rajputana state. The number grew to 99 by early 20th century. After the State of Rajasthan came into existence, many more municipalities were set up and by 1971 there were 145 local bodies. The number rose to 196 in the year 1986 and was subsequently reduced to 182 owing to the recommendation of the Mukharjee Committee.

The urban local bodies in Rajasthan till recently were classified as under :

1. Municipal Corporation—more than 5 lakh population,
2. Municipal Council—with a population of 1 lakh to less than 5 lakhs,
3. Municipal Board—with less than 1 lakh population.

The Municipal Boards were further subdivided into :

(a) *Class II Municipality* – Population between 50,000 to 99,000 or municipalities in district headquarters with a per capita income of Rs. 200.
(b) *Class III Municipality* – Population between 25,000 to 49,999 or per capita income of Rs. 150.
(c) *Class IV Municipality* – less than 25,000 population.

Presently, the statutory classification into Corporations (in larger urban areas), Councils (in smaller urban areas) and Municipal Boards (into transitional areas) exists. There is only one municipal Act viz. Rajasthan Municipalities Act, 1959 to govern the urban affairs in the State.

FUNCTIONS

The municipalities in Rajasthan are entrusted with special and secondary or optional duties :

Mandatory Duties

Every municipality is obliged to undertake following functions in its jurisdiction :

1. lighting roads and public places;
2. watering roads and public places;
3. cleaning of public roads, sewers and places of public importance ;
4. removal of filth, rubbish, etc. from toilets, urinals, cesspools etc.;
5. extinguishing fires;
6. regulating dangerous trades;
7. removal of projections from public roads or places;
8. securing of dangerous houses;
9. acquisition, maintenance and regulation of burials;
10. constructing and maintaining public roads, boundary marks, markets, slaughter houses, drains, sewers, bathing places, ponds, wells etc.

11. constructing public toilets and urinals;
12. additional and adequate supply of water,
13. naming the streets and numbering of houses;
14. registration of births and deaths;
15. public vaccination;
16. sheds for calves, cows for supply of animal lymph;
17. destruction of stray dogs;
18. preparation of annual report on the administration of the municipality;
19. meeting expenditure of police guards engaged for safety and security of municipal property;
20. organisation of volunteers for the safety and security of people and property;
21. preparing compost from refusals;
22. construction and maintenance of cattle pounds;
23. encouraging measures for controlling population, family welfare.

Special Duties

Every municipality has to make special arrangements for the following :

1. providing medical aid and relief during epidemics, prevention of dangerous disease;
2. providing relief during calamity.

Discretionary Functions

The municipality may, at its discretion, make provision for the following :

1. laying out of new streets and roads;
2. constructing, maintenance and contribution towards maintaining parks, libraries, museums, reading rooms, asylums, *dharamshalas*, rest rooms etc.,
3. constructing dwellings for poor,
4. dwelling units for municipal employees;

5. planting of trees on roadside;
6. conducting census;
7. providing receptacles for sewers;
8. disposal of filth, nightsoil;
9. recreation or music at public places;
10. public health and child welfare;
11. fairs and exhibitions;
12. regulating shops and markets;
13. supply of milk and milk products;
14. establishing labour welfare centres;
15. organising and contributing to municipal union;
16. maintaining ambulance service;
17. maintaining public hospitals and dispensaries;
18. providing antirabic treatment;
19. constructing shelter for poor, orphans, handicapped;
20. maintaining maternity and child welfare centres;
21. establishing and maintaining primary schools;
22. planning for economic development and social justice;
23. any function enumerated in Schedule XII assigned by the State Government.

TAXATION POWERS

Municipalities are empowered to impose obligatory as well as discretionary taxes, fees, tolls etc.

Obligatory Taxes

Every municipality is obliged to levy following :

1. a tax on buildings and lands or both,
2. octroi,
3. a tax on profession and trades.

Discretionary Taxes

Subject to authorisation by the State Government, the municipalities may impose any of the following :

1. a tax on vehicles
2. a tax on dogs
3. a tax on animals
4. a tax on vehicles and animals entering the municipal limits
5. a tax on boats
6. conservancy tax
7. a tax on cleansing of private toilets
8. a tax on constructing and maintaining public toilets
9. lighting tax
10. a water tax
11. a tax on undertaking trades or employment into municipal limits
12. a tax on sculptors
13. any other tax.

In Rajasthan, only two of the three obligatory taxes viz. octroi and lands and building tax have been levied. Profession tax is not levied by any of the urban bodies. Even amongst the obligatory taxes, house tax is not levied or collected by as many as sixty local bodies. The obligatory taxes assigned to the local bodies are not strictly obligatory because the State has the power to interfere in the levy of obligatory taxes. In other words, these taxes are imposed by the State government and levied and collected by the urban local bodies. The rate of these taxes and the date of imposition will have to be decided by the government in each case. This has resulted in non-levy of house tax by a number of local bodies and total absence of profession tax. In some cases, the State government had permitted the local bodies to withdraw the house tax.

Under these circumstances, most of the municipalities in Rajasthan are financially weak and they are in no position to meet the rising demand for municipal services. The municipalities are unable to discharge their obligatory functions satisfactorily, leave aside the discretionary functions. Rapid growth of cities and towns is not matched by a corresponding increase in their revenue. While the functional responsibilities of urban local bodies increased several folds inflating their resource needs, their performance was dismal on augmentation of revenue to carry out these functions. Even the statutory avenues provided for municipal revenue remained unexploited or under exploited. The constant fear of annoying the electorate loomed large and prevented the urban local bodies from tapping even the existing sources of income.

FISCAL DEVOLUTION

The Governor by his order dated 23rd April, 1994 constituted a four-member State Finance Commission. The Commission submitted its report in December 1995. The awards of the Commission are for a period of five years from 1st April, 1995.

AUGMENTING EXISTING SOURCES

Octroi

There is a need to devise a system for augmenting this important source of revenue. There is a considerable leakage in the octroi income. The Commission is, therefore, in favour of private collection of octroi. It feels that there should be a committee to go into the possible harassment of people by the contractor and suggesting measures to prevent the same.

Regarding the issue of a uniform rate schedule for octroi being applied to all urban local bodies, the Commission feels that the consumption pattern of goods and the industrial and commercial potentials of town widely vary and therefore the issue of uniform rate needs to be decided taking into consideration the views of all local bodies.

As far the grievances on non-payment of octroi on goods received by the Electricity Board and Public Health Engineering Department, the issue needs sympathetic consideration of the State government. If the government prefers to exempt octroi on the goods of these bodies, it may also consider introducing concessional charges for street lighting and water supply equivalent to the rates applicable to the domestic consumers.

Likewise any exemption by the government should have a built-in mechanism for compensating the loss of revenue to urban local body.

House Tax

The Commission recommends that the Department should demystify the house tax assessment procedures by simplifying them and by making them more transparent. Categorisation of areas on value of properties and a per square foot affordable rate of tax on the constructed and vacant area would reduce the inspector *raj* and the yield would improve.

The concept of self-assessment of house tax should be introduced after simplification of assessment procedure.

The exemption limit of house with a rental value of less than Rs. 180 per annum is too low and deserves to be increased to Rs. 1200 by amendment in the Municipal Act.

The local bodies with a very high growth rate in the housing sector can consider one time payment of house tax so that the staff could be deployed for new assessment and effective supervision.

As regards grant of exemption of tax on government properties, the Commission suggests that a lump sum assistance in lieu thereof could be given to the local bodies by the Central and State Governments.

Tax on Profession

Regarding the obligatory tax on profession, the Commission feels that the elected bodies should be left with the discretion to levy and collect this tax.

NEW TAX AREAS

Discretionary Tax

The discretionary taxes still remain unexploited or grossly under-exploited. Without covering the majority of inhabitants, taxes could be levied on selective sectors which strain the municipal services to its limits or substantially contribute to the sanitation problems of town. In this respect, the areas like *subzi mandies*, private hospitals/dispensaries, barber shops, *dhabas*, road side restaurants and industries may be considered for taxation. A sanitation tax could be levied on them.

Parking tax and Hoarding tax could also get good revenue to the big urban local bodies.

NON-TAX REVENUE

Sale of Land

The largest source of non-tax income to urban local bodies is sale of land which constituted about 8.91 per cent of the total income of local bodies. However, the Urban Improvement Trusts do not pass on 15 per cent of the proceeds from sale of land to the local bodies. The Commission recommends that the mechanism of transfer of municipal share from the procedure of sale of land by the Trust should be ensured by the government before according approval to Improvement Trust schemes for sale of land. In other words, the Local Self Government department in the government should insist on a 'no-due' to local bodies certificate from the Urban Improvement Trusts before according approval to their schemes.

Further, the State's powers could be delegated to the Divisional Commissioner after revising the scale of approval of sale of land from Rs. 5 lakh to Rs. 11 lakh. Only users of sales exceeding Rs. 10 lakh should come to the State government. Similarly, the powers of sanctions of the local bodies should be increased to Rs. 10 lakh for corporations, Rs. 3 lakh for councils and Rs. 1 lakh for municipal boards.

The Commission advises a policy direction in regularisation of old occupants of State owned properties without *patta* would enable the local bodies to raise additional resources.

The Commission feels that a clear and cohesive policy covering aspects like acquisition, conversion, development of house sites, transfer etc. for city development is required. There is also a need for reducing the number of government departments involved in the task of conversion and development of *abadi* land. There should be time bound clearance procedure for local bodies, proposals for development of house sites schemes.

The Commission recommends that the urban land in *mandi* areas should be transferred to the concerned local bodies and any cost in lieu of it is to be recovered from their earnings or on benefit from their grant.

Penalties etc.

The Commission suggests that the State government and the urban local bodies should examine the rates of fines, penalties, charges, fees etc. and use them to make them practical and effective.

DEVOLUTION PATTERN

Keeping in view the uncertain State assistance, the Commission feels proper to link the devolution of funds to total net tax proceeds of the State and fix a share of 2.18 per cent of the net State tax proceeds to be devolved on the local bodies. This amount would go to contribute to the divisible pool. The share of the Panchayati Raj Institutions and Urban Local Bodies in this pool would be according to their population ratio of 3.4 : 1.

The basic objectives underlying the funding pattern are (i) to accelerate local efforts in mobilising resources, (ii) judicious employment of funds bring about balanced growth, (iii) to recognise good work done by some local bodies to promote excellence in municipal administration. Unlike the villages, urban areas are populous and sustain in an economy which is predominantly non-agrarian. The *inter se* allocation of funds is based on population. size and resource mobilisation of urban local bodies and their managerial capabilities. Based on these principles the Commission recommends the following grants to urban local bodies from the divisible pool.

(i) General Purpose Grants

The service needs and the requirement of funds have direct bearing on the population of urban local bodies. It is, therefore, recommended that 60 per cent of the funds from the urban local bodies' share in the divisible pool should be allocated to different categories of local bodies proportionate to their population as general purpose grant.

(ii) Development Grant/Loan

Generally, the smaller urban local bodies have more resource constraint than the larger ones. The flexibility and elasticity that the larger local bodies have in their revenue earnings are rare in the case of smaller local bodies. The smaller local bodies have hardly any source to meet their huge funds requirements for capital investments. On the contrary, the larger local bodies confined funds for capital investments. It is, therefore, necessary that the perennial capital needs of urban local bodies can be met by a combination of loans and grant to satisfy the need of resource rich and resource poor local bodies.

For the purpose, the Commission recommends for creation of a State level Finance Corporation for urban bodies to advance loans at a concessional rate of interest. The major chunk of the municipal corporations and councils' developmental requirements could be met through loans while the resource poor boards can benefit from grant. The Commission proposes that this Finance Corporation could be a part of the Directorate of Local Bodies with the Director as ex-officio Managing Director and his staff to assist him without creating too many new posts. To build up the corpus, the Commission recommends that Rs. 1.5 crore should be contributed annually by the State government of its devolutions for the next five years. Till the time the Financial Corporation is set up, the amount should be disbursed as loan by the State government at a concessional rate of interest.

The Commission recommends that 20 per cent of the funds from the local bodies' share in the divisible pool should be earmarked for this purpose. After releasing Rs. 150 lakh annually to the corpus of the Municipal Financial Corporation, out of remaining 75 per cent should be earmarked for the Boards and 25 per cent for the Corporations and Councils. The Financial Corporation should earmark 75 per cent for its lendable resources to the municipal corporations and the councils and 25 per cent to the boards for advancement. Care should be taken to see that the Boards with poor financial and resource base get the development grant and Boards with good resource base and income are referred to the Corporation for loan.

(iii) Incentive Grant

With an aim to recognise and motivate urban local bodies to perform better, the Commission recommends for institutional cash awards to local bodies for development works within their areas. The Commission recommends the following awards at various levels :

State Level

(i) Corporation—1 award of Rs. 5 lakh
(ii) Councils—3 awards—First Rs. 5 lakh, Second Rs. 3 lakh and Third Rs. 1 lakh.

Divisional Level

(i) Class II—6 awards—one in each division for Rs. 5 lakh.
(ii) Class III—12 awards—First and Second in each division—First for Rs. 5 lakh and Second for Rs. 3 lakh.
(iii) Class IV—18 awards—three awards in each division—First of Rs. 5 lakh, Second of Rs. 3 lakh and Third of Rs. 1 lakh.

The selection of urban local bodies for the awards be made on the basis of their performance in revenue earnings and services rendered to the people in terms of quantity as well as quality. Development efforts of the local bodies are also considered for evaluating their performance. The State level awards are to be finalised by a Committee headed by the Secretary, Local Self Government and the Divisional Level awards should be finalised by a Committee headed by the Divisional Commissioner.

The Commission wishes to emphasise that it is essential for the local bodies to fulfil certain conditions for receiving these grants. They are :

1. the local bodies should achieve the additional resource mobilisation targets for them for the year;
2. the establishment expenditure under general administration and recovery of taxes should not exceed 10 per cent of total expenditure in the case of corporations, 15 per cent in the case of councils and 20 per cent in the case of boards. If these limits are exceeded, there will be proportional reduction in their grant;
3. norms for sanitation, street lighting and urban roads should be fixed for earning the award.

The amount of award should be spent on development works only and any violation of this condition should render the defaulting local bodies liable for deduction of the misspent amount from future devolutions.

(iv) Matching Grant

The Commission recommends that 20 per cent of local bodies' share in the divisible pool should be earmarked for incentive and matching grants. After deducting the award money, the remainder amount should be utilised for providing matching grant to local bodies for works of public utility in their respective areas against the Tenth Finance Commission grant.

Horizontal Distribution

The basis of distribution of allocated amount to municipalities within the same class would be population.

Sanction and Release of Funds

The Commission suggests that the funds should be released in two equal instalments — the first one in April and the second one in October of every year. The first instalment is a grant on population basis and, therefore, should be released to the local bodies straight away. The second instalment would be the development and incentive grant and, therefore, would require assessment of the previous year's performance to adjudge their entitlement. The amount may be released to the Collector to be kept at the district level. A Committee chaired by the Collector and other members nominated by the State government would adjudge the eligibility of the local bodies for release of funds. The award of money be retained by the State till the awards are finalised. The awards should be finalised before December every year.

The Local Self Government department and the Director of Local Bodies should be responsible for release of funds on conditions to the local bodies . They should ensure that the local bodies who receive the funds fulfil conditions laid down for such receipt. They should also closely monitor the additional resource mobilisation efforts of the local bodies and also the quality of services rendered by them.

MISCELLANEOUS

The Commission has suggested a number of other measures for improving the urban administration. Some of the important recommendations are :

1. It is imperative for the State government to formulate an urban development policy to mitigate the problems of urban poor and to strengthen urban infrastructure to

cater to their residents.

2. There is an urgent need to go into the human resource problems of the urban local bodies.
3. A Service Selection Board is to be set up to select municipal employees upto ministerial services level.
4. The State should play a promotional role with a right to interfere only in public interest.
5. It is expedient to decentralise powers to urban local bodies for revising the rates.
6. There should be a system for mid-term appraisal of financial position of the urban local bodies to provide them success in serious financial problems on account of conditions beyond their control.

10

TAMIL NADU

Tamil Nadu is situated on the southern tip of the Indian peninsula. The State has an old history and heavy antiquity. The State is successor to the old Madras Presidency which, in 1901, covered the bulk of the southern peninsula. The composite Madras State was later reorganised and the present Tamil Nadu was formed. It is bounded on north by Andhra Pradesh and Karnataka, on west by Kerala, on east by the Bay of Bengal and on south by the Indian Ocean.

The economy of the State depends largely on agricultural sector as more than 70 per cent of the population are engaged in agriculture. Tamil Nadu accounts for nearly one-fourth of the spinning capacity in India. One-fifth of cement, caustic soda and nitrogenous fertilisers and one-tenth of the nation's production of sugar, bicycles and calcium carbide are produced here.

The length of road network in Tamil Nadu is nearly 1.70 lakh km. There are five airports and four ports. The State is divided into 29 districts.

URBAN SCENARIO

Tamil Nadu accounted for about 8.76 per cent of the country's total urban population. The proportion of urban population to total population of the State was more than one-third (34.20 per cent) in 1991. Madras is the district with the highest urban population and with hundred per cent urban, followed by Coimbatore (53.20%) and Nilgiri (49.81%). Dharmapuri (9.41%) is the least urbanised district, preceded by Tiruvannamalai

Sambuvarayar (12.10%). Madras (100%), Nilgiri (49.81%), North Arcot-Ambedkar (31.76%), Coimbatore (53.20%), Madurai (44.99%), Kamarajar (37.55%), Chindambaranar (41.39%), Tirunelveli-Kattabomman (31.72%) and Chengai Anna (44.83%) are the districts with more than 30 per cent urban content. The level of urbanisation in the State is dispersed. One district falls between 50-60 per cent and four show 40-50 per cent and three between 30-40 per cent. Seven districts witness urbanisation between 20-30 per cent and four between 10-20 per cent while one is below 10 per cent.

The number of towns in the State has been found increasing over the years. There were 240 towns in 1971 which increased to 245 in 1981 and further to 260 in 1991. The corresponding number of class one towns was 16, 20 and 25 respectively. Majority of the urban population is concentrated in these class one towns increased with ranging proportion from 62.22 (1981) to 65.96 in 1991. The percentage figure in 1971 was 57.74.

There were seven Municipal Acts governing the urban affairs in the State. The city of Chennai (Madras) was administered by the Madras City Municipal Corporation Act, 1919, while other five Municipal Corporations were having their own separate Act enacted on the lines of the Madras City Corporation Act. The municipalities were governed by the Tamil Nadu District Municipalities Act, 1920. Recently, the State Government has repealed all the Acts and has enacted a unified Tamil Nadu Urban Local Bodies Act, 1998.

Powers and Responsibilities

The unified Act provides for obligatory as well as discretionary functions to be performed by the Urban Local Bodies.

Obligatory Functions

Every Council is obliged to perform following functions :

(a) construction and maintenance of roads, culverts and drains,

(b) execution and maintenance of water supply schemes required for domestic, industrial or commercial purposes, except in the municipality where there is a separate authority for the purpose,

(c) protection of public ponds and fountains,

(d) maintenance of sewerage and drainage schemes except in the municipality where there is a separate authority to which such functions are assigned,

(e) destruction of stray dogs,

(f) mosquito control,

(g) regulation of sale of meat, fish and other perishable food items,

(h) regulation of dangerous trades,

(i) licencing of eating establishments,

(j) disposal of unclaimed corpses or carcasses of animals,

(k) establishment of public comfort stations, latrines and bathing places,

(l) construction and maintenance of parks, gardens, play grounds, traffic islands in the urban areas,

(m) opening and maintenance of public burial and burning grounds and electric crematoria,

(n) registration of births and deaths,

(o) installation of street lights and their maintenance,

(p) providing parking places for vehicles,

(q) public health matters including vaccination and inoculation,

(r) maintenance of public markets, shopping complexes, bus stands, rest houses,

(s) solid waste management,

(t) prevention or removal of obstructions and projections in or upon streets, bridges etc.,

(u) numbering and naming of streets,

(v) regulation of hoardings and advertisements, put up for public view,

(w) civic reception to persons of distinction,

(x) organisation of fairs and exhibitions.

Discretionary Functions

The council may carry out any work delegated by the Government in relation to following matters :

(a) urban planning including town planning,
(b) regulation of land-use and construction of buildings,
(c) regulation of slaughter houses and tanneries,
(d) planning for economic and social development,
(e) fire services,
(f) urban forestry, protection of the environment and promotion of ecological aspects,
(g) safeguarding the interests of weaker sections of society, including the handicapped and mentally retarded,
(h) slum improvement and upgradation,
(i) urban poverty alleviation,
(j) promotion of cultural, educational and aesthetic aspects,
(k) cattle pounds, prevention of cruelty to animals.

TAXATION POWERS

The Council has the power to levy the following taxes :

(a) Property Tax,
(b) Water Tax,
(c) Sewerage Tax,
(d) Education Tax,
(e) Advertisement Tax,
(f) A duty on transfer of property.

DEVOLUTION OF FINANCIAL POWERS

The Government of Tamil Nadu constituted the State Finance Commission in December 1994, which effectively started functioning only with effect from March 1995. The five-member Commission consisted of one former MLA, the Commissioner of Municipal Administration and the Director of Rural

Development as ex-officio members and a Member-Secretary. The Commission was headed by a retired bureaucrat. The recommendations for augmenting the resources cover period of five years commencing from 1-4-1997. The Commission submitted its report in November 1996.

REFORMS IN EXISTING SOURCES

The State Finance Commission has undergone to suggest various measures reforming the existing sources of income with a view to optimise them.

Property Tax

For the optimisation of property tax, the Commission recommends switching over the determination of valuation from present annual rental value system to the area linked unit value system which ensures better acceptability by people and more revenue yield. General revision may be done once in three years and ARV may be revised based on inflation rate with reference to consumer price index.

The Commission recommends that in Town Panchayats, Property Tax should replace the present House Tax.

The total property tax may be divided into two parts, one as general purpose tax and other as service tax on 50 : 50 basis. Purpose in common like water supply, lighting, scavenging and drainage may be met from Service Tax with flexibility for utilising the income realised from service tax to the components with reference to top priority in the area. However, out of service component tax of 50 per cent, the local body should uniformly set apart at least half the amount towards water supply and sewerage/drainage.

For bringing transparency and reducing litigations, the Commission recommends that a directory of property tax be printed and made available to tax payers indicating the rate of taxation adopted area-wise with all exemptions/concessions and incentives and penal provisions.

The Commission has made certain important observations

about the exemptions. It says that total exemptions for all educational institutions from taxation is not equitable since the institutions avail all the civic facilities like roads, lighting, water supply etc. Instead of total exemption, concession may be given in the levy of general purpose tax by restricting the levy of service tax alone. In the case of Industrial Estates, the tax concession should not be available for more than a period of five years. Therefore, concession on service tax can be given proportionate to services locally provided but not on general purpose tax. In the case of Central Government buildings as also in the case of educational institutions and other charitable institutions, service tax may be levied in addition to the user charges. Public sector undertakings which have their own provision for services within their areas may be levied general purpose property tax in full and service tax in proportion to the services provided by local body from its funds in the locality.

There should be no restrictions, concessions, abolition or write off of tax or other revenue sources to local bodies by the government without consulting the local bodies. If intervention is found necessary by the government in the interest of public cause, compensation for loss of revenue should be simultaneously made available to local bodies.

For collection also, the Commission has recommended a foolproof system to avoid any harassment to the payers and loss to the local body. At the time of first assessment a pass book or a card be issued to the assessors. The passbook will contain particulars about tax levied, due dates of payment, grace time allowed, penalty for delayed payment separately for each half year upto the next general revision. The amount of tax indicated will be final, unless the tax is revised. It is the responsibility of the tax payer to pay the tax at the appropriate counters in the zones or in the specified branches of nationalised banks declared as the collecting agency. At the time of payment, entries will be made in the passbook and such entries will stand as proof for payment of tax.

A rebate of 25 per cent may be allowed for prompt payment before the expiry of the due date and 5 per cent for the advance payment of tax for more than a year. In the case of defaulters, a penalty of 5 per cent of tax may be added for each half year concerned and collected.

The Commission has recommended a minimum and maximum rate of tax for each class of municipalities to avoid the low level of taxation. The rates as recommended are as follows :

	Minimum	*Maximum*
Municipal Corporations	20 per cent	40 per cent
Municipalities (excluding education tax and library fee)	15 per cent	35 per cent
Town Panchayats	15 per cent	30 per cent

The main reform needed in case of the Town Panchayats is to introduce property tax by switching over from the House Tax presently levied under Tamil Nadu Panchayats Act, 1994.

The State Finance Commission recommends to create at State level a Tariff and Valuation Cell to help local bodies, in the valuation of properties and assist in determination of cost of service for user charges. A Tax Squad under the Valuation Cell may be created at Headquarters for making surprise checks to avoid evasion of tax mapping. The Squad may be given powers to direct assessment by the local body in cases of omission. It may consist of technically qualified people like Engineers, Town Planners and Revenue Officers.

A minimum performance of collection should be ensured. Government assistance to local body should be related to tax performance. Action may be taken for poor performance, against the concerned functionary, if no improvement is found even after direction. Tax collection machinery may be given incentive for higher collection of tax involved.

Reduction in tax for vacancy remission may be given for vacancy for a continuous period of 90 days, instead of 30 days presently adopted. Instead of suit in civil courts, all tax matters could be dealt with by a Special Tax Tribunal to avoid delay in disposal and to ensure uniformity in decisions. Initially, District courts may be the Tribunals. Based on the need and experience, Special Tribunals may be created.

Profession Tax

Profession Tax is another major tax levied by the local bodies. The Commission recommends that local body should take immediate steps for tax mapping of all kinds of assessees. Notices may be issued to those who have not registered themselves. Penal action may be initiated at least in a few cases which will make others to seek voluntary registration and enrollment. The Commission suggests a list of professionals to widen the tax base. The list includes the professionals dealing with computer, typewriter, shorthand, accountancy, training institutes, tutorial colleges, small scale garments/leather goods manufacturers and exporters, beauty parlours and beauticians, legal consultants, non-bank financial service companies, foreign exchange dealers, providers of transit/temporary offices, travel services/tour organisers, employment recruitment agencies, cable TV operators, ISD/STD/FAX operators, photocopying shops, commercially organised music parties, lending libraries, dry cleaners, petty traders etc. The present rates finally notified by the government after negotiations may be in force for the next five years and any revision can be considered later.

Vehicle Tax

The Commission recommends to abolish the tax on carts and bicycles. It further suggests that instead of totally deleting the provision of Vehicle Tax, local bodies may be allowed to levy tax on motorised vehicles and also on other two wheelers and tractors. The rate for levy may be as below :

Vehicle Type	*Tax (Rs.)*
Bicycles and Carts	Exempted
Two Wheelers	10-15
Tractors	15-30

Tax on Animals and Carriages

The Commission feels that tax on animals may be abolished. A uniform pattern of licencing of animals like dogs, pigs and other domestic animals may be introduced.

Tax on Timber

The State Finance Commission recommends that the tax on timber presently collected in Chennai Corporation may be continued and extended to other Corporations also.

Company Tax

The Commission suggests that the company tax available to Chennai Corporation may be continued and extended to other corporations as well.

Vacant Land Tax

The levy of Vacant Land Tax is considered necessarily since these lands derive the incremental price benefit due to basic amenities provided in the location for the existing inhabitants at high rate. The Commission suggests that the burden of tax should not be mulcted upon the buyer since the incremental benefits of price are mainly availed of only by the seller and not by the buyer. A one time vacant land tax may be levied for the specific period i.e., ten years on the promoters of a layout at the time when the promoter gets approval from the planning authorities. A tax rate of 0.5 to 1 per cent of the capital value is considered to be a normal rate on vacant urban land. The Registrar should collect the tax and pass it on directly to the local body concerned.

Pilgrim Tax

The Commission suggests that Pilgrim Tax or similar tax may be levied in respect of : (a) places of holiday resorts and seasonal specialities, (b) temple towns, and (c) places of geological or archaeological importance. This tax may be levied for the seasonal period at higher rates or can be uniformly levied at a lesser rate throughout the year. The scope of collection of Pilgrim Tax to cover both railways and bus passengers may be notified. The amount of tax may be collected in lump sum from Transport Corporations or fleet owners once in a month based on the capacity of the buses and the number of daily trips at Rs. 100-150 per trip (i.e. Rs. 2-3 per passenger on an average). The rate can be fixed after taking into account the average number of visitors to the place. A flat rate may be levied per bus per trip based on the seating capacity of the bus and the amount can be collected from the Transport Corporations or the fleet owners, allowing them to collect tax from pilgrims. Regarding people visiting the pilgrim centres in vans, lorries and private vehicles, cars etc., the local bodies may make their own arrangements to collect the tax. Rates recommended by the Commission are as follows :

Bicycles and two wheelers	no tax
Private Cars and Taxi cabs	Rs. 10-25 per trip
Vans, Lorries etc.	Rs. 25-50 per trip
Private Tourist Buses	Rs. 100-200 per trip

ASSIGNED TAXES AND REVENUES

Surcharge on Duties on Transfer of Property

The Commission recommends that the government may consider giving legal backing for issue of periodical guidelines on value of properties to be adopted for registration now being followed. Regarding flight of documents to neighbouring States for registration, the re-registration of the documents may be made compulsory as per the value of land. The government may also consider rationalising the rate of levy by widening the base to avoid flight of documents to nearby States.

Entertainment Tax

The Commission recommends the assignment of 90 per cent of the total realisations of Entertainment Tax. Any concessions/

remissions in the tax affecting local bodies may be resorted to by government after consulting the local bodies.

Surcharge on Sales Tax

Since the surcharge on Sales Tax has been merged with the compound Sales Tax, the Commission recommends that 15 per cent of the compounded tax may be assigned to local bodies and taken to a divisible pool.

NEW TAX DOMAINS

Advertisement Tax

In addition to assigning a few taxes to local bodies, the State Finance Commission has recommended to tap some new sources. The Commission suggests that all the hoardings should be under the control of the local bodies and the revenue earned should go to the local body concerned. The following is the suggested classification and rate of levy of tax :

Classification	*Basic Rate of Tax*
(a) Size	(i) below 200 sq. ft. Re. 1 sq. ft.
	(ii) above 200 sq. ft. Rs. 1.50 sq. ft.
(b) Location	(i) Chennai & Coimbatore 250 per cent
	(ii) Other Corporations 200 per cent
	(iii) Municipalities 175 per cent
	(iv) Town Panchayats 150 per cent
(c) Type	(i) High-rise Rs. 1000.00
	(ii) Others Rs. 500.00
(d) Message	(i) Social Rs. 100.00
	(ii) Commercial 500.00

Other types of advertisements on lamp posts and posters and writing walls should also be subjected to levy of tax/fee by local bodies. The levy on advertisement through slides in cinema houses may be revived. All types of advertisements except through newspapers and cut-outs should be brought under taxation.

Cable TV

In view of the mushrooming of Cable TV system, the Commission suggests that leeway rights in all roads in local body area for each Cable TV connection at Rs. 60 per year may be levied by local bodies. The collection may be done by the government alongwith Entertainment Tax and passed on to the local body.

TAX SHARING

Tax on Luxuries on Hotels and Lodging Houses

The Commission recommends that 25 per cent of the income accrued as tax on luxuries in hotels and lodging houses may be assigned to the local body.

Betting Tax

The Commission suggests that a share of at least 25 per cent out of this tax revenue may be distributed to Chennai Corporation and Udhagamandalam Municipality.

State Excise Revenue

The Commission considers that the local bodies may be allocated a share of the State Excise revenue as well. It suggests that 25 per cent of this revenue may be allocated for inclusion in general divisible pool for distribution to all local bodies.

Motor Vehicles Tax

The Commission recommends to set apart 40 per cent of the Motor Vehicle Tax collection by the government for sharing through divisible pool between the various types of local bodies.

Agricultural Income Tax

In view of the growing population scheme in urban areas, the Commission suggests that a share of 25 per cent of the tax may be allocated to the areas covered by plantations.

Sugarcane Cess

The Commission desires that the money allocated for roads in the area where the sugar mills situated should be passed on to the local bodies or in the alternative, the local body and the sugar mill concerned should be made jointly responsible for the upkeep of roads of the local body concerned which lead to the sugar mill.

Urban Land Tax

Land is a scarce commodity specially in urban areas. Moreso, the rise in land prices leads to more and more income on urban land. Hence the Commission recommends that a share of 50 per cent of the revenue earned on urban land may be allocated to concerned urban local bodies.

Surcharge on Bus Tickets

The Commission considers that to meet the problems involved due to floating population in specific areas, a surcharge may be collected on bus fare from persons travelling from a distance of 150 km. to metropolitan cities/important centres of trade and industry and made available to the concerned local body.

Local Body Cess on Passengers Travelling by Bus

The Commission recommends a levy of 5 paise on local town buses, 25 paise on mofussil buses and 50 paise on long distance buses in addition to ticket fare. This could be pooled and distributed on need basis to various local bodies.

Tax on Agricultural Lands

The Commission recommends that the government may permit the Municipalities/Town Panchayats to tax on the agricultural lands or pass on the land revenue collected in the area to the urban bodies concerned.

Local Cess

The Commission further recommends that a Local Cess and surcharge (as in the case of Rural Bodies) may be provided for in the Act and collected in Municipal/Town Panchayats areas and passed on to municipalities/town panchayats.

User Charges

The Commission considers that urban local bodies like Municipal Corporations and Municipalities of special and selection grade have scope for charging higher user charges under water supply at least 200 per cent more than what is collected at present. The local body should aim for full cost recovery of the services in the Corporations and Municipalities of special and selection grade area by cross subsidy against affordable community and by higher commercial and institutional rates. For clearance of septic tanks and cess pools, special charges should be levied and the local public may be advised to have cess pools cleaned rather than leave the sewage water on roads. Similar charges may be levied on hotels, lodges, hospitals, nursing homes and Kalyan Mandapams and other public places for clearance.

Licence Fees on Trades

The Commission proposes to revise rates for the various trades. Any industry not covered in the list may be brought in the schedule. If more than one trade is conducted in one premises, the higher rate should be collected. The penalty for default may be three or four times the normal licence fee. A grace time for renewal with penalty may be given for a period of three months. The licence fee should be suitably updated once in three years. The local body may also issue a licence for a period of three years on collection of licence fee in advance for those willing with a rebate of 10 per cent.

Income from Properties

The Commission recommends that the local bodies could resort to commercial line. The allottees of municipal properties could be selected in advance and the rent fixed in accordance with the prevailing market rate. The local bodies should take advance from intending allottees and this will reduce the financial burden substantially in the creation of assets.

Income from Special Services

The Commission considers that under town planning, there is a high potential for collection of development charges. In the case of new layouts, the cost of providing basic amenities like roads, lights and drainage can be met through development charges.

The Commission considers that the responsibility of local body to provide initial basic amenities in the newly developed areas is very heavy and, therefore, a portion of the development charge should be set apart to the concerned local body to meet the cost of provision of basic infrastructure. Wherever people of a particular locality want extension of certain services and are also willing to contribute a portion of the cost, the local bodies may be permitted to collect such contribution from the public in lieu of provision of services desired by the community.

Grants-in-Aid

The Commission recommends that specific purpose grants should be covered by devolutions and the funds allocated for the purpose should be passed on to the local bodies on the prescribed basis. It however feels that incentive and united grants are necessary to ensure additional resource generation.

Capital Fund

The State Finance Commission recommends to create a Capital Fund by transfer of contributions as under :

(a) Corporations, Special Grade and Selection Grade Municipalities — 15 per cent of total Revenue every year
(b) Other Municipalities, Selection Grade and Special Grade Town Panchayats—10 per cent of total Revenue every year.

From out of the Capital Fund, the local bodies can meet their future expenditure for taking up remunerative and entrepreneurial investments.

DEVOLUTION OF FUNDS

Quantum of devolution from the net tax revenue of the State has been proposed after considering the devolution that would be feasible due to constraints of State fiscal conditions. The Commission has fixed the overall percentage for devolution in a phased manner. The percentage of devolution proposed for each year with gradual increase is as below :

1997-98	8 per cent
1998-99	9 per cent
1999-2000	10 per cent
2000-2001	11 per cent
2001-2002	12 per cent

The Commission observes that if a general sharing is not accepted, the sharing of individual taxes will arise. For the purpose, the Commission recommends creation of following pools of taxes :

Pool A—This contains taxes which rightly belong to the local bodies but collected by the government (i.e. surcharge on stamp duty, local cess and local cess surcharge, Entertainment Tax)

Pool B—This forms the nucleus for General Devolution from Net Tax Revenue of the State to the Local Bodies (i.e., Sales Tax, Motor Vehicle Tax, State Excise Revenue, All others)

Special Reserve from Global Sharing

The Commission recommends that the quantum of general allocation from the divisible pool 'B' can be distributed after 15 per cent of that is set apart as Reserve to meet the post-devolution condition in the form of Equalisation and Incentive Fund. The remaining 85 per cent may be made available for distribution for sharing between urban and rural local bodies. The Special Reserve Fund may be kept at State level. The fund is created to correct deficiencies arising in the implementation of principles of distribution and Incentive Fund to continue the incentive grants for improvement of local tax collection efforts and the resources in the rural local bodies. A part can be utilised for rewarding performance in tax collection in urban local bodies as well.

VERTICAL AND HORIZONTAL DISTRIBUTION

From State to Local Bodies

The transfer of funds from State to local bodies is based on the population as per the last census. The ratio for the distribution of funds between the Rural and Urban local bodies would be 60:40.

Urban Local Bodies

The distribution of funds from the urban pool to different tiers is as under :

Town Panchayats	38 per cent
Municipalities	31 per cent
Corporations	31 per cent

Inter se Distribution

	Town Pan-chayats	*Muni-cipalities*	*Corpor-ations*
(a) Total Population (1991)	45	45	40
(b) Total SC/ST Population	20	10	10
(c) Financial Indicator per capita receipt under own resources (average of both Tax and non-Tax resources for the last three years)	15	15	15
(d) Service Sector (existing per capita expenditure on core civic servicces for the last three years)	20	30	35

Mode of Release

Funds should be released by the State government to the local bodies in three instalments :

Ist Instalment	April-May	25 per cent
IInd Instalment	Aug-Sept	50 per cent
IIIrd Instalment	Jan-Feb	25 per cent

The difference with actuals be adjusted during the release of first instalment of the following year.

TFC Award

The Tenth Finance Commission award alongwith investment by surplus local bodies will constitute a Corpus Fund, in which local body will hold shares and State government will give matching contribution. Over this market borrowing could be done for the Capital Fund. It could be accessed through matching contribution by the local bodies.

Privatisation

The Commission feels that privatisation can be aimed at by involving the local public or by forming NGOs. Local bodies can be encouraged to explore the system of contract for clearance of garbage and for solid waste management by private agencies.

11

UTTAR PRADESH

Uttar Pradesh occupies the central position in the Northern Great Plain of India. The history of Uttar Pradesh is very ancient and interesting. It is recognised in the later Vedic Age as Brahmarshi Desha or Madhya Desha. Several sacred books of the Aryans were also composed here. Uttar Pradesh preserved its intellectual leadership even under the ancient and medieval empires. British combined Agra and Oudh into one province and called it United Provinces of Agra and Oudh. The name was shortened to United Provinces in 1935. In January 1950 the United Provinces was renamed as Uttar Pradesh.

The State is surrounded by Tibet and Nepal in north, Himachal Pradesh and Uttaranchal in north-west, Haryana in west, Madhya Pradesh and Chhatisgarh in south and Bihar in east. Uttar Pradesh can be divided into two distinct regions — Gangetic plain and southern hills plateau.

Agriculture is the main occupation of about 78 per cent of the population of the State. The State is the largest producer of sugarcane and oilseeds.

The eastern region of the State is most populated but less urbanised and less industrialised, while western region is most urbanised and most industrialised.

Uttar Pradesh is the most populous State in the country accounting for a total population of 139.11 million according to 1991 census. It ranks fourth in terms of area, covering 9 per cent of the country's area and supports 16.5 per cent of total population of the country. As per praisional report of 2001 census, the population of the State has increased to more than

166 million, showing decadal growth of 25.80 per cent. However, the share to country's population has marginally decreased to 16.17 per cent. The State is divided into 70 districts.

The urban population of the State was about 19.9 million (17.9 per cent of total population) in 1981. It increased to 27.65 million (19.8 per cent of the total population) in 1991 and to 34.71 million (20.9 per cent of total population) in 2001. The analysis of level of urbanisation indicates that since 1961 the level of urbanisation in the State has been lower than that of the national average. Growth in urban population in the State has been quite rapid during the last two decades. Between 1971-1981, the State witnessed the highest growth rate of 60.62 per cent, which reduced to 38.97 per cent in 1981-1991 and to 25.5 per cent in 1991-2001. In these decades the growth was recorded more than that of the all-India level.

Consequent upon the growth in urban population, the number of urban settlements has increased from 293 in 1971 to 659 in 1981 and to 702 in 1991 and further 704 in 2001. The increase in number of towns has brought about significant changes in the proportion of population in each size class of towns. There were only two metropolitan towns viz. Kanpur and Lucknow in 1981, Varanasi was added in 1991 and Allahabad, Agra and Meerut because metropolis in 2001. These metro towns account for more than one-third of the total urban population of the State. The class one towns inhabit more than half of the urban population.

Presently, the State has 11 Municipal Corporations, 195 Municipal Councils and 417 Nagar Panchayats. The Municipal Corporations are administrated under the U.P. Municipal Corporation Act, 1959 and the other segments are governed by the U.P. Municipalities Act, 1916.

FUNCTIONAL RESPONSIBILITY

The municipal laws in the State provide for obligatory as well as discretionary functions to be performed by the municipalities.

Municipal Corporation

Obligatory Duties

It is incumbent on the Corporation to make reasonable and adequate provisions for each of the following matters:

1. erection of substantial boundary marks defining the limits of the city,
2. the naming or numbering the streets and public places and the numbering of premises,
3. the collection and removal of sewerage, offensive matter and rubbish and treatment and disposal thereof including establishing and maintaining farm or factory,
4. the watering, scavenging and cleansing of all public streets and places and removal of all sweepings,
5. the construction, maintenance and cleansing of drains and drainage works, and of public latrines, water closets, urinals and other conveniences,
6. supplying, constructing and maintaining receptacles, fittings, pipes and other appliances on or for the use of premises for receiving and conducting the sewage thereof into drains,
7. the management and maintenance of all Corporation water-works and the construction or acquisition of new works for a sufficient supply of water for domestic, industrial and commercial purposes,
8. guarding from pollution water used for human consumption and preventing polluted water from being so used,
9. the lighting of public streets, markets and public buildings and public places vested in the Corporation,
10. the construction and maintenance of parking plots, bus stops and public conveniences,
11. the establishment, maintenance or supports of public hospitals and dispensaries,
12. preventing and checking the spread of contagious, infectious and dangerous diseases,

13. provision for anti-rabic treatment,
14. maintenance of ambulance service,
15. establishing and maintaining a system of public vaccination;
16. the registration of vital statistics including births and deaths,
17. establishing, maintaining and assisting maternity centres and child welfare and birth control clinics and promoting population control, family welfare and small family norms,
18. the organisation, maintenance or management of bacteriological laboratories for the examination or analysis of water, food or drugs, for the detection of diseases or adulteration;
19. the reclamation of unhealthy localities, the removal of noxious vegetation and generally the abatement of all nuisances,
20. the regulation and abatement of offensive and dangerous trades, callings or practices,
21. the maintenance, fixing and regulation of places for the disposal of the dead and disposing of unclaimed dead bodies,
22. the construction and maintenance of public markets and slaughter houses, tanneries and their regulation,
23. the securing or removal of dangerous buildings and places,
24. maintaining hydrants and rendering such assistance including the maintenance and managing of a fire brigade,
25. the removal of obstructions and projections in or upon streets, bridges and other public places,
26. establishing, maintaining, aiding and suitably accommodating schools for primary education including nursery education,
27. establishing and maintaining or granting aid to institutions of physical culture,
28. maintaining and contributing to the maintenance of

veterinary hospitals,

29. the construction or acquisition and maintenance of cattle pounds,
30. the construction, maintenance, alteration and improvement of public streets, bridges, sub-ways, culverts, causeways and the like,
31. planting and maintaining trees on road side and other public places,
32. regulation of traffic and provision of traffic signs,
33. assisting by constructing and maintaining residential quarters, by giving loans to conservancy staff and all sections of working classes,
34. town planning and improvement including slum clearance and preparation and execution of housing schemes and laying out of new streets,
35. promoting urban forestry and ecological aspects and protection of the environment,
36. maintaining and developing the value of property vested in, or entrusted to the management of the Corporation,
37. safeguarding the interests of weaker sections of society including the handicapped and mentally retarded,
38. the promotion of cultural, educational and aesthetic aspects,
39. the construction and maintenance of cattle pounds and prevention of cruelty to animals,
40. the maintenance of a Corporation office and all public movements and open space and other property vesting in the Corporation,
41. the issue of a bulletin reporting proceedings of the Corporations and giving other information about the activities of the Corporation,
42. prompt attention of official letters and preparation and submission of return, statements and reports,
43. fulfilment of any obligation imposed by or under the Act,
44. slum improvement and upgradation,

45. urban poverty alleviation, and
46. providing urban amenities and facilities such as parks, gardens and playgrounds.

Discretionary Duties

The Corporation may, at its discretion, provide for all or any of the following matters :

1. the organisation, maintenance or management of lunatic asylums, leper homes, orphanages and rescue homes for women or for the care and training of blind, deaf, mute or otherwise disabled persons or of handicapped children,
2. the provision of milk to expectant or nursing mothers or infants or school children,
3. swimming pools, public wash houses and bathing places,
4. dairies or farms for the supply, distribution and processing of milk or milk products,
5. the construction and maintenance in public streets or places of drinking fountains or drinking sheds or standposts for human beings and water troughs for animals,
6. encouraging music and other fine arts and providing music in public place or places of public resorts,
7. making grants to educational and cultural institutions situated within and outside the city,
8. the provisions of recreation grounds, installing statues and beautifying the city,
9. the holding of exhibitions, athletics or games,
10. the regulation of lodging houses, camping and rest houses,
11. the construction, establishment and maintenance of theatres, rest houses and other public buildings,
12. the organisation or maintenance, in terms of scarcity of shops or stalls for the sale of necessities of life,
13. the building or purchase, and maintenance of dwellings for Corporation officers and servants,

14. the grant of loans for building purposes to Corporation servants,
15. any other measures for the welfare of Corporation servants,
16. the purchase of any undertaking for the supply of electrical energy or gas or the starting or subsidizing of any such undertaking in the general interest of the public,
17. the construction, purchase, organisation, maintenance or management of tramways, trackless trams or motor transport facilities for the conveyance of the public or goods,
18. the furtherance of educational projects and making grants to educational institutions,
19. the establishment and maintenance or the aiding of libraries, museums and art galleries, botanical or zoological collections and the purchase or construction of buildings thereof,
20. construction, establishment, maintenance or contribution to the maintenance of baths, bathing *ghats*, washing places, tanks, wells, dams and other works of public utility,
21. the construction or maintenance of infirmaries or hospitals for animals,
22. the destruction of birds or animals causing a nuisance or of vermin, and the confinement of destruction of stray or ownerless dogs,
23. contributions towards any public fund raised for the relief of human suffering or for the public welfare,
24. presentation of civic addresses and holding of civic receptions,
25. the acquisition and maintenance of grazing grounds and the establishment and maintenance of a breeding stud,
26. grant of loans or other facilities to any person, society or institution interested in the provision of dwelling or the execution of house schemes,
27. the provision of poor relief,
28. the building or purchase and maintenance of *gaushalas*

and of sanitary stables of ponies or cattle used in hackney carriages or cart,

29. surveys of buildings or lands,
30. relief measures to meet any calamity affecting the public in the city,
31. the adoption of any measure likely to promote the public safety, health or convenience,
32. the making of a contribution towards any public ceremony or entertainment in the city,
33. the establishment and maintenance of tourist bureau,
34. the establishment and maintenance of a press and workshop for Corporation work,
35. making arrangement for preparation of compost manure from nightsoil and rubbish,
36. taking measures to promote trade and industry and establishing a Corporation bank,
37. establishing Labour Welfare Centres for its employees and subsidizing the activities of association, union or club of employees,
38. organising or contributing to Municipal Boards Union,
39. making provisions for removal of social disabilities of scheduled castes and backward classes,
40. taking measures for the control and relief of beggary,
41. the setting up and maintenance of a Corporation police force for taking over and discharging police duties,
42. the undertaking of any commercial duty providing or promoting amenity or employment or removing unemployment, and
43. the doing of anything as desired by the State government or the Corporation.

Municipality

Obligatory Duties

It is the duty of every municipality to make reasonable provision within the municipality for :

1. lighting public streets and places,
2. watering public streets and places,
3. making a survey, and erection of boundary marks of the municipality,
4. cleaning public streets, places, and drains, removing noxious vegetation, and abating all public nuisances,
5. regulating offensive, dangerous or obnoxious trades, callings or practices,
6. confinement, removal or destruction of stray dogs and dangerous animals,
7. removing on the ground of public safety, health or convenience, undesirable obstructions and projections in streets or public places,
8. securing or removing dangerous buildings or places,
9. acquiring, maintaining, changing and regulating places for the disposal of the dead and making arrangements for the disposal of unclaimed dead bodies after ascertaining from the police in writing that there is no objection to do so,
10. constructing, altering, and maintaining public streets, culverts, markets, slaughter-houses, latrines, privies, urinals, drainage works and sewerage works,
11. reclaiming unhealthy localities,
12. planting and maintaining trees on roadsides and other public places,
13. providing water-supply for domestic, industrial and commercial purposes,
14. providing a sufficient supply of pure and wholesome water where the health of the inhabitants is endangered by the insufficiency or unwholesomeness of the existing supply, guarding from pollution water used for human consumption and preventing polluted water from being so used,
15. maintaining in addition to any other source of water supply, public wells, if any, in working condition, guarding from pollution their water and keeping it fit for human consumption,

16. registering births and deaths,
17. establishing and maintaining a system of public vaccination,
18. establishing, maintaining or supporting public hospitals and dispensaries, and providing public medical relief,
19. establishing, maintaining and assisting maternity centres and child welfare and birth control clinics and promoting population control, family welfare and small family norms,
20. maintaining or contributing to the maintenance of veterinary hospitals,
21. establishing and maintaining or granting aid to institutions of physical culture,
22. establishing and maintaining primary schools,
23. rendering assistance in extinguishing fires and protecting life and property when fires occur,
24. protecting, maintaining and developing the property vested in, or entrusted to the management of the municipality,
25. maintaining the finances of the municipality in satisfactory condition and meeting its liabilities,
26. prompt attention to official letters and preparation of such returns, statements and reports as the State government requires the municipality to submit,
27. fulfilling any obligation imposed by law upon it,
28. regulating tanneries,
29. construction and maintenance of parking-lots, bus-stops and public conveniences,
30. promoting urban forestry and ecological aspects and protection of the environment,
31. safeguarding the interests of weaker sections of society including the handicapped and mentally retarded,
32. promoting cultural, educational and aesthetic aspects,
33. constructing and maintaining cattle pounds and preventing cruelty to animals,
34. slum improvement and upgradation,
35. urban poverty alleviation,

36. providing urban amenities and facilities such as gardens, public parks and playgrounds.

Discretionary Functions

A municipality may make provision, within the limits of the municipality and with the sanction of the prescribed authority outside such limits, for :

1. laying out, in areas whether previously built upon or not, new public streets and acquiring lands for that purpose and for the construction of buildings, and their compounds, to abut on such streets,
2. preparing and executing Master Plan,
3. constructing, establishing, maintaining or contributing to the maintenance of libraries, museums, reading rooms, radio receiving stations, lepers homes, orphanages, baby folds and rescue homes for women, lunatic asylums, halls, offices, *dharamshalas*, rest-houses, encamping grounds, poorhouses, dairies, baths, bathing *ghats*, washing places, drinking fountains, tanks, wells, dams, and other works of public utility,
4. furthering educational objects by measures other than the establishment and maintenance of primary schools,
5. taking a census, and granting rewards for information which may tend to secure the correct registration of vital statistics,
6. granting rewards for information leading to the detection of evasion of tax imposed under this Act, or the detection of the causing of injury to or encroachment on property vested in or entrusted to the management and control of the municipality,
7. giving relief, on the occurrence of local calamities, by the establishment and maintenance of relief works or otherwise,
8. securing or assisting to secure suitable places for the carrying on of any trade or manufacture,

9. establishment and maintaining a farm or factory for the disposal of sewage,
10. making arrangements for preparation of compost manure from nightsoil and rubbish,
11. constructing, subsidizing or guaranteeing tramways, railways, railroads or other means of locomotion and electric (or gas) lighting or electric (or gas) power works,
12. promoting tourist traffic,
13. holding fairs and exhibitions,
14. preparing and executing House and Town Planning Schemes,
15. taking measures to promote trade and industry,
16. supply of milk,
17. establishing Labour Welfare Centres for its employees and subsidizing the activities of any association, union or club of such employees by grant or loan, for its general advancement,
18. organising or contributing to Municipality Unions,
19. adopting any measure likely to promote the public safety, health or convenience,
20. removing social disabilities of Scheduled Castes and backward classes in such manner as may be prescribed,
21. taking measures for the control of beggary,
22. the doing of anything whereon expenditure is declared by the State Government or by the Municipality with the sanction of the Prescribed Authority, to be an appropriate charge on the municipal fund.

TAXATION POWERS

The Municipal Corporations enjoy mandatory as well as optional powers to impose taxes :

Mandatory

The Corporation can impose the following mandatory taxes:

1. property taxes,
2. tax on vehicles other than mechanically propelled vehicles other than conveyances plying for hire or kept within the city or on boats moored therein, and
3. tax on animals used for riding, driving, draught or burden, when kept within the city.

Optional

The Corporation may also impose any of the following optional taxes :

1. tax on trades, callings and professions and holdings of public or private appointments,
2. tax on dogs kept within the city,
3. betterment tax,
4. tax on deeds of transfer of immovable property situated within the city,
5. tax on advertisements, and
6. theatre tax.

Municipalities

The laws provide for imposition of discretionary taxes only by the municipalities. The municipalities may impose all or any of the following taxes, fees:

1. a tax on trades and callings carried on within the municipal limits and deriving special advantages from, or imposing special burdens on municipal services;
2. a tax on trades, callings and vocations including all employments remunerated by salary or fees,
3. a theatre-tax, which means a tax on amusements or entertainments,
4. a tax on vehicles and other conveyances plying for hire or kept within the municipality or on boats moored therein,
5. a tax on dogs kept within the municipality,

6. a tax on animals used for riding, driving, draught or burden, when kept within the municipality,
7. a tax on inhabitants assessed according to their circumstances and property,
8. a water-tax on the annual value of buildings or lands or of both,
9. a drainage tax on the annual value of buildings leviable on such buildings are situated within a distance from the nearest sewer line,
10. a scavenging tax,
11. a conservancy tax for the collection, removal and disposal of excrementitious and polluted matter from the nearest sewer line,
12. a tax on deeds of transfer of immovable property situated within the limits of the municipality,
13. any other tax which the State Legislature has power to impose in the State under the Constitution.

FISCAL DEVOLUTION

The State Government constituted the State Finance Commission in October 1994. The three-member Commission was headed by the retired Secretary to the State Assembly. One member was a retired bureaucrat and Consultant to the Finance Department and the other was an academician and retired as Specialist from the State Planning Department. The Commission became functional in August 1995. In beginning terms of reference to the Commission were same as enshrined in the Constitution. Later on, the State Government added following additional terms of reference and required the Commission to recommend measures in those areas as well. The additional terms of reference were :

1. The Commission shall also examine and make suggestions regarding the maintenance of accounts and audit of the urban local bodies, and
2. make an assessment of the debt position of the Panchayats and urban local bodies at all levels as on March 31,1994 and suggest such corrective measures

as are declared necessary keeping in view the financial requirements of the State.

The Commission submitted its Interim Report in December 1995 and Final Report in December 1996. The Commission submitted its report for a period of five years from 1996-97 to 2000-2001. The State Government deferred the period by one year i.e. commencing from 1997-98.

AUGMENTING EXISTING RESOURCES

Restructuring of Property Taxes

The power to impose taxes is specifically conferred upon the Municipal bodies under the statutes. The power of taxation are to be exercised for the purpose of raising revenue of the municipal body so as to enable it to extend obligatory civic services. While the U.P. Municipal Corporation Act, 1959 makes the imposition of property tax obligatory, the U.P. Municipalities Act, 1916 has made property tax as an optional one. The municipal corporations can levy the following taxes on buildings and lands in the city :

(i) a general tax on graduated scale,
(ii) water tax,
(iii) drainage tax leviable in areas provided with sewer system,
(iv) conservancy tax in areas where the collection, removal and disposal of excrementitious and polluted matter from privies, urinals and cess pools is undertaken by the corporation.

These taxes are to be levied on the annual value of buildings or land, provided that the aggregate of property taxes in no case be less than 22 per cent and not more than 32 per cent of the annual value of building or land or both assessed to such taxes.

Keeping in view the new property taxes system obtaining in many other States, the Commission feels that it would be worthwhile and prudent if the State of Uttar Pradesh also embarks upon a revised and a rationalised pattern of property taxes. To this end in view, it appears more appropriate to adopt the carpet area as the indicator to assess the annual rental value.

The Commission makes following recommendations for determining annual rental value of a property :

(A) Location of Property
   (1) Property on the principal main roads,
   (2) Property on the main roads,
   (3) Property other than (1) and (2)

(B) Use of Property
   (1) Purely residential
   (2) Purely commercial/ industrial, whether self owned or otherwise,
   (3) Partly residential and partly commercial/ industrial,
   (4) Property other than (1), (2) and (3)

(C) Type of Construction
   (1) Pucca building with RCC/RBC roof,
   (2) Semi-pucca building with asbestos/corrugated sheet roof,
   (3) Other building not covered under (1) and (2).

The Mukhya Nagar Adhikari/Officer Incharge may get sample conducted of 20 per cent of buildings and collected data on the rental value of the buildings in a prescribed proforma. A draft notification be prepared, showing a monthly rent fixable per sq. mt. of carpet area. A District Level Body of officials may be constituted by the State Government to advise the monthly rental value. After advice of the District Level Advisory Committee is received, the monthly rental value per sq. mt. of carpet area of various types of buildings should be fixed, notified and published in the District Gazette and local newspapers. An opportunity be given to the public to place their objections/ suggestions within 15 days of the notification. The objection/ suggestion should be considered by the District Level Advisory Committee, and their final recommendations sent to the Mukhya

Nagar Adhikari/Officer Incharge. Therefore a final notification may be published in the District Gazette and local newspapers.

The following deductions may be allowed from the annual rental value attributable to the buildings only in lieu of all allowances for repairs :

	Age of building	*Deductions allowed*
1.	25 years and below	10 per cent of the annual rental value.
2.	About 25 years and upto 40 years	20 per cent of the annual rental value.
3.	About 40 years	30 per cent of the annual rental value

A rebate of 40 per cent of annual rental value may be allowed in respect of owner occupied residential buildings. This rebate will be inclusive of the rebatc allowed in respect of repairs.
The carpet area would be calculated as under :

1. Rooms – Full measurement of internal dimension
2. Covered Verandah – Full measurement of internal dimensions
3. Balcony or Corridor, Kitchen, Store – 50 per cent of measurement of internal dimension
4. Garage – 25 per cent measurement of internal dimension
5. Area covered by bathrooms, latrines, portico, staircase shall not form part of the carpet area for purpose of determining rental value.

The rates of property taxes may be :

1. Property tax – 2.5 per cent of annual rental valuc.
2. Water tax – 2 per cent of annual rental value.
3. Latrine tax or sewerage tax – 2 per cent of the annual rental value.

The Commission further recommends that tax collection should be made on self assessment forms and sufficient penalty may be fixed for default and wilful concealment of information, 10 per cent annual incentive may be provided for prompt payment within one month of the demand notice and penalty may be fixed for late payment after due date at the rate of 2 per cent per month. Service related taxes may be collected in most cases while exemption may be confined to the property tax only.

To hear the appeal against the assessment orders, a small committee may be constituted by way of a tribunal to hear and decide appeals.

The Commission has recommended to impose property taxes on that portion of the buildings and lands attached to the places of public worship which have been given on rent and are being used for the purposes other than public worship. Such portions of properties also be subject to water tax, latrine and sewerage tax.

The Commission further recommends that the existing provision for exempting the urban property having an annual rental value up to Rs. 360 per annum could be dispensed with and all the properties existing within the urban local body area could be brought in the tax net.

The Commission feels that the revision of assessment of annual rental value of buildings every five years may continue and wider powers should be given for ensuring speedy recovery of properties and other taxes.

The Commission has recommended that a crash programme for enumeration of houses in each local body is taken up and the houses not so far assessed are brought within tax net. It is also recommended that the data thus collected should be computerised.

In pursuance of the SFC recommendations, the State Government has introduced the carpet area system of valuation initially in the municipal corporation towns. The self assessment system is also initiated.

Non-Tax Revenue

The total resources of urban local bodies in the State comprise one-third revenue receipts from their own tax and non-tax revenues and the remaining two-third is in the shape of grants-in-aid from the State Government. It is also seen that in the two-third component of urban local bodies own tax and non-tax revenues, the share of non-tax revenue is practically 50 per cent thereof. The Commission, therefore, emphasises upon the tapping of more non-tax revenue sources in form of licence fee, charges etc. For the purpose, the Commission feels that it is necessary that the local bodies have, therefore, to educate and instil confidence in the public while revising user charges so that they get the much needed additional resources for improving the level of different civic services.

Assignment of Taxes

The Commission recommends that assignment of more taxes and duties to urban local bodies is not likely to be of great help and it would do more harm than good both to the urban local bodies and the State Government, as they are not able to collect more than half of the current demand of their own taxes.

Grants-in-Aid

The Commission recommends that the present system of grants-in-aid to urban local bodies be done away with. Instead they may be given a share in the net proceeds of the State taxes.

Devolution of Fund

The Commission recommends that 10 per cent (the State Government increased to 11 per cent) of the net own tax revenue receipt of the State Government should be shared with the local bodies every year from 1996-97 upto 2000-2001. Seven per cent of net proceeds of State's own tax revenue to be earmarked for urban local bodies. The Commission has further recommended that the urban local body should be informed in advance of certain performance indicators to be achieved by them for claiming 100 per cent share from 1997-98. In that year initially only 90 per cent of their share of the net proceeds may be passed on to the urban local bodies concerned and the remaining 10 per cent be given to them at the end of each year on the basis of their performance in the sphere of improving their resources.

The remaining ten per cent be given to them at the end of each year on the basis of their performance measured in terms of following criteria :

1. Each local body levies and collects all taxes and non-taxes items which are of obligatory nature.
2. Recovery of tax and non-tax revenue as percentage of the current demand is atleast of the order of 70 per cent in 1997-98 to be stepped up by 5 per cent each year so that it reaches the level of 85 per cent in the year 2000-2001.

The criteria of 80 per cent population and 20 per cent area for devolution of net proceeds of State's tax revenue have been recommended. The Commission has determined the *inter se* percentage share accordingly as 3.12 per cent of net proceeds earmarked each for Nagar Nigams and Nagar Palika Parishads and 0.76 per cent for Nagar Panchayats.

Release of Fund

The Commission recommends that the local bodies share in net proceeds of State's tax revenue be passed on directly to them by the State Finance Department. The State Government however released fund through the administrative department.

TENTH FINANCE COMMISSION

The grants-in-aid recommended by the Central Finance Commission will be available to the urban local bodies on the plan side as part of the State's annual plans. Similarly, matching contribution of the urban local bodies which they will raise should also be excused as part of the State's annual plans. The State Government has exempted Nagar Palika Parishads and Nagar Panchayats from matching contributions.

Debt Clearance

The Commission recommends that the amount of dues of electricity pertaining to electricity bills of urban local bodies (excluding Jal Sansthans) should be converted into grant to the State Electricity Board and the Electricity Board should in turn treat the amount as payment made by the urban local bodies towards electricity dues till 31-03-1996. The Municipalities will thereafter be responsible for payment of electricity dues.

The Commission recommends that the outstanding loans given for sanitation and water supply with interest upto 31-03-1994 be converted into grant.

As regards the loans given under Special and General component plan for Scheduled Castes and Scheduled Tribes etc., the Commission recommends that the loan outstanding upto 31-03-1994 alongwith interest thereon be converted into grant.

The Commission further recommends that loans advanced to urban local bodies for integrated development of small and medium towns alongwith the interest upto 31-03-1994 will also be converted into grant.

In relation to loans given for integrated urban development schemes, the Commission recommends that such outstanding loans as on 31-03-1994 with interest thereon be covered into outright grant.

While reviewing the recommendations, the State Government has raised the period in connection to all the above outstanding loans upto 31-03-1997.

Water Supply Scheme

Water supply is a major civic service which needs proper attention. The Commission has dealt with the scheme of water supply attentively. Presently, two systems are operative in regard to supply of potable water in urban areas. Firstly, there are Jal Sansthans in five KAVAL towns and one regional Jal Sansthan which cater to the local bodies falling within their region. In rest of urban local bodies supply of potable water is being carried out by the urban local bodies themselves.

Water supplied by Jal Sansthans is also being utilised by urban local bodies for their own use, like parks etc. In this connection, the Commission recommends that a mutually agreed percentage may be adopted for the purpose but, if no agreement is arrived at, then as a token measure, 5 per cent of water after transmission and distribution losses may be reckoned towards consumption of water by local bodies for their own use and for which the urban local bodies should make payment to the Jal Sansthan. If the local bodies fail to pay, the same should be recovered from the local bodies by the State Government out of devolutions to them from the State budget.

The Commission recommends that all the domestic connections should be made unmetered and the minimum flat rate should be raised gradually over the years so that a sustained revenue accrues to the urban local bodies. The non-domestic connections should be metered.

Municipal Infrastructure Development Corporation

The Commission has recommended for setting up of a Corporation for Municipal Infrastructure Development, on the line of one in Kerala, which will help urban local bodies to make the necessary investments. The proposed Corporation may be incorporated under the Companies Act, 1956 and its main objectives may be :

1. To prepare, formulate and implement projects, schemes and programmes relating to infrastructure development in the urban areas of the States, particularly land development, sanitation, road management, transportation and interconnected subjects.
2. To render financial assistance to urban local bodies by way of loans and advance for the execution of remunerative and non remunerative development schemes including town improvement and town planning schemes.
3. To provide technical and other assistance to urban local bodies for development schemes including implemen-

tation of Master Plans.

4. To provide assistance and guidance to urban local bodies for improving their administrative machinery and procedure.

The Commission has recommended that to begin with, such a Corporation may be set up in the State with an authorised capital of say Rs. 25 crore, 4/5th of this should be subscribed by the State Government and the remaining 1/5th by the urban local bodies. The State Government has however, rejected the recommendation for setting up such a Commission.

Miscellaneous

The Commission has deliberated upon various other factors of municipal administration in the State. It has made many important recommendations. Few of them are as under :

1. The Commission feels necessary that the State should enact one common legislation for all urban local bodies so that ambiguities are done away with and every urban local body should have the same set of legal provisions throughout the State.
2. The Commission has recommended a Committee of Experts to go into the question of reorganising the administrative structure etc. of the urban local bodies.
3. The Commission recommends that the Finance Commission Cell which is already existing in the Finance Department should suitably be strengthened. The staff and officers who are drawn for the Cell should have the background of economics and public finance. The Cell should also be put incharge of preparing annual review of the finances of the urban local bodies and Panchayati Raj Institutions. It should provide technical assistance to the next State Finance Commission.
4. The Commission recommends that the Development Authorities and Jal Sansthans operating in a municipal

area should be brought under the control of the elected urban local bodies. Also the power to sanction building plans in the areas following in the jurisdiction of local body should vest in the local bodies and not in the Development Authorities so that local bodies are able to administer in a better way the levy and collection of property tax. The State Finance Commission has issued notification for merging the Jal Sansthan with the Municipal Corporations. The move has touched a hornets' nest.

5. The Commission recommends that except in the case of Centralised Service, the Executive Officer and Mukhya Nagar Adhikari should be declared Appointing Authority in respect of subordinate staff and be given powers to inflict punishments including dismissal. The powers to hear and decide appeals against the punishment should be vested in the President and Mayor. The Commission recommends that for those categories of class III and IV employees who do not form part of Centralised Services in urban local bodies, necessary rules for recruitment of staff and their transfer within a division on the recommendation of the Executive Officer of urban local body be made.

RURAL LOCAL BODIES

For strengthening the PRIs, the Finance Commission has made certain valuable recommendations which are discussed as under.

Fiscal Devolution

The Commission recommended that three per cent of the net proceeds of the tax revenue, be parked with PRIs. The State Government has increased the share to four per cent.

The Commission has recommended that 20 per cent of district plan should be earmarked for Zila Panchayats and the remaining 80 per cent for Gram Panchayats. In case some activities and functions are devolved on the Kshetra Panchayats, ten per cent of the amount out of 80 per cent earmarked for Gram Panchayats should be made available to Kshetra Panchayats. i.e. 70 per cent may remain with Gram Panchayats and 10 per cent be earmarked for Kshetra Panchayats. The *inter se* distribution should be 80 per cent on the basis of population and 20 per cent on the basis of area.

Circumstances and Property Tax

The Commission does not recommend increase in the exemption limit but suggests that the maximum tax limit of Rs. 2000 should be done away with. The tax needs to be administered properly. Its coverage be increased and imposition be made obligatory for all the Zila Panchayats.

Non-Tax Revenue

The Commission recommends that the Gram Panchayats should be empowered to impose a levy on use of pump sets as also a levy on use of tractors in rural areas for carrying out agricultural operations.

Assignment of Taxes

The Commission recommends that assignment of more taxes and duties to urban local bodies is not likely to be of great help and it would do more harm than good both to the urban local bodies and the State Government.

The Commission recommends that the local body share in net proceeds of States' tax revenue be passed on directly to them by the State Finance Department.

As the Panchayat Raj institutions are not able to levy and collect tax and non-tax revenue for which they are already authorised, the Commission is of the view that assignment of new taxes to them will not be proper as on one hand, these taxes will meet the same fate and on the other hand the State Government might lose substantial part of their own revenues.

Grants-in-Aid

The Commission recommends that the present system of grant-in-aid to rural local bodies be also done away with. Instead they may be given a share in the net proceeds of State taxes.

The Commission suggests that a minimum population of 5000 be adopted as a norm for constituting a Gram Panchayat so that their number is reduced and they may become economically and administratively able units of local self government.

The Commission recommends that the outstanding loans given for sanitation and water supply may be converted into grants.

Miscellaneous

The State should enact one common legislation for all Panchayat Raj institutions to do away with ambiguities. Every Panchayat Raj institution should have the same set of legal provisions throughout the State.

12

WEST BENGAL

Bengal finds a coveted place even in pre-historic times. Bengal was ruled by various powerful kingdoms called Ganjaridai, Sasanka, Palas and Muslim rulers and governors till the Mughal period in sixteenth century. Battle of Plassey in 1757 changed the course of history when the English first gained a strong foothold in Bengal. In 1905 it was partitioned. After 1947, the merger of settlement began which ended with its final reorganisation in 1956 when some Bangla speaking areas were transferred to West Bengal.

The land frontiers of the State touch Bangladesh in east and is separated from Nepal in the west. Bhutan lies in the north-east, while Sikkim is on the north. On the west and south are the States of Bihar and Orissa respectively. Bay of Bengal washes its southern frontiers.

Agriculture is the mainstay of economy. However, State is one of the major industrial States in the country. The length of roads in West Bengal is 68,375 km. and of railway route is 3785 km. Calcutta is the most important port followed by Haldia. The State has good linkages by airways with the rest of the country.

The State has witnessed a steady increase in its population. West Bengal contained 7.97 per cent of country's population in 1981 which increased to 8.05 per cent in 1991. As regards urban population, the State contained in 1981 about 26.47 per cent of total population, ranking sixth in the country. The percentage increased to 27.39 per cent in 1991. The decadal growth in urban population was recorded 31.73 per cent in 1971-81 which reduced to 28.90 per cent during 1981-91 but the ranking remained static as thirteenth. Surprisingly, State recorded a 3.2 times increase in its total population between 1901 and 1991 but the increase in urban population during the period was found seven times. Calcutta is the total urban district, having the highest density, followed by Malda and Howrah districts. There has been a significant increase in number of urban centres as well. There were 112 towns in 1971, which increased to 130 in 1981 and further to 160 in 1991. The number of class one towns also increased manifold. In 1971, there were only five class one towns which became 12 in 1981 and further to 23 in 1991. Majority of the urban population in the State is contained in big urban centres. The urban component inhabited in class one towns in 1971 was 74.62, which became 77.04 in 1981 and further increased to 81.71 per cent in 1991. Except class two towns, all types of towns have been witnessing an increase over the decades.

LOCAL GOVERNANCE

Urban Local Government has an even longer history than Rural Local Government Institutions in Bengal. The East India Company obtained a Royal charter in 1726 for the establishment of a Corporation at Calcutta with a Mayor and nine Aldermen, all nominated. The charter was replaced by a statute in 1793 and, thereafter attempts were made to bring in a measure of popular representation but with a little effect. Following the Montague-Chelmsford Reforms, Local Government became a transferred subject and new Calcutta Municipal Act, 1923 was passed which replaced the three-tier system by a two-tier system of Commissioners and District Committees and resorting the domination of the elected representatives. After Independence, a new Calcutta Municipal Act, 1951 was passed setting up for the first time a Corporation based on universal adult franchise. Presently, the Calcutta Municipal Corporation Act, 1980 is in force. There are other Corporations as well and each has its own separate Act.

The smaller towns of Bengal Presidency saw a somewhat different pattern of municipalisation. The first Municipal Legislation outside Presidency towns was passed in the Bengal Presidency in 1842. Lord Mayo's resolution of 1870 recognised local self government as a conscious process of administrative decentralisation and led to the Act of 1876, which granted major tax powers to Municipal bodies but retained the District Magistrate as Chairman. Lord Ripon's resolution of 1882 further liberalised the Government policy and led to the Bengal Municipal Act of 1884, under which the post of chairman was reserved for elected councillors but strongest measures for State control were retained. The Bengal Municipal Act of 1932 increased proportion of elected members, reduced State control and delegated a wide range of civic functions to the Municipalities. The Act was amended in 1980 and reduced the minimum voting age from 21 to 18. This Act also provided for Notified Area Authorities which were set up with nominated Boards for newly developing towns or areas where new industries were being developed. Consequent upon the new West Bengal Municipal Act, 1993 all the Town Committees have been converted into Municipalities and the Notified Area Authorities have also been reconstituted as wholly elected bodies. By 1995, the State had 121 Municipal bodies; 5 designated as Corporations, 8 Notified Area Authorities and the rest classified as Municipalities. These bodies cover a wide range of population from 7,000 to 43,88,000 population density from 965 to 42,308 per sq. km. and number of holdings from 2099 to about 3,00,000.

There is one Act i.e. West Bengal Municipalities Act, 1993 for governing the urban administration in Notified Area Committees and Municipalities, whereas the municipal corporations are managed under separate Acts, based mostly on the Calcutta Municipal Corporation Act, 1980. The principal feature of the Calcutta Municipal Corporation Act, 1980 has been the introduction of Mayor-in-Council system in the country. Almost similar provisions prevail in other corporations. Similarly, the Chairman in Municipalities is assisted by a Chairman-in-Council consisted of certain elected councillors.

FUNCTIONAL DOMAIN

Municipal Corporation

The municipal corporations are empowered to discharge

obligatory as well as discretionary functions.

Obligatory Functions

The Municipal Corporations are obliged to make provision for :

(1) the construction and maintenance of water-works and providing, itself or by any agency, means for supply of water for public and private purposes,
(2) providing by itself or by an agency, means of supply of water for fire-fighting purpose,
(3) measures as may be required for fire prevention and fire safety under the West Bengal Fire Service Act, 1950,
(4) the construction, maintenance and cleansing of sewers and drains, sewerage and drainage works, and public latrines, urinals and similar conveniences,
(5) the scavenging, removal and disposal of filth, rubbish and other obnoxious or polluted matters,
(6) the reclamation of unhealthy localities, the removal of noxious vegetation and generally the abatement of all nuisances,
(7) the construction, maintenance, alteration and improvement of public streets and street furniture, bridges, culverts, flyovers, subways, causeways and the like,
(8) the lighting, watering and cleansing of public streets and other public places,
(9) the removal of obstructions and projections in or upon streets, bridges and other public places,
(10) the naming and numbering of streets and premises,
(11) the planting and care of trees on road-sides and elsewhere,
(12) the control of regular lines of streets,
(13) the control of building operations and securing or removal of dangerous buildings and places,
(14) the regulation of underground building operations,
(15) the co-ordination of overground rights enjoyed by

service agencies,

(16) the co-ordination of activities of agencies relating to laying and maintenance of underground railways, pipelines, tubes, cables and the like,

(17) the laying out or the maintenance of public parks, gardens or recreation grounds,

(18) a registration of births and deaths,

(19) the regulation of places for the disposal of the dead and the provision and maintenance of places for the said purpose,

(20) measures for preventing and checking the spread of dangerous diseases,

(21) public vaccination and inoculation,

(22) the organisation or management of chemical or bacteriological laboratories for examination or analysis of water, food and drugs for the detection of diseases or research connected with community health or medical relief,

(23) the construction and maintenance of municipal markets and slaughter-houses and the regulation of all markets and slaughter-houses,

(24) the regulation and abatement of offensive or dangerous trades or practices,

(25) the maintenance of all monuments vested in the Corporation,

(26) the maintenance and development of all properties vested in or entrusted to the management of the Corporation,

(27) the maintenance of a vigilance organisation in respect of its various functions,

(28) the compilation and maintenance of records and statistics relating to the administration and function of the Corporation,

(29) the fulfilment of any other obligation imposed by or under the Act or any other law in force for the time being.

Discretionary Functions

The Corporation may, at its discretion, provide either wholly or in part for all or any of the following matters :

(1) the furtherance of education (including cultural and physical education) and sports and the establishment and maintenance of, and aid to, schools for primary education,

(2) the establishment and maintenance of, and aid to, libraries, museums, art galleries and botanical or zoological collections,

(3) the survey of buildings and lands,

(4) the civic reception to persons of distribution,

(5) the providing of music or other entertainment in public places or public resorts and the establishment of theatres and cinemas,

(6) the organisation and management of fairs and exhibitions,

(7) the acquisition of movable or immovable property for any of the purposes herein before mentioned, including payment of the cost of investigations and surveys or examinations in relation thereto for the construction or adaptation of buildings necessary for such purposes,

(8) the construction and maintenance of—
   (a) rest houses,
   (b) poor-houses,
   (c) infirmaries,
   (d) children's homes,
   (e) houses for the deaf and dumb and for disabled and handicapped children,
   (f) shelter for destitutes and disabled persons,

(9) the construction and maintenance of cattle pounds,

(10) the building, or the purchase and maintenance of dwelling-houses for the officers and employees of the Corporations,

(11) any measures for the welfare of the officers and employees of the Corporation or for any class of them

including the sanctioning of loans to such officers and employees for construction of houses and purchase of vehicle,

(12) the establishment and maintenance of hospitals, dispensaries, maternity and child welfare centres, and the carrying of other measures necessary for public medical relief and family welfare,

(13) the organisation, construction, maintenance and management of swimming pools, public wash houses, bathing places, and other institutions designed for the improvement of community health,

(14) the construction and maintenance of warehouses and godowns,

(15) the construction and maintenance of garages, sheds and stands for vehicles and cattle biers,

(16) the provision for unfiltered water supply,

(17) the abatement of smoke nuisances,

(18) the provision of housing accommodation for the inhabitants of any area or for any class of inhabitants, and,

(19) any other measure not herein before specially mentioned, likely to promote public safety, health, sanitation, orderly urban growth, economic development and social justice and to prevent cruelty to animals.

MUNICIPALITIES

Obligatory Functions

It is the obligatory duty of every municipality to make reasonable and adequate provisions for the following :

(1) in the sphere of public works :
   (a) providing by itself or by an agency, means of supply of water for public and private purposes,
   (b) construction, maintenance and cleansing of sewers and drains, sewerage and drainage works,

(c) construction, maintenance and cleansing of public latrines, urinals and similar conveniences,

(d) construction, maintenance, alteration and improvement of public streets and street furniture, bridges and culverts, fly-overs, sub-ways, cause-ways and the like;

(e) naming of streets and numbering of premises,

(f) lighting of public streets and other public places,

(g) planting and care of trees on road-side and elsewhere,

(h) construction and maintenance of municipal markets and slaughter houses and the regulation of all markets and slaughter houses,

(i) maintenance of all monuments vested in the Municipality,

(j) providing by itself or by an agency, means of supply of water for fire-fighting purposes;

(2) in the sphere of public health and sanitation—

(a) collection, removal and disposal of solid wastes including filth, rubbish and other obnoxious or polluted matters,

(b) disposal of solid and liquid wastes consistent with effect to cause recovery and re-use of all that can be salvaged,

(c) reclamation of unhealthy localities, removal of noxious vegetation and abatement of all nuisances,

(d) regulating and abating offensive and dangerous trades or practices,

(e) cleansing of public streets and other public places,

(f) ensuring the wholesomeness of water supplied for drinking and domestic purposes,

(g) maintenance of all public tanks and regulating the re-excavation, repair and upkeep of all private tanks, wells and other sources of water supply on such terms and conditions as the Municipality may deem proper,

(h) provide places for the disposal of the dead and the regulation and maintenance of such places,

(i) measures for preventing and checking the spread of dangerous diseases,

(j) immunisation including public vaccination and inoculation,

(k) removal and disposal of the unclaimed dead bodies and carcasses of all dead animals,

(l) abatement of nuisance from birds and animals including dog menace,

(m) conversion of all service privies into sanitary latrines and providing adequate facilities for sanitation so that open defecation may be completely done away with,

(3) in the sphere of town planning and development—

(a) devising town planning within the limits of the municipal area in accordance with the laws relating to town planning for the time being in force,

(b) planned development of the borders of the municipal area in accordance with laws applicable for the purpose,

(c) improvement of *bustees*,

(d) control of regular lines of streets,

(e) control of all building operations and regulation of building uses,

(f) co-ordination of all over ground rights enjoyed by service agencies,

(g) co-ordination of activities of agencies relating to laying and maintenance of underground pipelines, tubes, cables and the like,

(h) laying out and maintenance of public parks, squares, gardens or recreation areas,

(i) re-development of congested areas for providing better living conditions,

(j) planned development of new areas for human settlement,

(k) preservation of monuments and places of historical, artistic and other importance,

(l) measures for beautification of the township by setting up fountains and statues, providing recreational areas, improving river banks, landscaping and the like,

(4) in the sphere of administration—

(a) survey of buildings and lands and preparation and maintenance from time to time of survey maps and plans of the town and other records relating to survey,

(b) removal of unauthorised encroachment on, or obstruction and projections in or upon, streets, bridges and other public places,

(c) securing or removal of dangerous buildings and places,

(d) registration of births and deaths,

(e) providing boundary marks for the municipal area,

(f) drawing up an Annual Administration Report on the activities and performances of the Municipality and submission, in the manner prescribed, of such report to the State Government,

(g) compilation and maintenance of records and statistics relating to the administrative functions of the Municipality,

(h) maintenance and development of all properties vested in or entrusted with the management of the Municipality,

(i) checking the construction of unauthorised buildings and pulling down unlawful construction,

(j) ensuring the stoppage of wastage of water supply and other civic facilities,

(k) protecting public properties in general and civic properties in particular,

(l) abatement of pollutions of all kinds,

(m) measures as may be required for fire prevention and fire safety under the West Bengal Fire Services Act, 1950, and the rules made thereunder,

(n) providing for adequate training facilities for the municipal employees and equipping and motivating them for public service,

(o) observance of occasions of national importance.

Discretionary Functions

A Municipality may, at its discretion, provide, either wholly or partly, out of the municipal property and fund, for the following matters within the limits of the municipal area :

(1) in the sphere of public works :

(a) giving relief to, and establishing and maintaining, in time of famine, flood and earthquake, relief works for destitute persons within the limits of the municipal area,

(b) construction or maintenance of, or providing or giving aids for, passengers' sheds, libraries, museums, community halls, offices, godowns, shops, markets, *dharmashalas*, rest houses, sports complex, place of entertainment swimming pools, public wash houses and bathing places and homes for the disabled and destitute and other public buildings designed for convenience of the community,

(c) construction and maintenance of old age homes and orphanages, domiciliary care of the sick, orphan, destitute and aged people,

(d) construction or maintenance of, or providing aids to hospitals, dispensaries, asylums, rescue homes, maternity houses, and child welfare centres,

(e) construction, purchase, organisation, maintenance, extension and management of mechanically propelled transport facilities for the conveyance of thc public,

(f) construction, maintenance, repair, and purchase of any works for the supply of electrical energy or gas,

(g) construction of dwellings for the inhabitants, specially low-cost dwellings for the social backward classes of citizens,

(h) providing accommodation for all classes of employees of the Municipality;

(2) in the sphere of education :

(a) establishing and maintaining pre-primary schools such as *balwadies* and creches,

(b) promotion of civic education, adult education, social education, non-formal education and the like,

(c) promotion of cultural activities including music, physical education, sports and theatres,

(d) advancement of civic consciousness of public health and general welfare by organising discourses, seminars and conferences,

(e) publication of municipal journals, periodicals and souvenirs, purchase of books, and subscriptions to journals, magazines and newspapers;

(3) in the sphere of public health and sanitation—

(a) construction and maintenance of cattle pounds,

(b) provision for unfiltered water-supply for non-domestic uses,

(c) promotion of the use of bio-gas and other non-conventional energy sources,

(d) provision for sewage treatment and preparation of compost manures from sewage and other refuse,

(e) abatement of smoke nuisances,

(f) setting up of milk dairies or farms (but not *khatals*) for supply, distribution and processing of milk or milk products for the benefit of the people,

(g) ambulance service for carrying patients;

(4) in the sphere of administration—

(a) civic reception to persons of distinction and paying homage on death to persons of repute,

(b) installation of statues, portraits and pictures in appropriate manner,

(c) organisation and management of fairs and exhibitions,

(d) organisation, establishment and maintenance of art galleries and botanical or zoological collections,

(e) construction and maintenance of garages and sheds and stands for vehicles,

(f) measures for eradication of addiction of all kinds like liquors and drugs,

(g) organising voluntary labour and co-ordinating the activities of voluntary agencies for community welfarc;

(5) in the sphere of dcvelopment—

(a) encouraging formation of co-operative societies and, in particular, housing co-operative societies, and assistance to such co-operative societies in construction of residential buildings,

(b) providing shelter for the homeless,

(c) undertaking manufacturing of building materials and their distribution at fair prices,

(d) reclamation of waste lands and promotion of society forestry,

(e) establishing and maintaining nurseries for plants, vegetables and trees and promotion of greenery through mass participation,

(f) organisation of flower-shows and promotion of flower-growing as a civic culture,

(g) promotion of agriculture, pisciculture, horticulture, poultry and improvement of cattle breed,

(h) assistance to small-scale and cottage and craft industries,

(i) programme for liberation and rehabilitation of scavengers and their families,

(j) income-generating activities, particularly for the women belonging to the socially backward classes of citizens;

(k) collection of statistics and data significant to the community,

(l) integration of the development plans and schemes of the town with the district or regional development plans, if any;

(6) generally, taking all measures not specified in the foregoing provisions, which were likely to promote public safety, health, convenience, education or welfare of the community.

Transferred Functions

The State Government may transfer to a Municipality such functions and duties as are performed by the departments of the State Government on any of the following matters :

(a) town and country planning,
(b) urban development,
(c) water supply and sanitation,
(d) transport system including regulation of traffic terminus;
(e) employment schemes and programmes,
(f) health and family welfare,
(g) relief and social welfare including social security schemes and programmes,
(h) public works including road construction and housing,
(i) cottage and small-scale industries, business and services including programme for skill development,
(j) education including primary education, adult education, vocational education, social education, non-formal education, audio-visual education, any library services,
(k) food and supplies including rationing and distribution,
(l) civil defence,
(m) fire protection and fire fighting,
(n) sports and youth services,

(o) welfare of the Scheduled Castes and Scheduled Tribes,
(p) environmental safety and improvement,
(q) social forestry and plantation programmes.

TAXATION POWERS

The Municipal Corporation can impose following taxes :

(a) a consolidated rate on lands and buildings,
(b) a tax on advertisement other than the advertisements published in newspapers,
(c) a tax on cart, and
(d) a tax on carriage.

The Municipality has power to levy following taxes :

(a) a property tax on lands and buildings,
(b) a tax on advertisements, other than advertisements published in the newspapers,
(c) a tax on cart,
(d) a tax on carriage,
(e) toll on—
    (i) ferry
    (ii) bridges, and
    (iii) heavy truck which shall be a heavy goods vehicle, and bus which shall be a heavy passenger motor vehicle, within the meaning of Motor Vehicle Act, 1988 (59 of 1988), plying on a public street.

FISCAL DEVOLUTION

In West Bengal, Property Tax, Advertisement Tax, Taxes on carts and carriages, tolls on ferries and bridges are levied by the Municipalities. Taxes on professions, trades and callings were levied by Municipalities till 1991 when a single point collection of Profession Tax through the State agencies was adopted. Non-tax revenue receipts have been quite significant for certain Municipalities. Major non-tax revenue sources are : Rents and fees from Municipal Markets, Building Plan sanction fees, Mutation fees, sales of forms, fees for tanker supply of water, fees for desludging septic tanks, sale of condemned materials, parking fees etc.

Own revenues of Municipalities have grown fairly fast (16.8 per cent per annum) but revenue expenditure has grown even faster and resource gaps have been projected to rise even more alarmingly in the years to come. The NIPFP study estimated that only 36 per cent of the Municipalities' revenue expenditure was met from their own resources (25 per cent from taxes and 11 per cent from non-tax revenue). The second Municipal Finance Commission assessed that, for the year 1989-90, only 4 of the 100 reporting Municipal bodies were financially self-sufficient on the basis of their own revenues, 24 on the basis of own revenues and tax transfers and 54 on the basis of own revenues, tax transfer and DA subvention grants. The rest had to divert plan resources to meet deficit.

In addition, the Municipal staff issue impinges on the Municipal revenue issue in five ways :

(1) A large contingent of unapproved/casual staff implies a steady drain of resources with no subventions coming from the State Government,

(2) Unlike the Panchayat bodies, the State Government only releases subvention grants covering 80 per cent of Dearness Allowance entitlements for the approved staff component and the rest of salary bill to be raised by the Municipality itself,

(3) At the instance of the State Government, the Municipalities had to introduce staff benefit measures and these have to be met entirely from Municipal resources,

(4) Pay revisions considerably enhance the salary bills of the Municipalities,

(5) A number of Municipalities run free primary schools but do not receive any grants-in-aid from the Education Department to meet the salaries of the teachers.

In bridging gaps, thus created, tax transfer from State

government played an important role. The net collection under Entry Tax was shared. Apart from Entry Tax, a small part (about 5 per cent) of Motor Vehicle Tax collection and a significant part of Entertainment Tax collections were also shared. Further, the State recompensated the Municipal bodies for the income foregone on Taxes on Profession, Trade and Callings out of State Profession Tax collections.

The West Bengal Finance Commission was constituted on 30th May, 1994. As required in Arts. 243-I and 243-Y of the Constitution of India, the Commission was to spell out the principles which should govern the distribution of resources between the State and Panchayats and Municipalities and also to suggest means through which own resources of these local self-government bodies may be increased. The four-member commission consisted of politician, academician and bureaucrat. The Commission submitted its report in 1995.

AUGMENTING EXISTING SOURCES

Tax Revenues

The Municipal tax base in West Bengal is very narrow and Municipalities largely depend on the Property Tax which is supplemented by other minor taxes and non-tax revenue but resource mobilisation efforts have obviously been inadequate. It has still not been generally enough to bridge the gap between revenue and maintenance expenditure. It is necessary to further stimulate resource mobilisation through local initiatives.

Property Taxes are the main source of income to urban local bodies in the State. There is a separate agency to valuate the properties for the purposes of assessment of taxes. The Commission in this regard recommends that periodical assessment by the Central Valuation Board should be made mandatory and the Board be strengthened adequately for the purpose. In connection with the realisation of service charges the Commission suggests that the State government should take up with the Union Government for timely payment of service charges for Union government properties.

Non-Tax Sources

There is considerable scope for increasing non-tax revenues. The Commission therefore recommends that Municipalities should be empowered to issue trade licences with fees at much higher level, to impose tolls at higher rates for heavy vehicles on Municipal roads, to levy imposts on tourists/ pilgrims, to impose water tax on large users and commercial and industrial undertakings, to introduce special conservancy charges for commercial and industrial establishments.

The Commission further recommends that resources generated in Regulated Markets should be brought within the purview of DPCs and the net proceeds ploughed back in the market hinterlands.

Incentive Scheme

To encourage the local bodies to increase their own incomes, incentive schemes separately for Municipalities and Panchayats have been suggested by the Commission. The purpose of this scheme is to encourage them to reduce deficits. The gap can be narrowed by increasing income or reducing expenditure or a combination of both. A Municipality will earn a bonus if it can increase its own total income by increasing returns from any of three components. The increase has to be at least five per cent in a financial year to earn a bonus of two-thirds of the incremental part. A common incentive fund for Municipalities and Panchayats will be created in a district by setting aside two per cent of the total entitlement due to the district in a year. The District Planning Committee will issue instructions as release of incentives after reviewing the performance of the local bodies every year.

Transfer of Taxes

The Commission feels that the entitlements do not depend on accretion of additional money but are only a deployment of funds which are now being spent for the districts already. The financing of entitlements is related directly to taxes. The

Commission, therefore, recommends that Entertainment Tax now collected by the State be handed over to local self government authorities. In addition, Urban Land Tax and Multi-storied Buildings Tax in Calcutta now collected by the State may be handed over to Calcutta Municipal Corporation. Steps may be taken to extend these two taxes to all Municipal Corporations.

Entitlement

The Commission recommends that in sharing of individual taxes 10 per cent of total net proceeds of taxes collected by the State in a year should be transferred to districts as entitlement. These will be untied funds at the disposal of the local bodies to maintain uninterrupted cash flow, somewhat less than half of the annual amount due may be remitted in the first two quarters and the rest in the last two quarters.

Grants-in-Aid

The Commission suggests that a substantial part of the grants-in-aid should be entitlement to the local bodies in the form of untied funds and the rest will continue to be grants. The Commission recommends that the State Government should distribute the fund collected as a surcharge on Sales Tax (in place of Entry Tax) to the Municipalities as grants. State grants on parts of collection of Profession Tax and Motor Vehicles Tax may be discontinued. It further recommends that DA subventions should cover the whole of the DA liability in respect of approved staff. The expenses on other benefits should be covered with grants. It feels that State and Central releases would continue to be grants and will not be part of the untied entitlement of the local body concerned. The Commission further recommends that covering of non-plan expenditure will also be grants.

Allocation of Funds

In the allocative exercise, two kinds of weights for the set of indicators for determining the composite index (entitlement percentage) have been used. Population has been taken as the single most important criterion for determination of allocation and 50 per cent weightage to it has been assigned. Having treated undifferentiated population size as the major basis, the Commission introduces an additional set of easily identifiable socio-economic indicators. Equal weightages have been assigned to all these indicators.

District Allocation

Fifty per cent of the total entitlement fund of the State is allocated to the district on the basis of population in each district. Besides, there is a need for allocation to compensate for varying levels of development. Some compensation for backwardness is common to most perspectives of the development process. The Commission has selected five criteria for identifying degrees of backwardness in a particular district, viz. area of a district, degree of illiteracy, proportion of backward population, proportion of rural population and paucity of bank deposit on per capita basis.

The Commission thus eschewed the path of the so called need based approach in determining untied entitlement allocation for the local self government. The State's contribution to each unit should be based on broad principles of equity rather than an assumed cost of services to be tendered.

Intra-District Allocation

After arriving at aggregate sum for a particular district, two per cent of the total entitlement of a district has been kept aside for funding an incentive scheme. The other 98 per cent has been split into three parts, namely (i) Municipal, (ii) Panchayat and (iii) Special area allocation solely on the basis of population accounted for by each segment.

The determination of the Municipal and Panchayat areas of a district has been done on the basis of the authority exercising administrative control on it, and the population calculated accordingly. Special areas are neither Municipal nor Panchayat.

Tea gardens, forest villages, factory colonies and defence establishments are examples of such entities.

Thus, the total percentage allocation for a district is represented as

$$A = 0.5\ D_1 + 0.1\ (D_2 + D_3 + D_4 + D_5 + D_6)$$

where

A = percentage allocation

D_1 = Percentage population of district to total population.

D_2 = Percentage of non-literates in district to total number of non-literates in the state.

D_3 = Percentage of the backward population of district to the total backward population to the State.

D_4 = Percentage of area of district to the total area of the state.

D_5 = Percentage of rural population of district to total rural population of the State.

D_6 = Proportion population per rupees one lakh of bank deposit in district to that of the total State.

Municipal Allocation

Fifty per cent of the District Municipal Fund is distributed to the Municipal Bodies on the basis of their population. The other half of the total District Municipal Fund is distributed according to the levels of backwardness of a particular Municipal area. These levels have been judged in terms of the following three criteria :

(1) Lack of literacy (weightage 0.1667),
(2) SC and ST population (weightage 0.1667), and
(3) Population density (weightage 0.1666).

Thus, $U = 0.5\ U_1 + 0.1667\ (U_2 + U_3) + 0.1666\ U_4$

Where,

U = Percentage allocation of municipality,

U_1 = Percentage of population of the municipality to total population.

U_2 = Percentage of number of non-literates in municipality to total number of non-literates in all municipalities in district.

U_3 = percentage of SC and ST population to the total SC/ST population in all municipalities in district.

U_4 = relative population density of municipality as compared with population densities of other municipalities.

District Fund

In pursuance of the Articles 243 H(d) and 243 X(d), the construction of a single fund, a District Fund is to be set up.

In 1995-96, 52 per cent of the plan fund was allocated for districts. Over the past decade, this proportion for district has increased gradually. As advised by the Commission, plan fund may now be divided into two parts; the first as grants and the second as entitlements going to districts. Entitlement of untied funds to local bodies would take care for locally perceived needs as also the problem of uncertainties of fund flow from above. Besides plan grants, the districts receive larger amounts of non-plan grants to cover committed expenditure.

The Commission further suggests that there should be a clear demarcation between the works under the State Plan Sector and the District Plan Sector and there should be lists of works entrusted to these sectors set forth in a Government notification. Funds for the State Plan Sector and the District Plan Sector may be desegregated according to these lists. Unless this is done, the local self government units will not be able to function effectively as a third tier of the Government.

Miscellancous

The Commission recommends a number of measures for bettering the municipal finances. Some of these are :

(1) The special areas be allotted funds in proportion to their population and the earmarked funds will be operated in consultation with the District Planning

Committee, which should be involved in supervising maintenance works.

(2) There should be some effective penal provisions for local bodies not following in line with financial discipline. Penal measures are also to be introduced for those Municipalities which divert development grants to meet revenue expenditure.

(3) Municipal Boards may try to involve the people to improve urban facilities.

(4) The State tax collecting officials should work in cooperation with LSG functionaries.

(5) Maintenance and development in towns be done by Municipal authorities with the help, when necessary, from the Zilla Parishad and the State.

APPENDICES

CHARACTERISTICS OF SFCs

State	*No. of Members*	*Academicians*	*Politicians*	*Bureaucrats*	*Others*	*Chairman*	*Whether Separate Act*	*Additional References*
Andhra Pradesh	5					Registrar of University		Yes
Assam	5	1		2	1 Advocate	Retired Bureaucrat	Yes	—
Karnataka	3	1		1		Academician		Yes
Kerala	3			2		Bureaucrat	—	—
Madhya Pradesh	5	2		2		Politician	Yes	Yes
Manipur	3	1		1		Bureaucrat	Yes	—
Orissa	5	21		2	1 Advocate	Academician	Yes	Yes
Punjab	5	1		3		Bureaucrat	—	—
Rajasthan	4		2	1		Politician	—	—
Tamil Nadu	5		1	3		Bureaucrat	—	Yes
Tripura	3	1		1		Bureaucrat (PT)	—	—
Uttar Pradesh	3	1		1		Judge	—	Yes
West Bengal	4	1		2		Politician	—	—

APPENDIX II

ADDITIONAL TERMS OF REFERENCE

Andhra Pradesh

(i) Resources of the State government on account of expenditure on administration, debt servicing etc.

(ii) Maintenance and upkeep of capital assets, and norms on the basis of which specified amounts are recommended.

(iii) Requirements of local bodies for modernising of expenditure on computerisation of accounts and upgrading the standards and non-developmental sectors, servicing and manner of monitoring expenditure.

(iv) Requirement of local bodies for meeting the non-plan expenditure on staff and administration.

Karnataka

(i) Manner in which the resources available to local bodies could best be utilised for meeting their expenditure.

(ii) Detailed analysis of repayment of loans and advances extended by government to local bodies and ways for repayment of government dues and the possibility of adjusting the dues against future devolution of revenue.

Madhya Pradesh

(i) Ways for yielding surplus for investment and reducing fiscal deficit.

(ii) Resources of State and demands on them.

(iii) Maintenance expenditure on plan projects, norms of expenditure on maintenance of capital assets and procedure for monitoring expenditure.

(iv) Deployment of additional funds for plan and determination of targets and possibilities of additional taxation.

(v) Possibility of better financial management.

(vi) Transfer of responsibilities and services by the State government to local bodies and correspondingly the transfer of services of employees engaged in such activities.

Uttar Pradesh

(i) Consider revenue resources of the State government and the demand thereon.
(ii) Consider the liabilities of panchayats and urban local bodies in respect of implementation of schemes.
(iii) Revenue resources of local bodies based on potential for raising resources.
(iv) Scope for better fiscal management.
(v) Maintenance and upkeep of capital assets and maintenance expenditure on plan schemes.
(vi) Assessment of debt position of local bodies.
(viii) Arrangement of funds for expenditure on plan and non-plan side.

Orissa

(i) Revenue resources of the State government and the demands thereon.
(ii) Functions and liabilities of local bodies.
(iii) Revenue resources of municipalities for five years, targets set for additional resources mobilisation and potential for mobilising additional revenue.
(iv) Scope for better fiscal management consistent with the need for speed, efficiency and cost effectiveness of delivery of services.

APPENDIX III

TIME HORIZON

Name of State	*Date of Constitution of SFC*	*Date of Submission of Interim Report*	*Date of Submission of Final Report*	*Duration*	*Recommendation Period*
Andhra Pradesh	21-06-1994	—	May, 1997	35 months	01-04-97 to 31-03-2000
Assam	23-06-1995	—	28-02-1996	8 months	01-04-96 to 31-03-2001
Karnataka	10-06-1994	—	January, 1996	19 months	01-04-96 to 31-03-2001
Kerala	23-04-1994	30-09-1995	29-02-1996	22 months	01-04-96 to 31-03-2001
Madhya Pradesh*	17-06-1994	—	30-06-1996	24 months	01-04-96 to 31-03-2001
Manipur**	22-04-1994	—	September, 1996	29 months	
Orissa **	21-11-1996	—	19-12-1998	25 months	01-04-98 to 31-03-2003
Punjab	25-07-1994	—	31-12-1995	17 months	01-04-96 to 31-03-2001
Rajasthan	23-04-1994	—	31-12-1995	20 months	01-04-95 to 31-03-2000
Tamil Nadu	06-09-1994	—	November,1996	26 months	01-04-97 to 31-03-2002
Tripura***	23-04-1994	—	January, 1996	21 months	
Uttar Pradesh	22-10-1994	26-12-1995	26-12-1996	26 months	01-04-96 to 31-03-2001 (State govt. has to implement from 1-4-1997)
West Bengal	30-05-1994	—	December, 1995	19 months	01-04-96 to 31-03-2001

Note: Submitted report on PRIs on April, 1995. * Report is related to PRIs only.
** Second SFC constituted. *** SFC reconstituted.

APPENDIX IV

NON-PLAN REVENUE SURPLUS/DEFICIT BEFORE TFC DEVOLUTION (1995-2000)

Item	Andhra Pradesh	Assam	Karnataka	Kerala	Madhya Pradesh	Manipur	Orissa
1	2	3	4	5	6	7	8
I. Receipts							
a. Tax Revenue	2747923	507202	3450797	2025890	2224072	16135	802092
b. Non-Tax Revenue	334672	204541	302458	161536	760091	11010	248023
c. Non-Plan Grants	2973	27448	22827	2748	12585	106	12521
Total	3085568	739191	3776082	2190174	2996748	27251	1062636
II. NON-PLAN REVENUE Expenditure	4604668	1513241	3372133	2563626	3698340	228485	1977890
III. SURPLUS/DEFICIT	-1519100	-774050	403949	-373452	-701592	-201234	-915254
IV. % SURPLUS/DEFICIT	49.23	104.72	10.70	17.05	23.41	738.45	86.13

APPENDIX IV *(contd.)*

Item	Punjab	Rajasthan	Tamil Nadu	Tripura	U.P.	West Bengal
1	9	10	11	12	13	14
I. Receipts						
a. Tax Revenue	1704598	1756214	3992583	35977	3839561	2541686
b. Non-Tax Revenue	193614	205098	317850	10830	401233	474409
c. Non-Plan Grants	15152	5367	19959	3863	57843	60541
Total	1913364	1967279	4330392	50670	4298637	3076636
II. NON-PLAN REVENUE Expenditure	2051861	2698234	4660335	328255	7451172	4077115
III. SURPLUS/DEFICIT	-138497	-730955	-329943	-277585	-3152535	-1000479
IV. % SURPLUS/DEFICIT	7.24	37.16	7.62	547.83	73.34	32.52

Source : Report of the Tenth Finance Commission, Government of India, December, 1994.

APPENDIX V

SUMMARY OF RECOMMENDATIONS OF THE STATE FINANCE COMMISSION

ANDHRA PRADESH

Shared Taxes

- Betting Tax—Ten per cent of receipts to Hyderabad Municipal Corporation.

Assigned Taxes

- Surcharge on stamp duty.
- Entertainment Tax—Amount collected in urban area after deducting collection charges.
- Profession Tax—95 per cent of collection be transferred.

Reforms in Existing

(a) Taxes

- Property Tax—General revision be made once in three years; Government should not interfere in taxation; no exemption to any house.
- Motor Vehicle Tax—More compensation.
- Entertainment Tax—Exemption/concessions be compensated by State Government.
- Octroi Compensation—May be increased by 10 per cent every year.
- Property Tax Compensation—Be enhanced by five per cent every year.

(b) Non-Taxes

- Water Rate—Municipalities be made empowered to increase

tap charges from Rs. 40 to cover total maintenance expenditure.

- New Source—To levy Rs. 50 per annum per telephone.

Grants-in-Aid

- Block Grant—Rs. 8 crore each to Hyderabad, Vizag and Vijayawada municipal corporations and Rs. 5 crore each to the remaining corporations to be utilised for their basic civic needs.
- To municipalities fixed on grade and to be distributed on population, area and slum area.
- Per Capita Grant—Be increased from Rs. 4 to Rs. 8.
- Incentive Grant—For propagating family planning and achieving highest target.
- Additional Grant—Rs. 50,000 when a Gram Panchayat is converted into municipality and Rs. 25 lakh when a new municipal corporation is constituted.

Fiscal Transfers

- Global Sharing—10.93 per cent of total tax and non-tax revenue of the State—9.14 per cent to rural and 1.79 per cent to urban local bodies.
- Entitlement—39.24 per cent of State revenue from tax and non-tax be entitlement to local bodies.

Miscellaneous

- No tax due certificate for applying for loan etc.
- Transfer of functions of Schedule XII.
- Rs. 31 crore per year for development works.
- Grants-in-Aid—Towards payment of pension to non-teaching municipal employees.
- Computerisation of local bodies.
- Creation of cell—In secretariat to monitor SFC recommendations.
- Increase in funds earmarked for SCs and STs to 18 per cent and 8 per cent.
- Preparation and publication of consolidated annual administration report on the accounts of local bodies.

- Rs. 18 crore per annum by setting off TFC award towards water supply schemes.
- Levying of Rs. 50 per annum per telephone.
- Introduction of social audit.
- Report on audit and accounts to be placed before Assembly.
- Second SFC to be appointed in early 1998.

ASSAM

Shared Taxes

- Share of State taxes for transfer and *inter se* distribution to be made on the existing basis.
- Existing rate of 30% M.V. Tax and existing units of taxes to continue for sharing.
- Share of Motor Vehicle Tax to be on the basis of number of vehicles in the urban area.

Reforms in Existing

(a) Taxes

- House Tax—House tax to cover the new households on the basis of floor area, revision and assessment of house tax in every five years, taxes should also cover all types of buildings including community halls, factories with highest rate for commercial type of buildings.

(b) Non-Taxes

- The subject for registration of birth and death certificate from Health & Family Welfare Department to local bodies be transferred. The local bodies may collect necessary fee per certificate.
- Municipality should levy user charges.

Grants-in-Aid

- Cost for maintaining registers and forms to be met by State Department out of plan fund as grants to local bodies at the rate of Rs. 1000 per local body for 1997-98 and Rs. 500 per local body for 1998-99, 1999-2000 and 2000-2001.

- Tenth Finance Commission—The award be distributed equally in each year from 1996-97 to 1999-2000 as grant by the State Government to each local body with basis of population as per 1971 census out of the fund allocated under the State Plan. Equivalent annual amount as in 1999-2000 may be given by the State Government as grants during 2000-2001 on the same basis out of plan fund.

Fiscal Transfers

- Total percentage of share of State Taxes for transfer should be 2% in each year from 1996-97 to 2000-2001 (Rs. 17.80 crore, 20.06, 22.50, 25.16 and 28.20 crore for urban and rural bodies.

Miscellaneous

- Outstanding State Government loan as on 31-3-1996 to be consolidated into a single block loan to be repaid in 30 annual equal instalments with interest of 5% per annum to be effective from 1996-97. Henceforth distribution of plan outlay between the loan component and non-loan component should be at the ratio of 1 : 30.
- High Power Committee headed by the Chief Secretary to be constituted to review the flow of funds in every six months.
- Permanent arrangement in the Finance Department be made to monitor the follow-up action with recommendations and to maintain the records for future SFCs.
- Tariff Commission to be set for streamlining the existing rates, taxes etc. and also to look into the service conditions and staffing pattern.
- Posting of regular Executive Officer for effective functioning is necessary.

KARNATAKA

Reforms in Existing

(a) Taxes

- Property Tax—Creation of Central Valuation Authority for

conducting periodical survey and valuing of property.
75 per cent of tax on properties of Union Government's Undertakings and State Undertakings as service charge.
Local bodies should be empowered to determine rate structure.

(b) Non-Taxes

- Licence Fee—Rates be revised to recover the cost of services.
- Parking fee—Levying parking fee on roads and towing charges for vehicles on public roads.
- User Charges—Full cost be recovered by increasing water charge.
- Municipal Property—Lower courts be barred to intervene, properties with litigations be disposed of.
- Cess—Different cesses like beggary cess, library cess, health cess, education cess, water cess etc. should be abolished.

Grants-in-Aid

- TFC Award—As recommended in addition to plan fund.

Fiscal Transfers

- Global Sharing—36 per cent of non-loan gross own revenue receipts of the State—15 per cent to urban and 85 per cent to rural local bodies.
  Criteria for allocation—population, area, illiteracy, road length and number of persons per hospital bed (5.4 per cent of ULBs and 30.6 per cent to PRIs).

Miscellaneous

- Enactment of one common municipal law.
- Creation of a permanent SFC Cell.
- Directorate of Municipal Administration be abolished.
- Urban and rural water supply be merged and Karnataka Urban Water Supply and Drainage Broad be entrusted the integrated water supply scheme.
- Fixation of water supply rates.

- Involvement of NGOs in solid waste management in big cities.
- Normative standard for street lights.
- Administrative Reforms Commission for restructuring municipal administration.
- Outstanding dues of Rs. 26.04 crore is KUWs & DB be recovered from share of ULBs.
- Development Authorities be merged with ULB.
- Town planning units be transferred to ULB.
- Outstanding amount of Rs. 102.95 crore to financial institutions be paid by the Government.

KERALA

Shared Taxes

- Court Fee Stamp—95 per cent of total collection from court fee stamp affixed on licences, permits, petition etc. be distributed among State government and ULBs.
- Building Exemption Fee—50 per cent be deposited by the applicant directly to ULBs and 50 per cent to treasury. The rate be increased by 100 per cent.
- Library Cess—Be continued to be collected by ULBs and be earmarked for improving the infrastructure of educational institutions under their control.

Assigned Taxes

- Building Tax—Presently levied and collected by State government should be assigned to ULBs.
- Tax on Sale of Properties—Revenue realised from urban areas be given as a statutory grant.
- Tax on Cable TV—Cable TV be subjected to Entertainment Tax levied and appropriated by ULBs.

  Annual licence fee of Rs. 500 or at the rate of Rs. 5 per connection.

  Entertainment tax on cable TV operators and proprietors of video parlours be levied @ 20% in corporations, 15% in municipalities and 10% in panchayats on the payment made by a customer.

Reforms in Existing

(a) Taxes

- Property Tax—The present system of assessing rental value be dispensed with and plinth area be adopted as basis, local body area be divided on the basis of civic amenities, proximity to shopping complex, to public offices, to medical institution and to factories and industries, buildings be classified on the basis of nature as ACC buildings with superior quality wood, with ordinary quality wood, tiled roof, huts and others, rebate is granted on the basis of age of the buildings and also for owner occupancy, general revision be made every four years instead of five years.
- Entertainment Tax—ULBs should be free to fix the rate above the minimum, rate be fixed on the basis of gross seating capacity; Additional Entertainment Tax be merged with entertainment tax.
- Show Tax—Surcharge on show tax be merged with show tax. Government should fix minimum and ULBs be made free to fix the rates above minimum.
- Profession Tax—Rate be uniform in urban and rural areas and slabs be reduced and rates rationalised.
- Advertisement Tax—The Government may fix minimum and ULBs be made free to fix rates.
- Octroi Tax—Be levied on goods sold in the locality instead of stopping vehicles for collecting tax.

(b) Non-Taxes

- Instead of constructing shopping complexes ULBs should get the real estate developed by private developers on tender basis.
- Government should fix minimum licence fee and ULBs be made free to fix rates above the prescribed limit.

Grants-in-Aid

- Entire non-plan non-statutory grants may be given as a single general purpose grant as one per cent of State revenue.
- Maintenance grant should be based on current cost of

construction.

- For maintaining roads the Vehicle Tax Compensation may be 25 per cent of net collection of Motor Vehicle Tax.
- TFC Award—One per cent is earmarked for fund for local development and 99 per cent be distributed. 85 per cent of grant to village Panchayats and 15 per cent to block and district Panchayats. Grant to ULBs on per capita basis.

Fiscal Transfers

- Creation of Urban Pool consisting of general purpose grant at one per cent of State revenue on the basis of population. 100 per cent of Basic Tax collected from urban areas and 25 per cent of surcharge on stamp duty collected from Municipal Council area.
- One per cent each of Rural and Urban Pools be credited to fund for local development. Remaining 99 per cent to be distributed among village Panchayats and Municipal Councils on the basis of population, population of SC/ST, financial needs of local bodies and tax efforts of local bodies.

Miscellaneous

- Constituting an Expert Group to suggest formats for budget and monitoring accounts.
- Commercial accounting system to be adopted.
- Constituting Local Development Fund consisting of one per cent each of TFC award, urban and rural pools, surcharge on stamp duty, non-statutory, non-plan grants Municipal Corporations, own income of all local bodies.
- Main purpose of fund is to leverage funds from market and to offer a scheme of interest subsidy on desirable non-remunerative schemes.
- Arrear upto 1-4-1994 relating to Kerala Water Authority be written off, the arrear accumulated during 1-4-1984 to 31-3-1991 be added to arrears from 1-4-1991 to 31-3-1996 and recovered from ULBs in 8 years out of grants.
- A special cell in Finance Department to watch the implementation of SFC recommendations be created.
- Unauthorised buildings be brought under network without conferring rights of regularisation.

- ULBs be empowered to execute civil works without government supervision.
- Repairs and maintenance of street taps be given to willing local bodies and a rebate be allowed by Authority.
- Unique Premises Numbering be adopted for tax mapping.
- 25 per cent of centrally sponsored poverty alleviation programmes be given to ULBs for implementing the programmes.

MADHYA PRADESH

Shared Taxes

- Entry Tax—Present sharing be continued.
- Vehicle Tax—Sharing be continued.

Reforms in Existing

(a) Taxes

- Entry Tax—The base be broadened and rate structure be rationalised.
- Evaluating the revenue raising capacity of ULBs.

(b) Non-Taxes

- User Charges—Cost of public utility services be recovered by charging appropriate user charges.

Grants-in-Aid

- Specific grants-in-aid in lieu of passenger tax be continued.
- Incentive Grant—An incentive grant to local bodies exceeding their targets of revenue mobilisation.
- TFC Award—To establish an Urban Development Finance Corporation with an authorised capital of Rs. 250 crore.

Fiscal Transfers

- Present amount of transfer from State government from 4.63

per cent of State's net tax and non-tax revenue be increased to 8.67 per cent.

- Share of different districts be based on urban population, actual receipt of Sales Tax, urban SC/ST population, and inverse of per capita power consumption.
- Rs. 407 crore be given from the State Consolidated Fund for rendering basic services.
- Rs. 203 crore be given through 1996-97 budget.

Miscellaneous

- Payment be made in twelve equal monthly instalments.
- Setting up of an Urban Infrastructure Development Fund for facilitating additional funds for proper allocation of funds for financing urban infrastructure projects.
- An Audit Committee at State level to consider all serious matters of audit reports and to take appropriate actions.
- Engaging private agencies in waste management on the principle of energy management.

MANIPUR

Reforms in Existing

(a) Taxes

- Holding Tax—The proposal is under the scrutiny of the Government. It is necessary to streamline the tax structure.
- Octroi—In the long run Octroi should be abolished and replaced by a surcharge on Sales Tax and the proceeds can be distributed as maintenance grants.
- Five Municipal Councils (excluding Imphal) should generate internal revenue @ Rs. 28 per head of urban population by the year 2000-2001. For the Nagar Panchayats, target for internal revenue generation may be fixed at the rate of Rs. 10 per head of their respective population.

(b) Non-Taxes

- Proposals for imposing separate charge/fee for drainage,

scavenging, street lighting etc., are under the scrutiny of the Government. It needs to be streamlined.

Grants-in-Aid

- Maintenance Grant—For Imphal Municipality, which imposes both Octroi and Holdings Tax, no maintenance grant. If the local body insists, it has to surrender Octroi and may be given Rs. 50 lakh per year for five years.
- For other municipal councils, grants may be retained at 1995-96 level of Rs. 26.33 lakh for 1996-97 with a 10 per cent annual increase.
- Maintenance Grant be worked out on the basis of internal resource generation target of each municipality on the basis of its population and deduct the same from approved annual expenses with annual increase higher than 5 per cent.
- Development Grant—Entire TFC funds may be passed on to the municipalities at the rate of Rs. 12.50 per capita per year.
- A per capita grant of Rs. 7 for Nagar Panchayats and Rs. 10 for Municipal Councils may be allocated per year till March 2001.
- Bonus Grant—Bonus Grants will be allocated to ULBs except Imphal on a 100 per cent matching basis for revenue generation beyond above.
- Half of the grant will be paid automatically on the basis of population and the balance along with entire plan funds on sanction of specific schemes and on receipt of utilisation certificate for the previous release of funds.
- Funds will be released quarterly.
- Entire amount has to be spent on schemes only. Special grant—A grant of Rs. 1 lakh per year to Mao to upgrade township to a respectable level as Mao takes care of the bulk of the passenger and freight traffic into or out of the State.
- A grant of Rs. 2 lakh per year for Moren which has a Small Town Committee and is gaining importance because of the recent opening of border trade.

Miscellaneous

- It will be appropriate if the State Government appears a range of rates for each type of tax-fee so that a local body staying within the range need not take approval of the Government in each case. In the alternate an amendment of the relevant laws may be carried out so that a proposal for imposition of fees/taxes could be deemed to be approved by the Government if the objections thereto are not conveyed within one month. A third alternative may be to allow local bodies to impose taxes/fees subject to the right of the State Government to issue directions.

- Assets created by Government departments roads and paths, streetlighting, drainage/sewerage facilities, community services etc. should be handed over to the ULBs free of cost and expect them to maintain by raising resources. It is for the inhabitants of the urban areas to pay for the upkeep of these assets.
- Comprehensive budget formats should be prepared and circulated.
- Directorate of Local Fund Audit be strengthened.
- Full time Executive Officer in each Nagar Panchayat be appointed.
- Other staff be given the minimum wages prescribed by the State Government.

ORISSA

Shared Taxes

- Surcharge on Entertainment Tax—Amount payable to municipalities be determined Rs. 44.85 lakh to each of six municipalities.
- Surcharge on Stamp Duty—Municipalities be also given a fixed share of stamp of duty, rates be uniform at 3 per cent.
- Profession Tax—50 per cent of gross collection.
- Motor Vehicle Tax—10 per cent of gross collection be given for maintaining roads. Share between Municipalities and NACs in the ratio of 60 : 40.

Assigned Taxes

- Compounding Surcharge on Entertainment—Whole of the surcharge on payments for admission to entertainment.

Reforms in Existing

(a) Taxes

- Octroi—Should not be abolished, system be made transparent in case of abolition, be replaced by Entry Tax. Regular monthly compensation with 10 per cent increase.
- Holding Tax—Rates be revised upwardly, periodical re-valuation be made mandatory, in case of non-valuation, 3 to 5 per cent increase in tax.

(b) Non-Taxes

Nil.

Grants-in-Aid

- Entire salary and terminal benefits liability pertaining to approved staff appointed prior to 1-1-1974 and 1-1-1976.
- Others case be also considered.

Miscellaneous

- Roads—All roads along with maintenance grant be transferred to ULBs.
- Drinking Water—Construction works be retained by the Government maintenance along with grant and staff be transferred to ULBs.
- Health—Staff dealing with public be placed at the disposal of municipalities along with allocation of proportionate salary and other grants.
- Electricity—Dual control be abolished. Municipalities be given skeleton staff along with funds for construction and erection of line and also maintaining it.
- Sewerage—Management and maintenance of sewer lines along with funds be transferred from PHED to ULBs.
- Sanitation—Private sector be associated to control unhealthy environment.
- Training—Regular training to staff and elected officials.
- Data Bank—Data bank at district level under the control of the Collector and at the State level with association of

Directorate of Economics & Statistics.

- Massive external assistance be provided to upgrade basic services.
- No dues certificate be insisted upon while sanctioning of loans by financial institutions.

PUNJAB

Shared Taxes

- Stamp Duty—20 per cent of the proceeds be distributed between ULBs and PRIs on the basis of derivation.
- Motor Vehicle Tax—20 per cent of the proceeds be distributed on the proportionate length of roads.
- Electricity Duty—20 per cent of the amount collected be distributed on the basis of collection.
- Entertainment Tax—20 per cent of amount collected from Entertainment Tax and Cinematograph Shows be distributed between ULBs and PRIs on 80 : 20 basis.

Assigned Taxes

- Profession Tax—Tax on professions, trade, callings and unemployment be levied and collected by ULBs.
- Advertisement Tax—Tax be levied on advertisements and hoardings.
- Licensing—Tubewells privately bored be taxed. In addition, a surcharge on water pumped be levied.

Reforms in Existing

(a) Taxes

- Octroi—System of Composite Permit be introduced. Inspection of warehouses or stores in rural areas be made by a joint agreement between ULBs and PRIs. Cost of collection should not exceed five per cent.
- Property Tax—Tax be delinked from rentals; vacant land and lands used for marriage parties be taxed at higher rates, surcharge of 50-100 per cent on commercial, industrial and other non-residential buildings; exemptions be reduced; any

exemption by Government be compensated, filing of assessment be made obligatory, Municipal Valuation Committees be formed to hear objections.

- Water Supply & Sewerage—Stand posts be abolished if not paid by consumer; rates be linked with power tariff with 10 per cent annual hike; sewerage charges be equal to water rates; different water rates for different uses; entire supply be metered; full cost recovery; maintenance, billing and collection be privatised.

(b) Non-Taxes

- Substantial increase in rates is desirable to recover cost escalation and improving the level of services.
- One time payment for disproportionate collection of charges may be introduced.
- Additional excise duty be enhanced from 7 to 10 per cent on country liquor and from 16 to 20 per cent on India made foreign liquor.
- Domain of user charges be extended to water supply, sewerage, parking and solid waste management.
- Full cost including operation, maintenance, billing and collection, capital cost and depreciation be recovered.
- User charges be fixed so as to provide cross subsidies to weaker sections.

Grants-in-Aid

- General Purpose Grant—Granted to remove fiscal imbalance amongst local bodies Rs. 30 crore annually for next five years on the basis of multiplying the difference between the average per capita income and actual per capita income with the population.
- Incentive Grant—Rs. 10 lakh to Nagar Panchayats, Rs. 15-25 lakh to Municipal Councils and Rs. 50 lakh to Municipal Corporations for efforts to make optimum use of their own fiscal domain, augment their resources and improve upon their fiscal administration.
- Specific Purpose Grant—Be given to meet the capital cost of augmentation and additional coverage of population by services and to stimulate specific local functions for

providing essential services. These grants be conditional and matching.

Fiscal Transfers

- Devolution be made through assignment and sharing of State taxes.

Miscellaneous

- For achieving better level of services, a contribution of 30 per cent of share by the ULBs as seed money for raising 70 per cent of the required amount through loan is provided.
- Pending transfer of assets, civic services be provided by private agencies.
- Improvement Trusts be abolished on transfer of functional domain to Punjab Urban Planning and Development Authority.
- Pre-Audit system be applied.
- Every Municipal Council should constitute its Municipal Accounts Committee from amongst its members to examine the accounts, scrutinise the audit reports and verify the works and records.
- State level Public Accounts Committee for Municipal Finance be constituted.

RAJASTHAN

Assigned Taxes

- Sanitation Tax—Be levied on *subzi mandies*, hospitals, barber shops, restaurants, industries etc.
- Parking Tax—Be introduced.
- Hoarding Tax—Be levied on hoardings advertising in public places.

Reforms in Existing

(a) Taxes

- Octroi—Private collection be introduced; a committee be set up to look into possible harassment of people by contractors and suggest remedial measures, in case of exemptions granted to goods of Electricity Board and PHED by the Government concessional rates for street lighting and water supply be charged from ULBs, all exemptions be compensated by Government.

- House Tax—Categorisation of areas on value of properties and per sq. foot affordable rate be applied; self assessment be introduced, exemption limit be increased, one time payment in certain cases be applied; simplification of system; more transparency.
- Profession Tax—This obligatory tax be made discretionary.
- Discretionary Taxes be levied on selective basis.

(b) Non-Taxes

- Sale of Land—No dues to local bodies certificate from Urban Improvement Trusts be desired before according approval of schemes; power be delegated to Commissioners; share of municipalities be transferred timely and fully.
- Penalties—The rates of fines, penalties, charges be enhanced to make them more effective.

Grants-in-Aid

- General Purpose Grant—60 per cent of urban bodies share from pool be allocated to ULBs in proportion of their population categorywise.
- Development Grant—Grants to Boards and loans to Councils and Corporations; 20 per cent of Urban Pool to be earmarked; payment through Finance Corporation.
- Incentive Grant—Cash awards to local bodies for development works in their areas.
- Matching Grant—20 per cent of Urban Pool be reserved for Incentive and Matching Grants. After deducting the awards money, the remainder be utilised for works of public utility on matching basis against TFC award.

Fiscal Transfers

- Divisible Pool—2.18 per cent of the net tax proceeds of the

State be given to local bodies—PRIs and ULBs on 3.4 : 1 ratio, distribution within the category be made on the basis of population. Funds be released in two equal instalments.

Miscellaneous

- A State level finance corporation for ULBs be set up to advance loan at concessional rate of interest. It should be part of the Directorate of Local Bodies with the Director as Managing Director. An annual contribution of Rs. 150 lakh for five years out of devolution; 75 per cent of funds be earmarked for Boards to be given as Development Grant and 25 per cent for lending to Councils and Corporations.
- To formulate an urban development policy to mitigate the problems of urban poor and strengthen urban infrastructure.
- To look into human resource problems.
- A Service Selection Board for municipal employees.
- Promotional role by the State.
- Decentralisation of powers of ULBs.
- Adoption of a system for mid-term appraisal of financial position of ULBs.

TAMIL NADU

Shared Taxes

- Tax on Luxuries—25 per cent of Tax on luxuries in hotels, and lodges be given to ULBs.
- Betting Tax—25 per cent of revenue be given to Chennai Corporation.
- State Excise Revenue—25 per cent of collection be given to divisible pool.
- Motor Vehicle Tax—40 per cent of revenue should be given to divisible pool.
- Agricultural Income Tax—25 per cent be shared to the areas covered by plantations.
- Sugarcane Cess—Amount allocated for roads be given to ULBs for constructing approach roads.
- Urban Land Tax—50 per cent of revenue to ULBs.

Assigned Taxes

- Tax on Animals—Licensing of animals like dogs, pigs etc. may be introduced.
- Tax on Timber—May be extended to other corporations.
- Company Tax—May be extended to other corporations.
- Vacant Land Tax—Tax burden be on seller; one time levy for ten years; may be applied.
- Pilgrims Tax—May be levied in places of resorts, temple towns etc.
- Surcharge on Transfer of Property—Rationalisation of rates; re-registration be made compulsory.
- Entertainment Tax—90 per cent of total realisation.
- Surcharge on Sales Tax—15 per cent of compounded sales tax be given to divisible pool.
- Advertisement Tax—All the hoardings be under the control of ULBs and revenue earned should go to them.
- Cable TV Tax—Rs. 60 per cent connection be collected annually by the Government and passed on to ULBs.

Reforms in Existing

(a) Taxes

- Property Tax—To switch over from present annual rental value system to area linked unit value system; general revision after three years; valuation linked with inflation; division as general purpose tax and service tax as 50 : 50; half of the service tax set apart towards water supply and sewerage/drainage; preparation of directory of property tax; no total exemption; exemption only on general purpose tax; passbook to rate payers; rebate for prompt payment and penalty for delay; creation of a tariff and valuation cell for valuation of properties; incentive to collection machinery for better recovery.
- Profession Tax—Increase of tax network by making registration compulsory.
- Vehicle Tax—Tax on motorised vehicles only.
- Tax on Carriages—To be abolished.
- Tax on Timber—May be extended to other corporations.

(b) Non-Taxes

- Surcharge on Bus Tickets—A surcharge on floating population be levied.
- Cess on Passengers—A cess on passengers travelling by bus be charged.
- Tax on Agricultural Land—ULBs be made empowered to levy tax.
- Local Cess—A cess on the pattern of PRIs be levied by ULBs as well.
- User Charges—User charges for water supply may be doubled, user charges on other services with an aim of full cost recovery.
- Licence Fee on Trades—Widening of network by including more trades; upward revision of rates.
- Income from Properties—ULBs should resort to commercial line on allotment of properties.
- Development Charges—To be levied on new townships for providing services, additional services to those who are willing to pay.

Grants-in-Aid

- Specific Purpose Grant—Should be covered by devolutions.
- Incentive and United Grants—Are necessary to ensure additional resource generation.

Fiscal Transfers

- Devolution of Fund is in phased manner, i.e. 8 per cent in 1997-98, 9 per cent in 1998-99, 10 per cent in 1999-2000, 11 per cent in 2000-2001 and 12 per cent in 2001-2002.
- In case general sharing is not accepted, two pools may be set up. Pool A contains taxes rightly belonging to local bodies but collected by Government. Pool B forms the nucleus for general devolution from net tax revenue of State.
- 15 per cent from Pool B is set apart as Reserve to meet post-devolution condition in the form of Equalisation and Incentive Fund.
- 85 per cent is distributed on 60 : 40 basis between rural and urban local bodies.

- Amount earmarked for ULBs be distributed as 38 per cent to Town Panchayats and 31 per cent reach to Municipalities and Corporations on the basis of population, SC/ST population, financial indicator, service sector etc.
- Payment be made in three instalments.

Miscellaneous

- Capital Fund—A Capital fund be created by transferring 15 per cent of total annual revenue in case of corporations, special grade and selection grade Municipalities and 10 per cent in case of other municipalities and town panchayats. ULBs can meet their future capital expenditure for taking remunerative and entrepreneurial investments.
- Special Tax Tribunal—Be set up to avoid delay in disposal and to ensure uniformity in divisions. All tax matters be dealt with by the Tribunal instead of civil courts. Initially District courts may function as tribunal.
- Corpus Fund—Be created by TFC award along with investment by surplus ULBs. State Government will give matching grant.
- Privatisation could be attempted in primary collection and depositions at bins, waste disposal, street light maintenance, maintenance of pumping station etc.

UTTAR PRADESH

Reforms in Existing

(a) Taxes

- Property Tax—Adoption of carpet area as the basis for assessing ARV. Following criteria for determining ARV: Location of property, use of property, Type of construction, Deductions from ARV on the age of building: 25 years—10 per cent, 25 to 40 years—20 per cent, above 40 years—30 per cent. Rebate of 40 per cent of ARV on owner occupied buildings/inclusive of deduction on age. For the purpose of calculation of ARV: Room—full internal dimension, covered verandah—full internal dimension, balcony or corridor—50 per cent of internal dimension, garage—25 per cent of internal dimension, bathroom, latrine, kitchen, portico, stairs not included. Rates recommended Property Tax @ 2.5% of ARV, water tax 2% of ARV and Latrine or Sewerage tax 2% of ARV. Service charges for Central/State Government buildings may be worked out *mutatis mutandis* and adopted in accordance with earlier provision. Tax collection on self-assessment forms. Tax collection on annual basis. 10 per cent incentive for payment within one month of the demand notice.

- Penalty of 2 per cent from due date or late payment. Exemption to be minimal. Service related tax to be collected and exemption to property (general) tax only. Exemption should not be granted on recommendation of State Government unless properly compensated.
- Carpet area rates to be determined by the State Government. Property Tax to be imposed on that portion of building and land attached to the place of public worship which have been given on rent and are being used for purposes other than public purposes.
- Such portions also be subject to water tax, latrine tax and sewerage tax. With switching over to the carpet area system the exemption of property with ARV upto Rs. 360 be dispensed with and all properties be brought under tax network. Revision of assessment after five years be continued. Wider powers be given for ensuring speedy recovery.
- The surplus octroi employees be deployed in updating the work of enumeration of houses. Number plate be allotted to each house. Data thus collected be computerised.
- Property Tax, Water Tax and Latrine Tax are to be collected by ULBs concerned and so long a decision to put Jal Sansthans and Development Authorities under one umbrella is not taken by the State Government, the receipts of Water Tax and Latrine/Sewerage Tax are to be passed on to the Jal Sansthans or executive body of the water supply and sewerage scheme.
- Water Tax—ULBs which do not produce and distribute potable water but use water supplied by Jal Sansthan for parks etc. should pay for water. A mutually agreed percentage may be adopted. If no agreement is arrived at, a

token 5% of water after transmission and distribution losses may be reckoned towards the consumption by ULBs for their own use. If local bodies fails to pay, the same should be recovered by State Government out of devolutions to local bodies. There is a need to enlighten the assessment machinery to ensure that illegal tapping of water is brought to book and necessary charges recovered therefor. Water Supply be maintained on commercial line. Water charges/rates be revised.

- Entire domestic water supply be unmetered and minimum flat rate be adopted and raised gradually over the years to accrue a sustained level of revenue. Non-domestic consumers be metered.
- It should be prudent to adopt certain performance indicators for ULBs which should be linked to release of Government funds to them as part of devolution and the local bodies which fails to do so should be suitably penalised.
- Rates of different taxes which have not been revised since long be revised immediately.

(b) Non-Taxes

- ULBs should raise the rates of the fee in case of those items in which fees were being levied earlier and certain new items of services.
- Rates of non-tax revenue be revised without further delay.

Grants-in-Aid

- In order to liquidate arrears of electricity dues till 31-3-1996 to enable ULBs to start with clean slate the State Government out of their outstanding wage and means advance against UPSEB convert the amount of dues to ULBs into grant to UPSEB.
- Loans given to different local bodies for water supply schemes and outstanding as on 31-3-1994 may be converted into grant.
- Loans given for integrated urban development schemes and outstanding as on 31-3-1994 with interest may be converted into outright grant.
- Loans given under Special and General Component Plan for

Scheduled Castes and Scheduled Tribes as on 31-3-1994 with interest thereon be converted into grant.

- Loans advanced for integrated development of small and medium towns and outstanding as on 31-3-1994 with interest may be converted into grant.
- Loans given for beautification which will not yield additional income but is in the nature of unproductive capital expenditure, be converted into grant.
- Tenth Finance Commission—The formula of devolution of non-plan funds to be applied.

Fiscal Transfers

- Seven per cent of net proceeds of State's total tax revenues may be earmarked for devolution of funds.
- Interest distribution be as under:
  Nagar Nigams—3.12%
  Nagar Palika Parishad—3.12%
  Nagar Panchayat—0.76%
- The share be passed directly to ULBs.
- Initially 90 per cent of amount of devolution be released and the remaining 10 per cent be given on following basis:
  (i) ULB levies and collects all taxes and non-tax items of obligatory nature.
  (ii) Recovery of their tax and non-tax revenue of current demand is at least 70% in 1997-98 and be stepped up by 5% each year.
- Criteria of 80% population and 20% area be adopted to determine their share.
- If and when decision is taken by the State Government to pass on functions enumerated in Schedule XII, the State Government will have to pass on accordingly necessary funds for the purpose also.

Miscellaneous

- A comprehensive enactment providing a uniform set of legal framework for all types of ULBs.
- To bring improvement in essential civic services, private participation be encouraged in ULBs.
- Necessary rules for recruitment of non-centralised staff and

their transfer within division on the recommendation of EO be made.

- Barring centralised services the EOs and MNAs be declared appointing authorities in respect of subordinate staff. They be given powers to inflict punishment including dismissal. The powers to hear and decide appeal against the punishment should vest in the Mayor/Chairperson.
- The employees of municipality should not be treated as Government employee and payment of their salary be ensured through augmenting the financial base including increased devolution and ensuring higher level of recovery of their demand.
- The Development Authorities and Jal Sansthans be brought under the umbrella of elected ULBs.
- The power to sanction building plans in the area should vest in the local bodies.
- Constitution of a committee of experts to go into the question of reorganising the administrative structure of the ULBs.
- Strengthening of the existing Finance Commission Cell in the State Finance Department for updating data and facilitating future SFCs. Cell be put incharge of preparing annual review of finances of ULBs and PRVs and their review report be placed before Legislature.
- A Corporation be set up which can be used for leveraging funds and subsidising the interest rate on non-remunerative but desirable schemes to strengthen civic infrastructure. Such a Corporation be set up with an authorised capital of Rs. 25 crore. 4/5 of which be subscribed by the State Government and the remaining by ULBs.
- A common detailed format for budget estimates is prescribed.
- Responsibility of audit of the accounts of Nagar Nigams and Nagar Palika Parishads be given to the Accountant General. The audit reports of AG be placed before State Legislature through Public Accounts Committee.
- Accounts of Nagar Panchayats be continued to be audited by Director, Local Fund. The audit report be sent to the Finance Department with a copy of Secretary, Urban Development.
- Municipal Accounts Code be suitably modified.
- Procedure for creation of posts and recruitment of personnel

should be followed strictly.

- The work of sanitation staff should be monitored closely and regularly. Dependence on the sanitation staff could also be reduced by encouraging private agencies to take up on contract basis work for sanitation and disposal of garbage.
- Some definite norms for sanction and recruitment of staff should be made.
- Budgets be prepared wardwise and operated upon by adopting a uniform pattern.
- There should be a uniform norm for the number of lamps/rods per km. of road length or per thousand population.

WEST BENGAL

Shared Taxes

- Entitlements will be financed by sharing of taxes.

Assigned Taxes

- Taxes on Entertainments now collected by the State should be handed over to ULBs.
- Urban Land Tax and Multistoried Building Tax should be handed over to Calcutta Municipal Corporation.
- Resources generated in Regulated Markets should be brought within the purview of DPCs and the net proceeds ploughed back in the market hinterlands.

Reforms in Existing

(a) Taxes

- Property Tax—Periodical assessment by the Central Valuation Board should be made mandatory and the Board be strengthened adequately.
- Water Tax—Municipalities be empowered to impose Water Tax on large users and commercial and industrial undertakings.

(b) Non-Taxes

- Municipalities should be empowered to issue trade licences with fee at a much higher level, to impose tolls at higher rates for heavy vehicles on municipal roads, to levy imposts on tourists/pilgrims; to introduce special conservancy charges for commercial and industrial establishments.

Grants-in-Aid

- 53 per cent of plan fund in 1995-96 was allotted. A substantial part of this should be entitlements in the form of united funds and the rest will continue to be grants.
- In place of Entry Tax, a surcharge on Sales Tax has been introduced. The State Government should distribute fund as grants.
- State grants on part of collection of Profession Tax and Motor Vehicles Tax may be discontinued.
- DA subvention should cover the whole of the DA liability in respect of approved staff. Expenses on various other benefits should be met by grants.
- State and Central releases in respect of centrally sponsored schemes would continue to be grants.

Fiscal Transfers

- Entitlements will be financed by sharing of taxes. 16 per cent of the net proceeds of all taxes collected by the State in a year be transferred to local bodies.
- Such funds may be released to districts in suitable instalments, quarterly or monthly.
- Distribution between municipalities is based on population, level of non-literacy, proportion of SC/ST population and population density.

Miscellaneous

- Municipal Boards may try to involve the people to improve urban facilities.
- Incentive Funds—Incentive Schemes have been suggested to encourage Municipalities to increase their own incomes. Two

per cent of entitlement due to a district set aside to operate on Incentive Funds.

- Inhabited areas which are the municipal jurisdiction will be allotted funds in proportion to their population and the earmarked funds will be operated in consultation with DPC.
- Works under the State Plan sector and District Plan sector should be clearly listed by the State Government.
- DPCs be involved in supervising maintenance works.
- There should be some effective penal provisions for local bodies not falling in time with financial discipline. Penal measures are also to be introduced for the municipalities which divert development grant to meet revenue expenditure.

APPENDIX VI

TAX SOURCES OF MUNICIPALITIES

Taxes / States	Andhra Pradesh	Assam	Bihar	Haryana	Karnataka	Kerala	Madhya Pradesh	Maharashtra	Manipur	Meghalaya	Orissa	Punjab	Rajasthan	Sikkim	Tamil Nadu	Tripura	Uttar Pradesh	West Bengal
1	2	3	4	5	6	7	8	9	10	11	12	13	14	15	16	17	18	19
House Tax/General Tax	√	√	√	√	√	√	√	√	√	√	√	√	√	√	√	√	√	√
Water Tax	√	√	√		√	√	√	√	√	√	√	√	√	√	√	√	√	√
Sewerage Tax	√	√	√		√	√	√	√	√	√	√	√	√		√	√	√	√
Drainage Tax	√	√				√			√	√	√	√					√	√
Education Tax															√			
Spl. Edu. Tax								√										
Advertisement Tax	√		√		√	√	√	√	√			√		√	√	√	√	√
Development/ Betterment Tax							√					√					√	
Tax on Professions, callings, circumstances			√	√		√					√	√	√	√			√	

(Contd.)

APPENDIX VI (contd.)

1	2	3	4	5	6	7	8	9	10	11	12	13	14	15	16	17	18	19
Fire Tax							√	√				√						
Tax on Vehicles/animals	√		√	√	√	√		√	√		√		√	√		√	√	√
Octroi	√			√				√	√		√		√	√				
Toll Tax											√							
Theatre Tax	√			√			√	√						√			√	
Water Benefit Tax								√										
Local Body Tax							√	√										
Sewerage Benefit Tax								√										
Street Tax								√										
Lighting Tax		√	√			√	√	√	√	√	√		√	√		√		
Environment Tax								√										
Scavenging Tax									√				√			√		
Tax on Transfer of Property	√					√			√					√			√	
Pilgrim Tax							√							√				
Passenger Tax														√				

APPENDIX VII

NON-TAX REVENUE SOURCES

Sources / States	Fee on Carts/Animals	Fee on Dogs	Fee on Boats	Betterment Fee	Fee on Fire Brigade	Fee for Social Services	Toll on Bridges	Toll on Animals/Goods	Fee on Platforms	Duty on Stamp	Water Cess	Fee on Pilgrims	Drainage Fee	Lighting Fee	Scavenging Fee	Cleaning fee for Latrines	Fee on Permits	Fee on building plan	Parking Fee	Entry Fee on Vehicles/ Goods	Market Fee	Fee for use of Street	Fee on animal sold.
1	2	3	4	5	6	7	8	9	10	11	12	13	14	15	16	17	18	19	20	21	22	23	24
Andhra Pradesh	√		√	√																			
Assam	√	√	√	√	√	√	√																
Bihar	√	√	√					√	√														
Haryana						√				√		√	√	√	√	√							
Karnataka										√	√												
Kerala	√							√		√													
Madhya Pradesh							√	√							√						√		√
Manipur				√																	√		
Meghalaya	√	√	√	√	√	√	√																

(Contd.

APPENDIX VII (contd.)

1	2	3	4	5	6	7	8	9	10	11	12	13	14	15	16	17	18	19	20	21	22	23	24
Maharashtra								√											√	√		√	
Orissa		√	√			√																	
Punjab																							
Rajasthan																							
Sikkim				√						√										√	√		
Tamil Nadu										√													
Tripura			√			√											√	√	√	√			
Uttar Pradesh	√	√	√				√			√	√								√		√		
West Bengal	√						√			√													

FUNCTIONS ASSIGNED TO THE MUNICIPALITIES

	Functions as per Schedule XII																		Additional Functions									
	1	2	3	4	5	6	7	8	9	10	11	12	13	14	15	16	17	18	19	20	21	22	23	24	25	26	27	28
Andhra Pradesh				M	D	M	M		D			M		M	M	M		M	M	M	M	M	M	M	M	M	M	M
Assam	D	D	D	M	M	D	M			D	D			M	M	M	M		M			D	D	M	M	M		D
Bihar	M	M	M	M	M	M	M	M	M	M	M	M	M	M	M	M	M	M	D	D			D	D	D	D		D
Haryana	D	D	D	M	M	M	D	D	D	D	D	M	D	D	D	M	M						M	M				M
Karnataka		M		M	M	M	M	D		D	D	D	D	M	M	M	M	M		M	M			M	M	M		M
Kerala	M	M	M	M	M	M	M	M	M	M	M	M	M	M	M	M	M	M										M
Madhya Pradesh	D	D	D	D		M	M	D	D		D	M		M		M	M	M	M	M	M	M	M	M	D			D
Maharashtra			M		M	M	M	M	M	D		D		M	D	M	M	M	M	M	M		M	M	M	M		M
Manipur				M	M	M	M					D		M	M	M	M	M	M	M	M		D		M	S		S
Meghalaya				D	D	D								D			D	M				D	D	D		D		D
Orissa	M		M	D	M	M	D	M	M	M	M		M	D	D	M	M	D				D	D	D		D		D
Punjab					M	M	M					M		M	D	M	M	M	M	M		M	M	M	M	M	D	
Rajasthan				M			M					D		M	M	M	M	M	M		M			M		S		S
Sikkim	M	M	M	M	M	M	M	M	M	M	M	M	M	M	M	M	M	M										
Tamil Nadu	D	D	D	M	M	M	D	D	D	D	D	M	D	M	D	M	M	D	M					M				
Tripura	M	M	M	M	M	M	M	M	M	M	M	M	M	M	M	M	M	M										
Uttar Pradesh	M	M		M	M	M	M	M	M	M	M	M	M	M	M	M	M	M	M	M	M		M	M	M	M	M	D
West Bengal	M	M			M	M						M	M	D	M	M	M	M				M	M	M		M	M	M

(*Contd.*

APPENDIX VIII (contd.)

	Functions as Per Schedule XII																		Additional Functions									
	29	30	31	32	33	34	35	36	37	38	39	40	41	42	43	44	45	46	47	48	49	50	51	52	53	54	55	56
Andhra Pradesh	M	D	D	D	D	D	D	D	D	D	D		D															
Assam	D	M			D	D	D	M		D		D							D		D							D
Bihar	D	D			D	D	D			D	D		D	D					D							M		
Haryana	M					M	M																			D		
Karnataka	M	D		D	D	D	D		D	D	M	M	M	M					D		D			D				
Kerala					M										M			M	M	M	M	M	M					
Madhya Pradesh	D	D		D	D	D	D	M	D	D	M	D		M		M			M								D	
Maharashtra	D	D		M	D	D	D	D	D	D	M	M	D	M					D		D							
Manipur	D	D	D	D	D		D							M														
Meghalaya	D				D	D	D			D			D						D									
Orissa	D	D			D	D	D			D			D	D		D		D									M	
Punjab	D	D	D	D	D	D	D			D				M	D				D	D	D						M	
Rajasthan	D	D		M	D	D	D	D		D	D	M	M													M	D	
Sikkim																												
Tamil Nadu							M					M	M	M	M	M	M											
Tripura																												
Uttar Pradesh	M	M	M	D	D	M	D	D	D	D	M	D	D	M	M	M	M		M				D		D		D	
West Bengal	D	D	M	D		M	D			D	D			M											M			

FUNCTIONAL CODE

1. Urban Planning including Town Planning.
2. Regulation of landuse and construction of buildings.
3. Planning for economic and social development.
4. Roads and bridges.
5. Water supply for domestic, industrial and commercial purposes.
6. Public health, sanitation, conservancy and solid waste management.
7. Fire services.
8. Urban forestry, protection of the environment and promotion of ecological aspects.
9. Safeguarding the interest of weaker sections of society including the handicapped and mentally retarded.
10. Slum improvement and upgradation.
11. Urban poverty alleviation.
12. Provision of urban amenities and facilities such as parks, gardens, playgrounds.
13. Promotion of cultural, educational and aesthetic aspects.
14. Burial and burial grounds, crematories, cremation grounds, and electric crematoriums.
15. Cattle pounds, prevention of cruelty to animals.
16. Vital statistics including registration of births and deaths.
17. Public amenities including street lighting, parking lots, bus stops and public conveniences.
18. Regulation of slaughter houses and tanneries.
19. Naming of streets/ roads.
20. Numbering of houses.
21. Boundary walls.
22. Maintenance of public monuments and open spaces.
23. Construction or acquisition and maintenance of public markets.
24. Public vaccination.
25. Reclamation of unhealthy localities.
26. Prevention of spread of infectious diseases.
27. Improvement of city.
28. Providing relief works.
29. Maintenance of asylums, hospitals and house for lunatics.
30. Maternity and infant welfare houses.
31. Analysis of water, food and drugs.
32. Swimming pools, wash houses etc.

33. Milk dairies, farms.
34. Planting trees.
35. Public resorts, exhibition, gardens, rest houses, entertainment etc.
36. Ambulance service.
37. Public transport.
38. Libraries, museums, etc.
39. Maintaining schools for primary education.
40. Public ponds and fountains.
41. Destruction of stray dogs/mosquito control, public nuisance.
42. Regulation of dangerous trades.
43. Licensing of eating establishments, small scale industries.
44. Disposal of unclaimed corpses or carcasses.
45. Regulation of hoardings and advertisements.
46. Improvement of model agricultural farms, animal husbandry, minor irrigation, fisheries etc.
47. Veterinary hospitals.
48. Housing.
49. Electricity, non-conventional energy, etc.
50. Public distribution system.
51. Employment.
52. Cooperation.
53. Maintaining vigilance/Police Organisation.
54. Planning for social justice.
55. Control of begging.
56. Maintenance of band, orchestra.

EPILOGUE

India is a "Cooperative Federation" with three-layer governments — the Union Government, the State governments, and Local governments. But the local governments are directly under the State governments, no separate allocation of taxation rights has been provided to them. The Constitution envisages separate tax jurisdictions for the Union and the State governments, though proceeds of certain Union taxes are sharable either wholly or in part with States. The basis of division of taxing powers between the Union and the State governments is "quite unambiguous". There is no tax which can be levied by both the Union and State governments. In other words, the most significant development in the financial relationship between the Union and the States is the high degree of centralisation of resources and greater reliance of States on the Centre for financial assistance as a result of growing inflexibility in the scheme of devolution.

The centralisation of resources is the product of four major considerations. Firstly, the division of tax resources and functions made at the transfer of power mainly on the provisions of Government of India Act, 1935 could not visualise the implications of planned development for sources of revenue under the successive Five Year Plans. Secondly, it was implicit that great stress was being placed for establishing tax structure on the basis of the need to develop a strong Federal Government. Thirdly, the requirement of economic development was regarded as more significant than fiscal autonomy of State. Fourthly, no comprehensive study of the tax structure of each State, tax compliance and the expenditure programme was made to take note of the widening gap between resources and functions of the State brought about mainly by the planning process and consider what adjustments should be made in Union-State financial relations which would add strength both to the Union and the States. In this context, probably the Constitution prescribes for devolution of financial powers to the States.

PRINCIPLES OF FEDERAL FINANCE

Prof. B.P. Adarkar lays down three principles governing the working of federal finance. These are :

(a) *Independence and Responsibility* — According to Prof. Adarkar, full freedom of financial operations must be extended to all units of federation in order that they may not suffer from a feeling of cramp in the discharge of their normal activities and in the achievement of their legitimate aspirations for the promotion of social and economic advancement. It means that each unit must have its own independent financial resources to carry out its exclusive functions. Each should be independent within its own sphere.

(b) *Adequacy and Elasticity* — The resources should be adequate so that each layer of government can discharge its obligations laid upon it. It stands for sufficiency of resources for the discharge of functions and duties assigned. Besides adequacy, there should be elasticity in the financial resources. Resources should be capable of expansion in response to rapidly growing needs and responsibilities.

(c) *Administrative Economy and Efficiency* — The sources of revenue should be fully exploited. The administrative cost should be minimum and there should not be any evasion.

Thus, the Constitution and the principles of federal finance put greater emphasis on equity in transfers of funds and financial powers from the Union to the States. An important direction of inquiry in the Union-State financial relations is whether the transfers from the Union to States have satisfied the basic principles of equity. The Directive Principles of State Policy enshrined in the Constitution require that the State should strive to minimise inequalities amongst groups of people residing in different areas. In the country, both inter-State and intra-State disparities are glaring and persistent in the backdrop of overall underdevelopment. Lack of adequate financial resources has been recognised to be the basic constraint in the development of the backward areas. Provision for necessary administrative services, social and industrial and infrastructural facilities is crucial for mitigating regional disparities.

Thus, in our peculiar system of multi layer government, mobilisation, sharing and utilisation of financial resources play a very crucial role. It can give rise to difficult problems of inter-governmental relations unless handled in a spirit of mutual accommodation and understanding. The main problem of Centre-State-Local finance is to deal with the overall revenue expenditure imbalances, which is the resultant of any given distribution of functions and resources among the respective units. The upper layer government is bestowed with correspondingly more resources. The lower layers invariably experience revenue gap in their budget. This gives rise to vertical fiscal imbalance. The gap between the revenue and expenditure of the lower layer is required to be filled by the respective upper layer government under certain obligatory and discretionary conditions by transferring portion of the resources raised by it respectively.

URBAN FUNCTIONS AND FINANCES

The long history of evolution of public finance in India shows very complex factors at work. However, one clear discernible trend is that while it is wholly possible to divide the taxation powers and allocate resources, it is extremely difficult to establish a balance between needs and resources.

Urban governments in developing and industrial countries

alike complain about the lack of resources to provide sufficient services to their populations. Any observer of city life can quickly see that urban public resources are usefully deficient. The gap between the perceived need for services and the financial resources to provide them can be attributed in many cases to demand for unrealistically high standards of service which are beyond the financing capacity of an urban economy. Efforts by urban governments to provide services at levels which are not affordable commonly result in an inefficient and inequitable allocation of public resources.

The fiscal gap also may have its origin in the misallocation of functions and revenues to urban governments by high level authorities. Urban population has grown rapidly in recent years and is likely to continue to do so. This growth has led to concomitant increase in the demand for a minimum level of public services for each new urban dweller. Rising incomes in urban areas have also increased the demand for public services, yet the revenues of local authorities most directly affected have not usually increased commensurately. The primary reason for this situation is that urban governments are often restricted in their revenue raising authority to income inelastic sources such as property taxes, fees and fines and transfers from higher level governments. In such cases, the fiscal gap is the result of mismatch between urban government's responsibilities to provide services, on the one hand and their authority to raise revenue, on the other.

There is often a mismatch between urban government's responsibilities for public service provision and their revenue raising authority. The gap is filled with some form of governmental transfers, a grant, a shared tax or a subsidy. Certainly, there is justification for inter-governmental transfers as part of the urban local financing structure. Transfers from higher level governments are an appropriate way to finance these local government functions which have regional or national spill-over benefits. A realistic view is that transfers are untimely to resolve fully the local problems of local authorities.

A comparison of the conformity legislations of the States

reveals that there exists wide variations in the perceptions of the State governments regarding the assignment of non-traditional municipal functions given in the Twelfth Schedule. The assignment of functions requires that they are matched by adequate sources of finance. Bahl and Linn identifying revenue sources appropriate to financing municipal expenditure opine that where the benefits of services are measurable and accrue to readily identify individuals, user charges are the appropriate source. Taxes on local residents can be levied for providing local services whose benefits and costs to individuals and identification of beneficiaries are difficult. The costs of services with spillover jurisdiction should be financed by substantial inter-governmental transfers. Borrowing is an appropriate source for financing capital costs on utilities and roads.

While transferring functions, the State Government should transfer appropriate and adequate revenue sources as well. Both the transfers be simultaneous. The mismatch between the functional responsibilities and financial authority may lead to a situation wherein urban local bodies may not be able to cope with the provision of the services.

With the aim of financially strengthening and functionally fattening, the Constitution prescribes for constituting State Finance Commission every five year and annexing a separate schedule of functions for the grassroot urban institutions.

FINANCE COMMISSION

The Constitution envisages the setting up of Finance Commissions at two levels — Union and State. There is, however, an ambiguity in constituting the State Finance Commission. While Article 280 specifies the number of members of the Central Finance Commission, Articles 243-I and 243-Y do not throw light on it, leaving the matter to the State Government. This has resulted in variation in composition of State Finance Commissions. The number of members of the State Finance Commission varies from one to five. The pattern of composition also differs from State to State.

It is observed that the first State Finance Commissions were generally dominated by bureaucrats. Except Kerala, Tamil Nadu and Rajasthan, all other State Finance Commissions had at least one academician. Madhya Pradesh consisted academicians and bureaucrats, two each. In Rajasthan, it was a show of politicians. Orissa was the only State where the Commission was headed by an academician.

Assam, Madhya Pradesh, Manipur and Orissa were the States which enacted separate Act for the respective Finance Commission. In other States the enabling provisions were incorporated in the Municipal Acts itself.

Terms of Reference

Although Articles 243-I and 243-Y prescribe the terms of reference for State Finance Commissions, Andhra Pradesh, Karnataka, Madhya Pradesh, Tamil Nadu, Uttar Pradesh and Orissa were the States which framed additional terms of reference, while others directly mentioned them. In Andhra Pradesh, it was clearly mentioned that the Commission should indicate the norms on the basis of which specified amounts are recommended for the upkeep and maintenance of capital assets. In Tamil Nadu, the terms of reference specified that the financial position of the urban local bodies must be reviewed with reference to their revenue receipts and expenditure, tax efforts and level and adequacy of existing devolution. The Commission was also to suggest changes in the classification of urban local bodies on the basis of financial position. There was a specific mention of the optimum utilisation of the available resources and detailed analysis of the repayment of loans and advances extended by the Government from time to time. In Madhya Pradesh the Commission was asked specifically to review the resources of the State and demand thereon, maintenance expenditure on plan projects and norms therefor besides suggesting transfer of responsibilities and services by the State to local bodies and also the corresponding transfer of employees engaged in those activities. The Commission in Uttar Pradesh was given the responsibility of considering revenue resources of the State and demands thereon besides ensuring the liabilities of local bodies, maintenance of capital assets, assessment of debt position and arrangement of funds for plan and non-plan expenditure. In Orissa, the Commission was asked to review the functions and liabilities of local bodies and also the revenue resources of the State Government and set the target for additional resources mobilisation and potential therefor.

Time Horizon

Except in Assam and Orissa, the State Finance Commissions in other States were constituted in 1994. In Assam and Orissa, the year of setting up was 1995 and 1996 respectively. In Orissa and Manipur, the Commissions were reconstituted. As is evident, the Commissions took 8 to 35 months in submitting their reports. The reports in Assam, Karnataka, Madhya Pradesh, Manipur, Tamil Nadu and Uttar Pradesh were submitted in 1996, while the Commissions in Punjab, Rajasthan and West Bengal finished their jobs in 1995. In Andhra Pradesh, it was 1998.

Kerala and Uttar Pradesh were the States where Commission submitted preliminary (interim) report in 1995. The Finance Commissions of Madhya Pradesh and Tripura submitted reports pertaining to the Panchayat Raj Institutions separately.

In a few States, the reports were submitted just couple of months prior to commencement of the period for which the recommendations were made. In Andhra Pradesh, Madhya Pradesh, Orissa and Uttar Pradesh the reports were submitted even after the commencement of the recommendation period. Thus, most of the State governments were left with a little time to study and scrutinise the pros and cons of the recommendations. The haste in implementation was the only option.

Further, the State Finance Commission adopted different time frames for projections and estimating the financial requirements of the local bodies. Surprisingly, the Orissa State Finance Commission was given a time frame of four years commencing from 1998-99 and the Commission in Andhra Pradesh covered only three-year period from 1997-98 to 1999-2000. In Uttar Pradesh, the Commission recommended the period as 1996-97 to 2000-2001 but the State Government deferred it by one year and adopted for the period from 1997-98 to 2001-2002.

Coordination with Planning Commission

"Need for great coordination between the Finance Commission and the Planning Commission has been emphasised by many experts. The Administrative Reforms Commission had recommended that in order to ensure greater coordination between the two bodies, one member of Planning Commission should also be nominated as Member of Finance Commission. A precondition for smooth coordination between the two bodies, is the synchronisation of Five Year Plans with the period of Finance Commission". These observations of the Commission on Centre-State relations pave the way for discussion on the relationship of these two bodies. The Finance Commission is constituted to distribute the revenue income of the Union Government between Union and States, the Planning Commission, a non-statutory body, allocates the plan funds. The Tenth Finance Commission remarks that "while there is intense jostling amongst States for more and more new projects, the zeal is not matched by corresponding attention to the upkeep of the assets created at great expenses...... though successive Finance Commissions have provided for this purpose and the actual expenditure has exceeded the provisions, most of it has got diverted to payment of salaries and wages rather than to material and equipment necessary for maintenance work."

In this light, it is necessary to establish a relationship between the State Planning Board and the State Finance Commission. It becomes more relevant when it is observed that "the States have no elastic sources of revenue excepting the general sales tax. Even in respect of the general sales tax, certain inhibitive factors arise from additional excise duties in lieu of sales tax. It is found that indirect taxes also dominate the State governments' tax structure and it has been very important source of revenue of these governments during the planning period."

Taking into account the plan and non-plan requirements of

the State governments and their budgetary and revenue deficits, it is necessary that the State has to tighten its belt and spare some additional sum of its net tax proceeds for the local bodies. It may be that with the combined efforts of these institutions and the State government, the resource gap that comes in the way of meeting the service needs of people in the urban and rural areas could be gradually narrowed and substantial improvement in delivery of services could be brought about.

The foregone discussion necessitates that the Central Finance Commission, State Finance Commissions, Planning Commission and the State Planning Boards act in collaboration and active association of one another. The functioning of any of these in isolation may hamper the spirit of the Constitution.

Congruity with Central Finance Commission

The Constitution (Seventy-fourth Amendment) Act, 1992, established a linkage between the Central Finance Commission and State Finance Commission by amending Article 280. It provides that the Central Finance Commission shall also make recommendations as to "the measures needed to augment the Consolidated Fund of the State on the basis of the recommendations made by the Finance Commission of the State". Such a linkage paves the way of the State Finance Commission to appreciate the financial needs of the municipalities and develop adequate financial resources to them. The extent of fiscal transfer from the Centre to State will thus be linked with the corresponding transfer from the State to local government units. This indirectly enthuses the States to financially strengthen the municipalities and devolve sufficient fiscal resources to make themselves (States) entitled for the corresponding funds from the Centre.

The Tenth Finance Commission has also elaborated the importance of congruity between the Central and State Finance Commissions as under :

> "Because of the 73rd and 74th Amendments to the Constitution, Finance Commissions will be required in

future to suggest measures in the light of the recommendations of the State Finance Commissions. We believe it is important that the Panchayati Raj Institutions are firmly established and strengthened. Equally it is necessary to guard against generation of dependency for resource at each sub-national level. The three-tier structure with two layers of Finance Commissions, may generate expectations that in the end it will be the responsibility of the Centre to channel resources through the State governments to the Panchayats and urban local bodies. The fiscal system can scarcely meet such expectations. Panchayats and urban local bodies need to have well defined sources of income and taxing powers on a matching basis. Decentralisation of the development process is a desirable objective. But it can prove effective only if local resources are mobilised for local development thus ensuring minimum leakage and cost effective deployment."

Despite these observations by the TFC, there is hardly any congruity between the State Finance Commissions and the Eleventh Finance Commission, which was constituted on 3rd July, 1998. The period of the Eleventh Finance Commission commences from 1st April 2000, while the corresponding date in case of most States falls one year later to that. The State governments should come forward and constitute Finance Commissions in congruity to the next Central Finance Commission and direct them to submit recommendations earlier than the Central Finance Commission submits its report. For better appreciation of the problem, the Central Finance Commission should consider the recommendations of the State Finance Commissions while recommending transfer of resources to the States. The recommendations of the Central Commissions be made on the basis of indent of transfer affected by the State Finance Commission to the local government units. In absence of congruity, the Eleventh Finance Commission experienced difficulties and observed to re-amend the Art. 280 and remove the necessity of considering the recommendations of State

Finance Commissions while suggesting fiscal devolutions.

Review of State Finances

The Constitution delineates the need of strengthening the State finance to enable them to transfer adequate funds to local government units. The Tenth Finance Commission observed that under Article 280(3), "The Finance Commission has 'the duty' to make a recommendation to the President regarding the 'measures needed to augment the Consolidated Fund of a State', once the recommendations of State Finance Commission become available to it. On the basis of recommendations made by the State Finance Commissions, the Finance Commission would have to first ascertain the 'need' for augmentation of the consolidated fund of a State and then recommend 'measures', which may not necessarily involve any transfer of resources. It is obvious to us, however, that once the State Finance Commissions complete their task, it would be obligatory upon the Finance Commission to assess and built into the expenditure stream of the States, the funding requirement for supplementing the resources of Panchayats/municipalities. This would be necessary to determine the measures needed for augmentation of the State Consolidated fund."

In the circumstances, it is pertinent to discuss briefly the conceptual framework of State finances. It is felt that the Union Government has been raising bulk of the financial resources. Of the combined aggregate resources during the period 1951-85, Union Government raised 71.5 per cent and States 28.5 per cent sources. State taxes have shown widely different growth rates. Some like land revenue, have hardly grown. But the important taxes like Sales Tax, State Excise Duties and Entertainment Tax have shown considerable buoyancy. The growth rate in States' own tax revenue has been significant and indeed, somewhat high than that of the Union.

The Tenth Finance Commission has observed that "while tax revenues of the States have been generally more buoyant than estimated by successive Finance Commissions, non-tax revenues have consistently fallen behind. This has been a major reason for the yawning gaps between receipts and expenditure which have eroded the revenue resources of the States and crippled their efforts at providing reasonable services in many vital sectors like power, transport, irrigation and water supply. All these constitute vital elements of infrastructure and hold the key to development factor in the new economic regime."

The State Finance Commission in most of the States studied and reviewed the financial position of the respective State governments. The reviews bring out one common factor that is widening gap in revenues and expenditure on the revenue accounts. Another important factor is increase in non-plan expenditure mainly on account of salaries, pensions and loan payments. The Commissions had to keep all these factors while recommending additional devolutions to local bodies. The situation is, no doubt, grim but the needs of the local bodies also must be considered.

REFORMS IN EXISTING SOURCES

One of the salient features of local self-government is that a major portion of revenue of a local body is derived from the taxes it imposes on the people and properties of the locality. Thus local government is allowed to have a share through taxes over the properties of the people as its purpose is to serve the people intimately. The proceeds derived by the local government through a variety of taxes and other fees have to be spent on the services and amenities which go to make town life healthy and comfortable. But here lies the heaviest civic responsibility of the local authority to administer the civic affairs efficiently and satisfactorily and while doing so, it must prove itself competent to assess the properties correctly, to impose the necessary percentage of tax rate and to collect the tax revenue in time without causing any difficulty to the tax collector as well as to the rate payer and also to spend the proceeds properly on the welfare of the civic community. If local body fails to discharge its duties in respect of assessment and collection, it reflects very badly on the civic electorate.

Further, of all the factors that cut into the financial resources of urban local bodies, the laxities and disabilities or the processes and procedures for the imposition, assessment, collection and proper administration of taxes are by no means the least. Levy of high rate of tax on lands and buildings alone cannot bring the desired revenues, if the assessment of annual value of properties is outmoded or influenced by extraneous considerations. Poor organisation and inept administration may result in low collections and high costs. In a large number of local bodies in various States, the collection is often found to be below 50 per cent. The reasons for the failure of the urban local authorities to take full advantage of their powers of taxation can be traced both to the complex provision of laws and rules made thereunder as well as the machinery for assessment and collection of revenues existing in various local bodies. The various commissions and committees while recommending broadening of the tax base have emphasised the need of increasing efficiency in tax administration by adopting suitable personnel particularly at the higher executive levels.

Moreso, in some of the State municipal laws, the procedure for the imposition of a new tax or the enhancement of the rate of an existing tax is extremely complicated and dilatory. The cumbersome procedure often takes years before a tax is finally approved to be imposed or even the rate is increased.

In the backdrop, the State Finance Commissions have emphasised upon mobilising the existing sources of urban local bodies. This is congruent to the present status of local finance in the country.

Tax Revenue

Property tax is one of the earliest tax sources and the backbone of local finance in municipalities where octroi is not levied. As such, performance of obligatory and discretionary functions of these local bodies depend very much upon this lucrative source of revenue. Property tax is the most common and generally the most important tax collected by the urban governments. However, the property tax revenue have generally not kept pace with the growth of urban incomes or property values and often not even with the growth of urban population. Urban property tax systems vary widely among States, but the systems seem to suffer from a number of common problems : assessment practices are inadequate, professional expertise for evaluating urban properties is in short supply, the necessary data base to support assessment and enforcement is not in place, collection and enforcement problems abound, and tax payer resistance is a universal obstacle to more effective property tax administration.

Notwithstanding these practical obstacles, urban property tax is clearly among the few sources of local public revenue that can carry a significant share of the financing requirements for urban expenditure. Substantial efforts and ingenuity, however, are required to mobilise the technical and administrative resources to develop accurate urban property registration and property tax valuation rolls, to update them at regular intervals, and to bill and collect property taxes effectively.

Property tax administration concerns with the properties to be taxed, the manner in which they are to be taxed, the basis on which the assessment is to be made, the rate of tax to be fixed and the targeted amount of tax to be collected every year from the assessees. Further, almost as corollary, tax administration also includes tax collection, enforcement of penalties for delay and non-payment and the revision of assessment.

Generally, there are two methods adopted for evaluating the properties after they are identified. These are capital value system and rental value system. Broadly, properties used for industrial and commercial purposes are evaluated on their capital cost and the value of residential properties for tax purposes is determined on the basis of rental value. The latter system inherits discretion at various levels, hence prone to shortcomings, lapses and corruption. The State Finance Commissions have emphatically recommended the reformatory measures for removing these loopholes in the administration of this major tax. Most of the States have been advised to switch over from value derived on the basis of rent to the value determined on area basis. Further, the commissions all over the country have felt the importance and need of regular and timely revision. They have also suggested to review the exemptions granted to the properties.

The Karnataka Finance Commission has recommended the creation of a Central Valuation Authority for conducting periodic survey and valuing of properties, while the West Bengal Commission suggests the revamping of the existing Central Valuation Board. The Commissions have suggested to increase the rates and reduce the government interference in tax administration. They have exhorted the need of widening the tax network by identifying, at regular interval, more and more properties. They have noted astonishingly the lacking increase in properties in proportion to urbanisation and urban sprawl.

Other Urban Taxes

Local government can reasonably impose a productive set of non-property taxes. The policy objectives to be considered in formulating the system of non-property taxes may be sub-divided into the usual four broad goals of revenue policy : economic efficiency, fairness, revenue performance, and low administrative cost. The Commissions have therefore favoured to optimise water tax, vehicle tax, entertainment tax, show tax, lighting tax etc.

Non-Tax Sources

With the growing urbanisation, the local urban population demands more and more services—quantitatively as well as qualitatively. The people are ready to even pay for better and prompt services. Thus, an effective administered set of user charges should be desirable source of local revenues. User charges do not compete with government revenue base, are largely non-exportable, can have desirable effects on revenue, efficiency and equity and are administratively feasible at the local level, hence, be preferably adopted by municipalities.

There can be little doubt about the usefulness and desirability of developing broadly based changing systems for urban public services. The application of properly designed service charges, or more generally the recovery of urban service costs from beneficiaries, can contribute to an improvement of resource allocation within and between urban areas. Service charges can also contribute to equitable urban growth. Recouping the costs of public services from beneficiaries is a fair way to finance a service, and windfall gains may be minimised. User charges are not only a tool for ensuring efficient use and equitable financing of public services, but they also serve as an investment guide because consumers' willingness to pay for services is in many instances the only way by which the benefits of a service can be ascertained and compared with the cost of providing service.

The State Finance Commissions have felt that the urban local bodies are not bestowed with many taxes. Hence, they have emphasised upon mobilising non-tax revenue resources available with them. The Commissions have strongly recommended to enhance the rates of licence fees, parking fee, user charges, stamp duty, water rate, surcharges, local cess, development charge etc., besides suggesting tapping of various potential sources of income, e.g. charges on cable T.V. network, fee on trades and callings, fee on floating population etc.

Compensation

The Commissions all over the country have felt the need of increase in compensation in lieu of octroi, entertainment tax etc. They have emphasised upon upward revision of rates under Entertainment Tax, Show Tax, Profession Tax etc.

SHARING OF TAXES

Unlike the sharing of tax revenue between the Union and States, the State Finance Commissions have not given more importance on sharing of taxes between the States and the urban bodies. In Andhra Pradesh, the Commission has recommended the sharing of Betting Tax with the Hyderabad Municipal Corporation. In Assam, the Commission awards the continuance of sharing of Motor Vehicle Tax. The local bodies in Kerala have been favoured with a share from Court Fee Stamp, Building Exemption Fee, Library Cess (all non-tax revenue sources). The Madhya Pradesh Commission has suggested the continuance of sharing of Entry Tax and Vehicle Tax. In Orissa, sharing of surcharge on Entertainment Tax, Surcharge on Stamp Duty, Profession Tax and Motor Vehicle Tax has been recommended. The Punjab Finance Commission advises the sharing of Stamp Duty, Motor Vehicle Tax, Electricity Duty and Entertainment Tax. The States of Karnataka, Rajasthan, Uttar Pradesh and West Bengal have not been suggested to share their revenue sources with their junior partners in the federation.

Advantages of Shared Taxes

There are three important advantages to pure shared taxes. First, in comparison with allocation by formula or ad hoc arrangement, undersharing the amount of transfer to local unit, is certain and the fiscal planning of local government is improved by this certainty. Second, the sharing might give the local government access to an income and inflation elastic revenue base and thereby improve the adequacy of the revenue raised by local government. Third, if conditions are not imposed on the use to which the funds are put, local fiscal autonomy might increase significantly.

Though local government is a State subject, the Constitution has recognised that local government institutions are essential part of National Government (Article 12). The subject of local government appears under Entry No. 5 of List II of the Seventh Schedule of the Constitution. They are the creation of the State governments who have responsibility for providing adequate finances to them because there is no local list along with Union, State and the Concurrent Lists. They possess those powers and functions which are specifically delegated to them by the Acts passed by the State Legislatures. They are also subject to statutorily defined supervision and control by the State governments. The Constitution, however, prescribes for limited autonomy to those grass-root institutions. The autonomy can be granted only if the local governments share the tax base of the State government. Interestingly, none of the State Finance

Commissions has recommended the local tax base despite principally agreeing to that. This may be due to having been the First Commission. The subsequent Commissions may think on and suggest the exclusive tax base to local government units.

ASSIGNMENT OF TAXES

The Finance Commission in Andhra Pradesh has assigned Surcharge on Stamp Duty, Entertainment Tax and Profession Tax to local bodies. In Kerala, the Commission has recommended to assign Building Tax, Tax on sale of properties, and Tax on Cable TV operators. The Madhya Pradesh Commission suggests the assignment of the Compounding Surcharge on Entertainment only, while in Punjab, Profession Tax, Advertisement Tax and Licensing have been assigned to local bodies. In Rajasthan, Sanitation Tax, Parking Tax and Hoarding Tax have been assigned to the local institutions. The Commission in Tamil Nadu has assigned Tax on Animals, Tax on Timber, Company Tax, Vacant Land Tax, Pilgrim Tax, Surcharge on Duties on Transfer of Properties, Entertainment Tax, Surcharge on Sales Tax, Advertisement Tax, Cable TV Tax and Tax on Luxuries, whereas, the taxes on Entertainment and Urban Land are shared in West Bengal. Contrarily, the State Finance Commissions of Assam, Karnataka, Madhya Pradesh and Uttar Pradesh have not recommended the assignment of any tax revenue to urban local bodies.

GRANTS-IN-AID

Interestingly except Uttar Pradesh, all the State Finance Commissions have recommended the continuance of the existing grants-in-aid and also the introduction of additional heads of grants-in-aid. Many Commissions have suggested the Incentive Grants for performing better and Block Grants to few leading urban local bodies. In Uttar Pradesh, the Commission has recommended grants-in-aid only to liquidate the outstanding electricity dues and other outstanding loans.

In many States, the award of the Tenth Finance Commission

has been pooled as a corpus for constituting a Municipal Finance Corporation for creating infrastructural assets in urban areas.

FISCAL TRANSFERS

In Andhra Pradesh, the Commission has recommended the global sharing of 10.93 per cent of State revenue to local bodies. The Assam Finance Commission has favoured urban government with two per cent of State taxes, while in Karnataka the share has been fixed as 36 per cent of non-loan gross revenue receipts of the State. The Madhya Pradesh Finance Commission advises the transfer of 8.67 per cent of State's tax and non-tax revenue yield. In Tamil Nadu general devolution in phased manner from 8 to 12 per cent has been recommended. The Uttar Pradesh Commission had suggested ten per cent of net proceeds of total tax revenue of State but the State Government raised it to 11 per cent. In West Bengal the local bodies have been made entitled to 16 per cent of the net proceeds of all taxes collected by the State. Orissa and Punjab are the States which have been suggested to devolve only through sharing of tax/non-tax sources and not by global sharing.

MISCELLANEOUS

All the State Finance Commissions have discussed many other aspects of financial management in urban local bodies. Some have felt the need of setting up of an Urban Infrastructure/ Development Corporation, while a few have suggested constitution of Audit Committee. An emphasis has been laid upon preparation of balanced and rational budget and creation of a cell for monitoring the status of recommendations of State Finance Commissions. The improvement in level of services and encouraging the private sector participation have also been suggested by the Commissions. There is a felt need to computerise the municipal working and create a data base with a view to make the municipal administration effective and efficient. Except a few, none of the Commissions has standardised the civic services, although all recognises the low status of services and feel upgradation.

The State Finance Commissions have felt that while the potential for raising resources is inadequately utilised by the urban local bodies, expenditures have continued to mount. It is of utmost importance that the growth of expenditure on revenue account is curbed and a serious attempt is made to contain it within the revenue receipts. Fiscal discipline does not stop at bridging the revenue deficit. Equally important is to ensure that resources are not diverted from the purpose for which they are allocated. The Commissions further observe that it is not the purpose of any system of resource transfer by grant-in-aid to diminish with the responsibility of the local government units to balance their own budgets. The extent of self-help of an urban local body evidenced by its tax effort in relation to the general scope for additional taxation and economy in expenditure should determine the eligibility for, as well as the amount of help from the State.

The foregone analysis illustrates the strategy of fiscal transfers from States to urban local bodies in the country. Surprisingly, most of the Commissions have either ignored willingly or inadvertently the prescription of the Constitution for Central Finance Commission. The lack of political will and administrative motive at the State level to transfer adequate revenue to local government units may lead in proportional devolution from the Centre. Such a situation calls more and more transfer of funds by the State to local bodies to entitle them to get more revenue from the Centre. Further, the Commissions have adopted population as the main criterion for devolution of funds. The weightage given to population size, which is essentially a scale factor, as a major criterion in the formulae of devolutions, when combined with other criteria may result in lower per capita transfers to the less developed local bodies. Such a situation happened in Uttar Pradesh. This needs to be reviewed as poor local bodies need more funds to enable them to perform properly, efficiently and satisfactorily as a unit of local government, while other units, however, should not be demotivated.

The recommendations of the first Finance Commissions, however, may provide a framework to future Commissions. It is a welcome step for future betterment and development. Despite loopholes, the measure is a landmark in the history of local finance in the country.

BIBLIOGRAPHY

Argal, Municipal Government in India, Agarwal Press, Allahabad, 1955.

Bharadwaj, R. K., *The Municipal Administration in India*, Delhi, Sterling, 1970.

Bhattacharya, Mohit, *Management of Urban Government in India*, New Delhi, Uppal, 1976.

Chelliah Committee Report, Government of India.

Datta, A., *Urban Government : Finance and Development*, Calcutta, World Press, 1970.

Five Year Plan Documents, (Seventh and Eighth), Government of India.

Hicks, U., *Development from Below*, Oxford, 1961.

Jakaria Committee Report, Government of India.

Local Finance Enquiry Committee Report, 1951.

Maurya, R.D., *Fiscal Policy and Economic Development in Developing Countries*, Chugh, Allahabad, 1989, 87-140.

Nanjundappa, D. M., Trends in Resource Transfer from the Union to the States, in R.K. Sinha (ed.) *Economic Development Planning and Policy in India*, Deep & Deep, New Delhi, 1989, 260-283.

National Commission on Urbanisation Report, Government of India.

Raipuria, K. M., *State-Local Fiscal Relations in India : Some Vital Issues,* IIPA, New Delhi, 1980, 76-83.

Rural-Urban Relationship Committee Report, Government of India.

Sarkaria Commission Report, Government of India.

Sastry, S.M.Y., *Local Finance*, Mumbai, AIILSG, 1974.

Sharma, G.D., *Financing Urban Government*, Mumbai, Himalaya, 1978.

Singh, P., *Municipal Finance in India*, Local Finance, 3(4), August, 1974, 32-33.

Singh, P., *Municipal Finance in Punjab*, Nagarlote, 5(2) (April-June, 1973), 16-20.

Singh, U.B., *Urban Local Government*, Jaipur, Rawat, 1997.

Strategy Paper for Ninth Five Year Plan, Government of India.

Venkatraman, K., *Local Finance in Perspective*, Mumbai, Asia Publication House, 1964.

REPORTS OF STATE FINANCE COMMISSIONS

1. State Finance Commission, West Bengal, 1995.
2. State Finance Commission (Panchayat Raj and Urban Local Bodies), Uttar Pradesh, 1996, Vol. I-III.
3. Summary of Recommendations of State Finance Commission for Local Bodies, Tamil Nadu, Vol. I.
4. State Finance Commission, Assam, 1996.
5. State Finance Commission (Report for Urban Local Bodies), Madhya Pradesh, 1996.
6. State Finance Commission, Punjab, 1995.
7. State Finance Commission, Rajasthan, 1995.
8. Recommendations of the Cabinet Sub-Committee on State Finance Commission, Kerala, 1997.
9. State Finance Commission, (Urban Local Bodies), Karnataka, 1996.
10. State Finance Commission, Orissa.
11. State Finance Commission, Manipur.
12. State Finance Commission, Tripura.
13. State Finance Commission, Andhra Pradesh.

MUNICIPAL ACTS

1. U.P. Nagar Nigam Adhiniyam, 1959.
2. U.P. Municipalities Act, 1916.
3. Madras City Municipal Corporation Act, 1919.

4. Tamil Nadu District Municipalities Act, 1920.
5. Tamil Nadu Urban Local Bodies Bill, 1997.
6. Karnataka Municipalities Act, 1964.
7. Karnataka Municipal Corporation Act, 1976.
8. Punjab Municipal Corporation Act, 1976.
9. Punjab Municipal Act, 1911.
10. M.P. Municipal Corporation Act, 1956.
11. M.P. Municipalities Act, 1961.
12. Manipur Municipal Act, 1994.
13. Tripura Municipal Act, 1994.
14. Guwahati Municipal Corporation Act, 1969.
15. Assam Municipal Act, 1956.
16. Kerala Municipality Act, 1994.
17. Rajasthan Municipal Act, 1959.
18. Andhra Pradesh Municipal Corporation Act, 1956.
19. Andhra Pradesh Municipalities Act, 1965.
20. Report of Decentralisation Committee, Government of Kerala.
21. Action Taken Report on SFC, Government of U.P.
22. Action Taken Report on SFC, Government of Kerala.
23. Action Taken Report on SFC, Government of Assam.
24. India Yearbook, 1997, 1998, 1999, 2000 and 2001.

INDEX